"The Stranger, the Native and the Land"

Perspectives on Indigenous Tourism

Claudia Notzke

Captus Press

"The Stranger, the Native and the Land":
Perspectives on Indigenous Tourism

Captus Press Inc.
Units 14 & 15
1600 Steeles Avenue West
Concord, ON
Canada   L4K 4M2
Phone: (416) 736–5537
Fax: (416) 736–5793
Email: Info@captus.com
Internet: www.captus.com

Cover Photos: 1. Inukshuk near Pangnirtung, Nunavut; 2. Reggie Crowshoe of the Piikani (Peigan) First Nation, Alberta; 3. Author with Blackfoot Spanish Mustangs in Montana.

Library and Archives Canada Cataloguing in Publication
Notzke, Claudia, 1952–
   The Stranger, the Native and the Land : Perspectives on Indigenous Tourism / Claudia Notzke.

Includes bibliographical references and index.
ISBN 1-89571-269-6

   1. Culture and tourism 2. Heritage tourism 3. Indigenous peoples. I. Title.

G156.5.H47N68 2006   338.4'791089   C2006-902287-9

Canada⬥ We acknowledge the financial support of the Government of Canada through the Book Publishing Industry Development Program (BPIDP) for our publishing activities.

0 9 8 7 6 5 4 3 2 1
Printed in Canada

This book is dedicated
to my mother.

Contents

List of Figures

List of Tables

List of Illustrations

The book *"The Stranger, the Native and the Land": Perspectives on Indigenous Tourism* shines a critical light on the opportunities and constraints that indigenous people[1] face when engaging in tourism, while trying to maximize the benefits and minimize the threats to their culture, their land and their communities. This book is based on my personal travel experience and observations on four continents, on fieldwork, and on a synthesis of published and unpublished literature in the field. It primarily explores indigenous tourism phenomena that capitalize on an Aboriginal identity and sense of place (rather than just any kind of tourism venture indigenous people may choose to get involved in, including casino gambling, hotels, golf courses etc.). I have also omitted the topics of tourist arts and cultural institutions (see Notzke 1996).

Aboriginal/Indigenous cultural tourism always involves a cultural encounter between "the Stranger" and "the Native". Generally speaking, "the Land" is at the very heart of native culture and, in northern Canada in particular, this bond is alive and well. Even in southern Canada, where people no longer depend on the land for survival, their cultural and political identity is still derived from their bond with the land. These circumstances apply equally to other parts of the world. Consequently I have chosen the title of a CNATA (Canadian National Aboriginal Tourism Association) video, *The Stranger, the Native and the Land* as the name for this book. Barry Parker, former president of CNATA, graciously agreed to my use of this title, for which I would like to express my sincere gratitude.

This book is of interest to the general reader — both host and guest — to the tourism professional and practitioner, and to the educator. It should alert indigenous decision makers to the fact that significant negative impacts may occur if tourism is not approached in a cautious, comprehensive and knowledge-based manner. On the other hand, it also shows that if employed wisely, tourism may aid in aboriginal people's economic, political and social emancipation. The book encourages visitors to aboriginal territory to be responsible travellers rather than consumers of culture. For tourism professionals and practitioners the book highlights issues characteristic of the indigenous context rather than generic for rural areas or the underdeveloped world. It should be of interest to educators in the fields of tourism, development studies and native studies. Educators are advised, however, that this volume is not intended as an "Introduction to Tourism." Students will derive a greater benefit from it,

---

1 The terms "indigenous" and "aboriginal" are used interchangeably. The plural "peoples" is used when a collectivity or political unit is emphasized; "people" refers to individuals.

if they have at least a rudimentary knowledge of the tourism industry, particularly its basic structure, economics, impacts, marketing issues and different types of tourism.

The people I owe thanks to are too numerous to individually mention by name. Many have already been thanked on other occasions. First and foremost I want to express my gratitude to the many indigenous hosts I have encountered on my travels near and far. Aboriginal people throughout North America, Africa and Australia have graciously shared their culture and the magic of their land with me. In Canada, many of them have become friends. Heartfelt thanks are owed to the many travellers who so generously shared their ideas and thoughts with me, through interviews and questionnaires, as well as informally on the trail and in camp. Members of the travel trade and government officials have shown extraordinary generosity and patience in answering my many questions and discussing critical issues with me. My students in the Aboriginal and International Management Programs at the University of Lethbridge, as well as graduate students from other institutions, have been a source of inspiration and encouragement. I am also appreciative of the intellectual exchange with my peers at conferences, workshops, and on other occasions throughout my work on this project. Finally, many thanks are extended to the University of Lethbridge, the Faculty of Management and the BESS-Program (Business Enterprises and Self-Governing Systems of Indian, Inuit and Metis Peoples) for supporting and facilitating my travel and research activities.

A Note to the Reader

This book provides a global perspective on issues of indigenous tourism development. It also offers a closer look at aboriginal tourism in Canada. Chapter One provides a brief overview on both scales. Many of the examples and concepts introduced here are revisited in subsequent chapters. Chapter Two discusses the operational environment of indigenous tourism, exploring different scenarios in North America and other parts of the world. An understanding of these frameworks is crucial to an appreciation of the challenges faced by indigenous peoples, which are not necessarily the same as those faced by rural populations and the underdeveloped world in general. Chapters Three, Four and Five explore the closely intertwined elements of indigenous tourism, the stranger, the native and the land. These elements are, in fact, so closely interconnected that a clear

Introduction

An April 2000 edition of the news magazine *TIME* (Vol.155, No.14) envisioned us travelling back or forward in time, taking vacations in space, visiting other planets and discovering another universe. Such ideas might be considered more reflective of mankind's vivid imagination than a realistic assessment of our foreseeable future, if it was not for the fact that the first year of the new millennium witnessed the first tourist travelling into space (Smith 2000:10). In spring 2001 American investment broker Dennis Tito became the first person to purchase his own ticket, worth US$20 million, to spend one week on a space vacation, and established the precedent for elite space tourism. At the same time, through her serious engagement with the topic, veteran tourism scholar Valene Smith established space tourism as a legitimate subject for academic inquiry.

The preceding journey bears witness to the dynamic character of tourism and its never ending quest for new geographical and conceptual frontiers. Tourism is on its way to becoming the largest industry in the world and is one of the fastest growing industries. It is constantly changing and evolving. Tourism is touted as a panacea for destination regions' economic woes and as a means to promote peace (D'Amore 1990) and cultural understanding. Alternatively, tourism is discredited as a scourge, destroying culture as well as nature. The truth is that tourism is a complex and volatile phenomenon with tremendous potential for creating benefits as well as for doing harm. While as a concept modern tourism is firmly rooted in the cultures of the Western industrialized world, it has become a force that is likely to touch the lives and homelands of people virtually everywhere on earth.

As a socio-cultural phenomenon tourism may be a product of the First World, but some of its most important ingredients are integral parts of many and varied indigenous cultures. Mankind has always traveled, be it in search of food, to avoid conflict, to trade or to attend celebrations or social gatherings. Even though the appreciation and experience of something new and out of the ordinary as an intrinsic value appears to be the hallmark of the modern leisure person while being absent in most cultures, a penchant for travel has been recorded for non-Western groups. There seems to have been a tradition among the Blackfeet of Alberta and Montana to travel long distances along the Old North Trail, not only for trade and plunder but also for adventure: in other words, that is for the sake of travelling. McClintock (1910, 1968:3), citing the testimony of Mackenzie in 1800, mentions Blackfoot expeditions taking several years and travelling as far as Mexico, before returning and stimulating a younger generation to emulate their adventures. Author and world traveller Eric Hansen (who founded *Penan Guides*, a small tour operation that provides rural employment for the Penan) calls northeast Borneo's (Sarawak's) Penan the "world's best travellers": "They don't go from point A to point B, but by the most interesting route. Destination is the byproduct of the journey. And quite often there is no destination at all. That's why I sought them out" (Dworski 1994:16).

On the other hand, the legendary "walkabout" of many Australian Aborigines served to reaffirm and reinforce their ancient ties to the land, not the experience of something new and exciting. More than likely, all cultures have bred the occasional "footloose" individual with an unusual penchant for travelling. Such "eccentrics" may have served as scouts and pioneers for their group's more utilitarian travels, but in most cases, travel for the sake of travel and the titillation of novelty is not a trait present in many cultures. However, the protocol of hosting guests is an almost universal societal trait. Hospitality is a celebrated tradition in many cultures and is something that most communities, no matter how small or big, take considerable pride in. Furthermore it is often overlooked that indigenous societies had developed coping skills to deal with outsiders — not just visitors, but also intruders — long before the first "tourist" stumbled onto their lands, be he called Erik the Red, Christopher Columbus or Captain James Cook. There are many elements in indigenous people's cultural tool kits that they can capitalize on when developing strategies to deal with tourism, but the fact remains that most aboriginal people have great difficulty understanding the tourist's psyche and behaviour.

Questions of Definition and Scope

What are we referring to by the term "indigenous tourism"? An acquaintance of mine jokingly remarked that the first indigenous tourists in North America came via the Bering Strait, referring to the (no longer universally accepted) theory that the ancestors of today's Amerindians entered the continent by crossing the Bering Strait land bridge. This comment highlights one element of common confusion: When we talk about indigenous or aboriginal tourism, we are usually not referring to indigenous people being tourists (though this may well be the case), but to tourism using indigenous peoples, their culture, their lands, their facilities or all of these as attractions. This, however, addresses only part of the confusion.

The favouring by an African political elite of settled agriculture over hunting, gathering and nomadic cattle-herding has been instrumental in both stigmatizing and marginalizing certain groups and inspiring them to identify themselves as indigenous peoples (Ibid.). This has endowed them with a certain collective political identity and forum for political expression. East Africa's Maasai are the best known example. The International Labour Organization (ILO) Convention 169 of 1989 adopted the following definition of indigenous peoples: "Peoples .... are regarded as indigenous on account of their descent from the populations which inhabited the country, or a geographical region to which the country belongs, at the time of conquest or colonisation or the establishment of present state boundaries and who, irrespective of their legal status, retain some or all of their own social, economic, cultural and political institutions." Further: "Self-identification as indigenous or tribal shall be regarded as a fundamental criterion for determining the groups to which the provisions of the Convention apply" (quoted in Dahl & Waehle 1993:2).

Such an approach sidesteps yet another complication, namely that of legal indigenous status in some countries, which may derive from blood quantum, documented descent from an ancestor listed on a tribal or voting list at a certain point in time, recognition by a tribal government, documented association with a historical land base, or community recognition, to name but a few of the many different criteria adopted for the recognition of legal status.[1]

In view of the above discussion this book shall not adopt an unnecessarily narrow or dogmatic approach to indigenous tourism. However, the ILO concept of indigenous people has been used to guide the selection of examples and materials highlighted in this book. There are many common issues and lessons to be learnt from each other, when we consider indigenous peoples in either the broadest sense (as defined by Hinch & Butler 1996) or in the more restricted definition by the WCIP and the ILO, but the fact remains that certain issues central to the tourism debate come into much sharper focus when we consider indigenous peoples in the more restrictive sense of a Fourth World: issues such as control over land and resources, intellectual property rights, cultural revitalization, cultural commodification, use of indigenous cultural images for national tourism marketing campaigns, stereotyping, economic leakages and control over tourism. With this in mind, indigenous people's involvement in the tourism industry shall be explored with

---

1 For a critical engagement with the indigenous-peoples movement see Kuper 2003. For a further interesting perspective on Africa see Woodburn 1997.

particular attention to their efforts to nurture and protect their communities, culture and land.

Indigenous Tourism: A Worldwide Phenomenon

The establishment of indigenous tourism as an object of scholarly research was marked by Valene Smith's 1977 seminal collection of papers entitled *Hosts and Guests* (Smith 1977, 1989).[2] Contributions to this volume explored the impact of tourism from an anthropological perspective. During the last decade there has been exponential growth in the body of literature dealing with a variety of issues in indigenous tourism. In 1996 editors Richard Butler and Thomas Hinch compiled a volume on *Tourism and Indigenous Peoples* (Butler & Hinch 1996), which clearly demonstrated the growing sophistication, breadth and variety of issues in this emerging field of research. Special issues of the *Cultural Survival Quarterly* Journal have also tackled indigenous tourism with an emphasis on critical advocacy of indigenous peoples' interests in relation to tourism (Johnston 1990 and Epler Wood 1999). Comparison of the respective titles of these special issues which are almost a decade apart, "Breaking out of the Tourist Trap" in 1990 and "Protecting Indigenous Culture and Land through Ecotourism" in 1999, illustrates an interesting evolution: from the notion of being trapped by tourism to the idea of using tourism to protect land and culture. While the contributions in the more recent issue are critical and tell tales of tourism gone wrong, many of them also clearly contain indications of indigenous people being empowered to shape and employ the industry for their own purposes.

Tourism does not happen in a vacuum. Context and framework for indigenous tourism are particularly complex, as illustrated by Hinch & Butler (1996):

> Indigenous tourism occurs within the context of a global tourism industry that is dominated by non-indigenous actors. Yet, even this global industry does not exist within a vacuum. It is part of a broader environment which influences, and in turn is influenced by, non-indigenous and indigenous tourism activity. This interaction of the

---

2 These two editions were followed by *Hosts and Guests Revisited: Tourism Issues of the 21ˢᵗ Century* (Smith & Brent 2001), virtually a new book with a broader tourism focus.

Sharing a Way of Life

When old Martha handed us the raw, still-warm caribou kidney, we knew it was a special honour. This choice bit of fresh kill is usually reserved for the camp elders. She sliced a third off the slippery, dark brown organ, then cut that into small chunks and handed them around. We looked at her. We looked at each other. And then we ate. It tasted a bit like liver, but with a hint of gamey flavour and a dense feel. We wondered about the etiquette of wiping fresh blood on someone else's hair shirt.

Standing outside our igloos, dressed in caribou skins and eating raw meat, we had stopped being just observers. We were beginning to live the way of the Inuit.

We'd come North to Baker Lake [Nunavut, Canada], near the Arctic Circle, to see how Inuit live in winter. We figured it would be a staged show; a tourist demonstration like so many you can see farther south, where locals play at a way of life long past. But that is not what we found at all.

We found a final generation of these people of the land, living a way of life that still exists. And they were willing to share that way of life with us for several days.

Source: Cardozo & Hirsch 1994:19

which operate within the context of indigenous society, and which may or may not exhibit cultural identity and sense of place. More commonly, however, indigenous tourism is understood as being focused on indigenous culture, with indigenous people being culture providers or culture managers (Zeppel 1998).

Frequently, indigenous people's relationship with their land takes centre stage in their cultural expressions and the visitor's indigenous tourism experience. This is well demonstrated by Valene Smith's "Four Hs" of indigenous tourism. Smith (1996) has developed a set of analytic tools to assess the indigenous tourism potential in a specific setting as a first step in policy decision making and management. These tools are easily used and global in application. Smith's Four Hs are derived from the Four S acronym (sun, sea, sand and sex) that is often used in tourism literature to describe beach resort tourism. Aboriginal tourism is based on four interrelated elements: the geographical setting (habitat), the ethnographic traditions (heritage), the effects of acculturation (history), and the marketable handicrafts. These elements describe the indigenous tourism phenomenon as a culture-bound visitor experience, which, quite literally, is a micro-study of man-land relationships (Smith 1996:287).[3]

Invariably it is a communal identity on a defined land base that accounts for tourist interest in indigenous groups. As Fagence

---

3 See Notzke 2004 for an application of the Four Hs to identify aboriginal tourism potential in southern Alberta, Canada.

(2000:83) points out, what may be described as "the urban component" of such groups is hardly ever of special interest to tourists.[4] Fagence also calls our attention to what he perceives as subtle differences between ethnic tourism in developed countries and in the developing world. Using the United States and Australia as examples, he observes that distinct communities such as Native Americans and Australian Aborigines are becoming the target for "popularized tourism with many of the trappings of commercialized mass tourism" (Ibid.:77). The latter is characterized by "gazing upon" or merely shopping or gambling rather than "participating" in the lifestyles of the targeted groups, more characteristic of ethnic tourism. Arguably, both forms of tourism are encountered by indigenous peoples in First and Third World countries, where both mass tourism and smaller scale special interest tourism occur. Examples are the American southwest (Chiago Lujan 1993) and Uluru-Kata Tjuta National Park in Australia's Northern Territory (Altman 1989; Altman & Finlayson 1993), on the one hand, and Indonesia's Tana Toraja (Crystal 1989; Adams 1995; McGregor 2000) and Cuzco, Peru (van den Berghe & Ochoa 2000) on the other.

Providing a comprehensive quantitative and qualitative overview of indigenous tourism on a global scale is impossible as the availability of information is uneven at best. The following pages provide a cursory sketch of the state of indigenous tourism development around the world along with information on bibliographical resources for readers who want to explore selected regions in more depth.

North America[5]

Browne and Nolan (1989), Lew (1996) and Martin (1998) each offer interesting and comprehensive perspectives of tourism development on Indian lands in the **United States**, highlighting its history, issues and management structures. Economic gain is the dominant motivator for Native Americans to get involved in tourism development but is far from being the only force driving the manner of this development. Tourism growth in Indian country has been slow. A report by the Travel Industry Association of America (TIA) states that only one million Americans visited Native communities in 2001 (Tirado

---

4 An interesting departure from this notion is offered by Hinkson (2003). She describes how during the past decade urban sites of pre-colonial, colonial, and contemporary significance to Aboriginal people have been identified in Sydney, Australia, and made publicly accessible and suitable for visitation.

5 Canada will be discussed in a separate section of this chapter.

problems. Compulsive gambling, economic dependence, loss of privacy and distrust of tribal officials were other voiced concerns with respect to casinos (Davis & Hudman 1998:91).

The topic of Indian casinos has engendered extensive commentary by academics (Stansfield 1996, Baron 1998, Davis & Hudman 1998, King & McIntire 1998, Pitts & Guerin 1998) as well as the popular press, including a highly controversial *TIME* magazine article in December 2002 (Barlett & Steele 2002). For the time being, revenues from Indian gaming far exceed those derived from cultural or ethnic tourism:

> Fuelled by the success of Indian gaming, the Native American tourism sector has grown to the point where it offers serious competition to mainstream tourism elements. Why else would Donald Trump and Senator Torricelli from New Jersey pick a fight with Indian gaming in the halls of Congress? Why else would Nevada gaming interests put up millions of dollars to fight Indian gaming in California? And why would Indian gaming be under such broad attack today across North America? (Sherman 2003:25)

The long-term future and profitability of gaming is doubtful, however. Most critics express serious concerns about its sustainability. They anticipate cyclical boom and bust patterns (Lew & Van Otten 1998:219) and increased competition, which will result in an erosion of the comparative geographical advantage that these operations might initially have (Stansfield 1996:143f). There is likely to be a window of perhaps a decade or two in which tribes must reinvest gaming profits to create balanced reservation economies for the future when gaming competition in a saturated market will probably erode Indian casino revenues and marginal Indian casinos may go out of business.[7]

Australia and New Zealand

Altman (1989, 1993), Altman and Finlayson (1993; 2003), Burchett (1991), Finlayson (1991), Hollinshead (1996), Whittaker (1999) and Zeppel (1998a) effectively illustrate the uneasy relationship between **Australia**'s Aboriginal populations and the tourism industry, as represented by tourists, government stakeholders, industry representa-

---

7 For a useful review of Native American tourism websites see Mosser & Turco 2000.

tives and the economics of tourism. Whitford, Bell and Watkins (2001) provide us with interesting insights into 25 years of indigenous tourism policy in Australia. One of their key findings is the existence of a sharp contrast between federal and state governments' emphasis on "economic rationalism" in their policy design, and the social and environmental aspirations of Aboriginal and Torres Strait Islander People.

While there are some very successful Aboriginal tourism enterprises (many of them joint ventures, like the world famous Tjapukai Dance Theatre and Aboriginal Park), and there has been a recent proliferation of Aboriginal ventures in the industry, too many of them are short-lived and fail to penetrate the market deeply enough and to provide a satisfactory livelihood for their owners. There is still a widespread reluctance on the part of Aboriginal people to engage directly with the visitor and a preference for "indirect tourism" (Altman & Finlayson 1993:45; 2003:85) through the production of crafts. Furthermore, as Hollinshead (1996:309) notes, "It is simply a fruitless task to try and project traditional Aboriginal societies without taking pains carefully and appropriately to explain something of the mysteries of the Aboriginal inner dreaming of and about the earth." While there may be an increased openness to an alternative world view among certain types of travellers, it remains extremely problematic to introduce such fundamentally different ways of knowing and experiencing in the tourism marketplace.

Sharing the Dreaming

Eric Naylor, a tribal elder with the Yuin people, an Aboriginal Group living near Wallaga Lake on the south coast of New South Wales, tells the Dreaming story of Gulaga as he mixes a paste of white ochre in a small tin bowl. "This mountain is Gulaga, the mother," he says to visitors standing near the top of a peak known to white Australia as Mount Dromedary. "In the Dreaming, she had two sons." Naylor explains how her sons ran toward the sea, though Gulaga pleaded with them to stay. The younger son, Najanuga, who was slower and more cautious, became a rocky headland, later named Point Dromedary by Europeans. The elder son, Barunguba, swam out to sea, where today he stands as the windswept outcrop known to settlers as Montague Island. Naylor dips his index finger in the bowl and carefully paints a single line down a visitor's forehead. "This is your third eye. It will let you experience the spirits who live here. And this" — he dabs the ochre on the left cheek- "is to allow you to open your mind." A simple mark on the right cheek "will help you to listen," and a touch of ochre on the chin "will help you to be quiet." As he paints, Naylor relates how for thousands of years the Yuin people have made the arduous five-hour trek up the mountain to this spot to learn from elders "how to look after and respect the land and all its creatures." Their faces suitably daubed, the visitors enter the sacred site. Behind thick scrub, hidden from the hikers

Continued.

who trek the local trails, lie huge, round, moss- and lichen-encrusted granite monoliths, ancient rocks worn smooth and sensual. The spiritual aura of the site is immediately obvious, and Naylor's timeless stories ensure that no visitor can fail to sense it.

Source: Elder 2000:31f

Similar to Australia and Canada, national tourism authorities in **New Zealand** have for a long time followed a policy of using indigenous images to highlight the uniqueness of their destinations for distant markets. Aotearoa's (New Zealand's) original inhabitants, the Maori, have become increasingly frustrated by this appropriation of their identity and the stereotyping and image creation that went hand in hand with it, but which failed to provide true economic benefits and opportunities to participate in the industry on their own terms (Hall 1996; Ryan 1997). The Maori have been proactive in countering this trend since the mid-1970s and have assumed increasing control over tourism ventures by investing in mainstream businesses and by establishing their own tourism enterprises. Despite much progress, Maori tourism is still embryonic (Ryan 1997:263). In no other country would it appear that the future of tourism in general, and indigenous tourism in particular, is so dependent on the interpretation and implementation of a historical treaty between indigenous populations and the British Crown: The 1840 *Treaty of Waitangi* effectively recognizes Maori ownership of natural resources and cultural treasures and icons, both central to New Zealand's assets for tourism development. However, despite this treaty, many issues pertaining to both natural and cultural resources for tourism remain unresolved to the present day.

Asia

In **Russia** indigenous tourism is at a truly embryonic stage. Lack of infrastructure in the country's northern and eastern regions, lack of tourism education and training and an overabundance of bureaucratic hurdles to travelling "off the beaten track" create numerous problems for special interest tourism in general. But above all, it is extreme economic deprivation coupled with political and legal powerlessness of Russia's indigenous peoples which renders the very notion of indigenous tourism development or indigenous involvement in nature, adventure or ecotourism extremely problematic. Nevertheless, indigenous peoples like the Nenets, non-governmental organizations (the World Wildlife Fund's *Linking Tourism and Conservation in the*

Arctic Project), and a small number of intrepid tour operators are trying to change that.

In Asia there is a broad kaleidoscope of relationships between the tourism industry and indigenous peoples, but information and research reports on these developments are sketchy. On one end of the spectrum are the Sherpas of **Nepal**'s Sagarmatha (Mount Everest) National Park (Adams 1992; Robinson 1993, 1994; Weber 1991) who have developed a relatively successful accommodation with the tourism industry, having assumed the roles of owners and managers rather than just that of employees and service providers. This was made possible by a certain degree of political and economic autonomy (Nepal's national system of panchayat or village government), the Sherpas' unique skills, and their success in accommodating the tourism industry within their traditional system of reciprocity, which managed to embrace visitors.

Another tourism example that has been studied repeatedly (Cohen 1989, Dearden & Harron 1994) is that of "Hill Tribe trekking" in Northern **Thailand**, which started in the 1970s. In contrast to the trekking tourism in the Himalayas, where the Sherpas act as "travel facilitators" by providing guides, porters, food and lodging, in Thailand it is the "Hill Tribes"[8] people come to see, and visitors are guided by northern Thai as well as by tribesmen. The trekking companies are faced with the challenge of providing their clients with the desired experience in a rapidly changing tribal environment, and resort to elaborate staging and distortion of tribal reality. Notwithstanding recent changes in the nature of Hill Tribe trekking, options for adaptive strategies and control over the industry on the part of the tribes have remained limited. Tourism development there has followed a "boom-and-bust approach" (Dearden & Harron 1994:88), with more acculturated villages being abandoned by the trekking companies in favour of more "authentic" and "untouched" communities. Obviously such an approach to development is not sustainable.

An extreme case of tribal members being exploited as a tourist commodity is constituted by the Padaung Tribe, famous for its "long necked women." Their long necks are created by heavy brass rings weighing down collar bones and shoulders and resulting in such weak neck muscles that women are rendered almost incapable of supporting their head naturally if the rings are removed later in life (or as

---

8 Hill Tribes consist of some 23 ethnic minorities (nine in Thailand) who occupy the Highlands extending across several countries including Myanmar, Laos, Vietnam, and China, as well as Thailand (Dearden & Harron 1994:83). Most of them are traditionally swidden agriculturalists and ethnically, culturally and linguistically distinct from the lowland northern Thai peasants.

Iban Longhouse Tourism

At each longhouse, tourists are conducted through a standard program to experience Iban culture. These structured activities include a guided tour of the longhouse building, cultural dances (*ngajat*), handicraft sale, games, blowpipe demonstrations, cockfighting demonstration and a jungle walk with an Iban guide. Depending on the tour company, other activities may also be included to enhance visitor appreciation of traditional Iban culture. These include Iban bards chanting ritual poems (*mengap*), informal social songs (*sanggai...*), group drumming (*gendang pampat*), masked clowns .... martial arts (*kuntau*) and the *miring* ceremony, a ritual food offering. Additional Iban lifestyle activities included in some tour programs may include a jungle picnic with rice cooking in bamboo, visiting a farm or garden or fishing. Tourists may also witness special events such as a traditional Iban wedding (*melah pinang*) or be present at a longhouse during a *gawai* or ritual festival.

Source: Zeppel 1995:111f

punishment for adultery). While this tradition is falling into disuse in Burma (Myanmar), it is reportedly being revived in neighbouring Thailand, where many Padaung are living as refugees (Prior & Fry 2003:137). The Thai government, usually reluctant to accommodate refugees, has welcomed this tourist attraction with open arms, and in some villages, parents have started again to weigh down their children with heavy metal rings for the sake of tourist dollars. *Tourism Concern* reports that businessmen from the resort area of Phuket in southern Thailand have approached the Padaung Tribe with a business proposition involving the "purchase" of up to five Padaung families as tourism exhibits (*Tourism in Focus* 49/50: *Tourism Concern Campaigns,* Spring 2004). Padaung tribal members were said to favour the offer, as they felt that the promised tourism income would be more substantial than what they currently received as tourist attractions in Mae Hong Son in northern Thailand. The provisional governor of Mae Hong Son intervened, stating the Padaung need to remain there as refugees so they can return to Burma if conditions improve. Clearly, the Padaung have become pawns of the tourism industry.

Cohen (1996) investigated hunter-gatherer tourism in Thailand. This type of tourism is far less developed than Hill Tribe trekking and, with few exceptions, consists in a zoo-like touristic display of mostly deculturated, socially and economically deprived people. They are passively exposed to tourists and derive marginal to no economic benefits from this exposure. The same must be said of **Sri Lanka**'s Wanniyala-Aetto (better known as Veddha), who, under the guise of "ecotourism", experience not only cultural and economic disruption, but also exposure to alcohol (IWGIA 2000:327ff).

Another *cause célèbre* of indigenous tourism in Southeast Asia is Iban longhouse tourism in Sarawak (East **Malaysia**, Borneo). The

Iban, the largest ethnic group in Sarawak, are just one of several indigenous rice cultivating groups in Borneo, who live in longhouses and have become well known for hosting visitors. We owe much of our knowledge about Iban involvement in tourism to the work of Heather Zeppel (1995, 1998b). Iban longhouse tourism sharply contrasts with Hill Tribe trekking tourism in Thailand, since the Iban have considerable input in how the industry conducts itself. As illustrated by Zeppel with three examples, Iban involvement ranges from the community acting as a service supplier to one tour operator, to a partnership with an ecotourism company, and community control of tourism and guesthouse facilities. This continuum illustrates the changing role of Iban hosts in Sarawak's longhouse tourism, from being entertainers to entrepreneurs, from being culture providers to culture managers (Zeppel 1998b).

The Tana Toraja on the neighbouring Island of Sulawesi (**Indonesia**) constitute a unique case. In the 1970s they moved within half a decade from very modest beginnings of elite ethnic tourism to being a target for cultural charter tourism without passing through any intermediary stages (Crystal 1989:153; see also McGregor 2000). The main attractions are elaborate funerary rituals according to *Aluk to Dolo,* the traditional religion of the Tana Toraja. In the 1970s the "tourist ethic" — i.e., recognition, by those in power, of the economic potential of tourism attracted by the traditions of the Tana Toraja — resulted in an empowerment of this traditional culture and its adherents. Nevertheless, tourism has been a "mixed blessing" for the Tana Toraja, who have derived only limited economic benefit from the industry, but who have also learnt to manipulate touristic images for their own internal power struggles (Adams 1995). There are numerous other small scale indigenous tourism ventures, which have not been documented and are hardly known (like the aforementioned Penan Guides). Many indigenous rain forest groups in Malaysia, Indonesia, and the Philippines have their livelihoods threatened due to unsustainable industrial resource extraction practices in their traditional territory, particularly logging. Involvement of such groups in ecotourism[9] could assist them in raising international awareness of their situation.

Latin America

The use of tourism for their own purposes is an opportunity that has been recognized by several indigenous groups in the Amazon region

---

9 See Chapter Six for a definition of ecotourism.

olent, redistributive, non-exploitative, community-oriented and non-capitalist. Conversely, *indigenismo* vilifies the Spaniards and other Europeans as the "scourge of the Americas" and the purveyors of epidemic diseases, slavery, capitalist exploitation, racism, tyranny, and environmental devastation (van den Berghe & Flores Ochoa 2000:10). As van den Berghe & Flores Ochoa (Ibid.:7) observe in Peru, *incanismo* and tourism have quite different roots, but they feed symbiotically on one another: both are elite phenomena.

Africa

On the African continent, particularly in eastern and southern Africa, many recent developments in indigenous tourism have occurred within the framework of new initiatives in community-based natural resource management, specifically wildlife management. **Kenya** represents the best and the worst of nature tourism, and for many years was notorious for excluding its people from its celebrated national parks and alienating them from the country's most treasured tourism resources. In Kenya 75 percent of the wildlife exists outside of protected areas, many of which are hopelessly overrun by tourists. East Africa's Maasai have always coexisted with wildlife, but have nevertheless been displaced by the creation of national parks. The Kimana Wildlife Reserve near Amboseli National Park is a Maasai Group Ranch and the first game reserve to have been turned over to local people (in 1996). This new approach aims at making wildlife a part of the local economy. At the same time it enables visitors to experience wildlife as well as culture. The Maasai are involved in managing the reserve (as community scouts) and profit from its revenue, which enables them to finance services such as schools. Other initiatives have been implemented in the Masai Mara (Epler Wood 1999, Honey 1999, Olindo 1991, Western 1997). In neighbouring **Tanzania** a similar but more tentative trend can be observed. Development initiatives here have been hampered by a lack of resource security, skills, and management devolution (Goodman 2002).

> ### Protecting Maasai Culture
>
> "Most of all it is our culture we must protect. Before the people will agree to opening up our land for wildlife tourism, thereby changing so radically our farming habits and risking our livelihood, it must be made clear how the negative impacts will be overcome by the positive ones. If we can be sure we shall be better off by changing, then we shall welcome tourism."
>
> *Source:* Paul Ntiati, a Maasai leader from Kenya, in an interview with David Lovatt Smith, Smith 1997:13

Illustration 1.3

Visiting remote Berber villages in Morocco's High Atlas: Insourene, with mountain guide Mohammed.

In **Namibia** the year 1995 witnessed the formation of the Namibia Community-Based Tourism Association. This grassroots membership organization has been an important catalyst in involving some of Namibia's San communities in community-based tourism, thus enabling them to benefit from visits by outsiders to their traditional land base, now organized into a communally managed area conservancy (Schalken 1999). In neighbouring **Botswana** community-based natural resource management has given rise to tourism opportunities for the country's Basarwa/San/Bushmen (Gujadhur & Modshubi 2001; Van den Berg 2001; Vosa Flyman 2001).

North Africa's Berber people have also become involved in tourism. In **Morocco**'s High Atlas, Berber villages provide guides and accommodation to trekkers from all over the world and, prior to the civil war in the 1990s, **Algeria**'s Tuareg supplied desert travellers with guides, camels and logistics. In both cases (which I had the opportunity to participate in) the indigenous groups worked with major international adventure travel wholesalers like *Explore* and *Guerba Expeditions*. After travelling with Tuareg in **Niger**, Robin Hanbury-Tenison explains their motivation very fittingly:

> The salt trade is dying, as have all the other reasons for crossing some of the most hostile regions on Earth by

sentatives of the provincial and territorial governments and the tourist industry.

With this shift came a change in focus with respect to aboriginal tourism, away from that of the late 1980s and early 1990s. During those decades the "native" dimension was essentially seen as "ethnic." Native culture was seen as an integral part of outdoor and adventure tourism, and aboriginal tourism was described as "an added dimension to Canada's product line" (Tourism Canada 1988:4). The fact that the Canadian Tourism Commission undertook an Aboriginal Marketing Program in the late 1990s shows that aboriginal tourism began to be viewed as a force in its own right. This changed outlook was a direct result of the increasing global interest in indigenous cultures and environmentally benign tourism. The CTC marketing plan's overview refers to "other destinations (such as Australia, New Zealand, and the US) that have successfully utilized their aboriginal cultures to create strong international branding images." Some of the major perceived challenges for marketing aboriginal tourism were consumer research and an overall lack of integration and communication among the different stakeholders:

> The product is known to the consumer, the wholesaler and the retail market. The corollary is the lack of knowledge and awareness on the part of Aboriginal operators of the business opportunities, realities and practicalities, as well as marketing venues available to them. The Aboriginal tourism industry as a whole has developed largely in a vacuum, with little or no coordination among various groups. Most Aboriginal operators work on an individual basis and linkages between Aboriginal groups and other non-Aboriginal tourism operators have been virtually nonexistent (The Canadian Tourism Commission 1995:1).

For several reasons, the Canadian National Aboriginal Tourism Association (CNATA) was short-lived, and from its ashes came another attempt in 1996 by government bodies and some Aboriginal tourism officials to form a national strategy group and association to be known as Aboriginal Tourism Team Canada (ATTC) and more recently, simply as Aboriginal Tourism Canada (ATC). With approximately 10 regional aboriginal tourism organizations formed in Canada (half of them quite recently), ATC continues to be loaded with government officials and native consultants and solely dependent on government funding. As a result there is the challenge of effective communication between this national organization and the grassroots. In the past, with national organizations, there has been a lack of clear direction and mandate. Most of the regional tourism association directors believe that front-line native tourism operators must be the major stakeholders in the group, and must drive the organization's objectives and agenda.

Despite representation by the regional organizations, many difficulties are encountered in reflecting and addressing the huge differences that exist across this vast country in the character and level of development and product readiness in aboriginal tourism, as well as the major issues and problems perceived by the key stakeholders. Not surprisingly, the challenges and issues faced by aboriginal people involved in the industry in Canada are vastly different depending on whether they live in northern communities, where a land-based way of life is still prevalent, or whether they are residents of southern reserves. The following points (Figure 1.2, pp.28–30) highlight some of the differences. They are mostly observations from this author's experiences and fieldwork in the western Arctic and in southern Alberta, and they are offered to stimulate further discussion and research. Many of these ideas will be revisited and elaborated on in the following chapters.

In industry terms, aboriginal tourism in the North and South shares the challenges of a niche product. There is an overall lack of knowledge of and expertise in this kind of product on the part of the travel trade. At the same time, the importance of partnerships between local product suppliers and travel trade intermediaries cannot be overstated.

On the positive side tourism has a tremendous potential to serve as an educational vehicle for cultural exchange and understanding. There is a great potential in tourism for alleviating, as well as entrenching, stereotypes. Mythology, imagery, and stereotypes have dominated the relationship between the North and the South of Canada, and between aboriginal and non-aboriginal people, for a long time, with disastrous consequences for northerners and aboriginal people. As tourism makes its inevitable way to new geographical and conceptual frontiers, it is only fair that it should contribute to a reversal of this historical process.

To date, aboriginal tourism development in Canada falls far short of its potential. As Virginia Doucette, executive Director of Aboriginal Tourism Team Canada, points out, Aboriginal people constitute approximately four percent of Canada's population. If aboriginal people were to share in the tourism industry in proportion to their population, aboriginal tourism would be a $1.6 billion industry, providing 30,000–40,000 jobs. The reality is that the

Figure 1.2 Continued

North	South
Issues	**Issues**

North

Issues

- The Inuvialuit have responded to challenge number one proactively with the development of "Tourism Guidelines" for beluga-related activities. They clearly stipulate that subsistence hunting takes priority over tourism activities. In contrast, there appears to be an "unwritten policy" in Pond Inlet/Nunavut to conceal hunting from tourists.

- The hosting of ecotourists and cultural tourists, as well as sport hunters, is fitted within the annual cycle of land-based activities. The cross-cultural experience is used as a vehicle to teach outsiders about the northern way of life.

South

Issues

- Aboriginal people are facing the challenge of sharing their culture without compromising its integrity. Certain cultural "icons" are particularly vulnerable: the sundance and sweatlodge ceremonies, and spiritual elements in general.

- These challenges are addressed by enforcing strict cultural boundaries; by intense soul-searching and consultation with Elders and spiritual leaders; and by following cultural protocol.

aboriginal tourism industry is currently estimated at $270 million employing only 14,000–16,000 people with half of these seasonal or part-time. This is less than one-half of one percent of the Canadian industry (Doucette 2000). It is also estimated that the Canadian aboriginal tourism industry comprises 1,200–1,500 businesses, the majority of which can be described as small or micro businesses. Outside of the arts and crafts sector most of these tend to be culture and/or nature based (Hounsell 2002:1). It must be pointed out, however, that the compilation of data on aboriginal tourism is extremely problematic. There have been repeated attempts to prepare a directory of aboriginal tourism enterprises at national and provincial scales, which were eventually abandoned due to the constant fluctuation of new businesses making their appearance and others going out of business. There are also successful aboriginal

Illustration 1.6

"A Blackfoot on horseback, with a rifle", by Karl Bodmer, 1833–34.

Illustration 1.7

Aboriginal tourism in southern Canada: Many tourists seek "the past in the present." Blackfoot images ca. 150 years apart: "Blackfoot on Horseback" by Karl Bodmer, Vignette No.19 for Maximilian, Prinz zu Wied, *Reise in das Innere Nordamerika*, 1833, and Chief Nelson Small Legs Sr. at Nelson Small Legs Jr.'s Memorial Powwow, 1980, Peigan Reserve.

and the close connection between indigenous tourism initiatives and community-based wildlife management in Africa. The reader will have a chance to return to all of these way stations in subsequent chapters.

Finally, the reader is taken to Canada, a country of continental proportions. Here, the past two decades have witnessed a redefinition of the relationship between aboriginal and non-aboriginal Canadians and a restructuring of power over, and responsibility for, natural and cultural resources. A concurrent development has been the emergence of aboriginal tourism as a force in its own right. Not surprisingly, in such huge country no unified picture of aboriginal tourism reveals itself. A major division exists between aboriginal tourism in northern and southern Canada. Some highlights of the differences are presented in point form, contemplating the context, contents and selected issues of aboriginal tourism development in the territorial North (primarily represented by the western Arctic) and the southern provinces (represented by southern Alberta). No claims are made as to the representative character of these observations.

Due to road access, tourism development in the western Arctic is farther advanced than in the central and eastern Arctic, but context, contents and issues in tourism development across this vast region exhibit more similarities than differences. The same cannot necessarily be said for the southern provinces, which exhibit far greater variety of cultural expression and economic status than the North. However, there are essential similarities in the context of the tourism setting for aboriginal people in the southern provinces, and the differences are less substantive than evident in cultural and socio-economic detail. The contrast between the North and South becomes blurred in most parts of the northern provinces, where people may pursue mixed economies without the benefit of co-management regimes engendered by the claims process. This has implications for tourism development. The reader will return to various Canadian aboriginal tourism destinations in the following chapters.

2

The Operational Environment of Indigenous Tourism

may only seek part-time, occasional or seasonal participation in the tourism industry, and that such a level of participation may be necessary for the cultural sustainability of Aboriginal tourism ventures." The structure of such a mixed economy, its viability, its cultural and social base, and people's aspirations for the future, vary from case to case and warrant further study. By and large, however, it appears, that the indigenous people in question retain the traditional land- (or water-) based elements of their mixed economy as a matter of choice rather than out of necessity (but often both).

Depending on whether indigenous communities have suffered a total loss of their traditional economic base along with the cultural and social consequences accompanying such loss, or whether they engage in some form of mixed economy — which may be thriving or destitute — the implications for tourism can vary considerably. The seasonal nature of tourism, for example, can be an asset or a liability, depending on its intended role in a community's economy or a family's livelihood. The challenges and opportunities encountered by the tourism industry are likely to be different from community to community. In the following pages both scenarios will be examined in more detail, with Canadian Indian reserves representing the situation of underdevelopment as a result of loss of economic base and political disenfranchisement, and northern mixed economies constituting an example of an "alternative economic system." It should be pointed out that there is by no means a sharp division between these economic patterns. Even in situations where the traditional mode of economy has been totally displaced, there may well be traditional distribution patterns or rules of reciprocity as well as a sizeable "informal" or "invisible" economy in terms of exchange of goods and services. All of this has important implications for indigenous tourism.

Indian Reserve Economies

In Canada there are 884 occupied Indian reserves, the large majority of which are located in rural areas (RCAP 1996:807). They have their own governments and a clearly defined membership and land base. Compared to non-aboriginal communities, a private sector is less evident and not likely to be organized in a chamber of commerce or board of trade, nor is there usually a bank or trust company on a reserve.[1] Most important, in the majority of cases there are no clearly understood rules of the game about the relation-

---

1 See Record 2003 for an interesting case study of the Pine Ridge Area Chamber of Commerce, one of the first reservation-based chambers of commerce in the United

ship between the private sector and government (Ibid.). While Indian reserves have a defined land base, title to it rests ultimately with the Crown. As stipulated by the *Indian Act*, a reserve is a "tract of land, the legal title to which is vested in Her Majesty, that has been set apart by Her Majesty for the use and benefit of a band." (*Indian Act*, R.S.C. 1985, c.I-5, s2(1)). Reserve lands and the personal property of an Indian or a band are not subject to seizure under legal process and cannot be mortgaged or pledged, which severely restricts access to financing for economic development. Reserve lands and the personal property of a First Nation individual or a band are exempt from all forms of taxation except local taxation. This provision can result in an economic advantage for individuals and businesses located on reserves, but does not apply to corporations owned wholly or partially by First Nation people. Systems of land tenure vary from reserve to reserve. Individual band members may obtain possession and use of a defined parcel of land according to the "custom" of the band or by being allotted a portion of the land by the band council and given a certificate of possession or a certificate of occupation by the minister according to the provisions of the *Indian Act*. None of these systems provides security of tenure or protection from political interference. Furthermore, there is a profound shortage of land on virtually all reserves.

As already mentioned, reserve communities have their own government. The nature and composition of these governments, however, and their powers are defined outside the communities (RCAP 1996:811). The *Indian Act* stipulates the composition of a band council, the manner of its election, and its term of office (two years). The powers of band councils are limited to passing by-laws and enforcing them within the reserve boundaries. These by-laws are subject to ministerial approval and must conform to the act and its regulations. Band councils may pass by-laws, for example, with respect to taxation of land and interests in land, and the licensing of businesses, trades and occupations. The *Indian Act* has effectively turned Indian lands and property into enclaves and removed them from the Canadian economic realm (Ibid.:812). Here, creditors and bankers are reluctant to enter because they have no recourse in case of default; provincial governments are reluctant to get involved because it is an area of exclusive federal jurisdiction; and private entrepreneurs are reluctant to enter because they perceive that reserves are inhospitable to their interests.

States, which assists small businesses in negotiating Pine Ridge's unstable political environment.

Illustration 2.1

Tourism businesses on Indian reserves often face challenging conditions: a short-lived venture on the Peigen Reserve in southern Alberta.

There are no easy or straightforward solutions to these problems. On the one hand there are growing opportunities for proactive, resourceful and more aggressive communities to remove themselves from the strictures of the *Indian Act*, even though the terms and conditions still tend to be defined outside the communities. At the turn of the new millennium about 80 different negotiations on self-government were ongoing, concerning a wide variety of issues such as education, powers over the judiciary, policing, child welfare and health care (Purvis 1999:19). Under the *First Nations Land Management Act*, 14 First Nations are in the process of withdrawing their reserve lands from the land management provisions of the *Indian Act* and replacing them with their own land code. On the other hand, notwithstanding the widespread dissatisfaction with the *status quo* of the *Indian Act* regime, there are in many native communities unease, fear, uncertainty and a reluctance to take risks and assume responsibility for their own future. There is also a deep-seated distrust of the fairness of the negotiating process with governments, and frequently there is a lack of trust in their own leadership.

It cannot be denied that the operational environment for tourism development on Indian reserves is often an unsupportive one. Individuals who are trying to make a go of a tourism venture as owners and operators of their own business often complain about problems related to land tenure and political interference. Access to government funding, even for private business, often depends on a band council resolution, which opens the door to political interference and crippling delays. The same problems apply to the operation of band or tribal enterprises, which are frequently hindered by the lack of a system of checks and balances, preventing political interference with business. These problems are in addition to a still widespread lack of training and industry knowledge, and issues related only indirectly to the operational framework of a reserve environment, such as marketing problems and preconceptions of tour operators and other members of the travel trade. Nevertheless, there are success stories, as exemplified by a local operator on the Tsuu T'ina Reserve on the outskirts of the City of Calgary, Alberta:

> *EagleStar Tours* is owned and operated by Hal Eagletail. He specializes in customized tours of the Tsuu T'ina community where visitors are given an authentic reflection of reserve life. He stresses the cultural heritage of the Tsuu T'ina as well as highlighting the tribe's modern achievements. Popular tours feature visits to the modern and impressive tribal administration complex, the nation's bison herd, the explanation of murals depicting Tsuu T'ina history and prehistory, a visit to the museum, dance presentations and the serving of bannock (fry bread). Others involve tourists in hands-on activities like setting up a tipi or making bannock. There is great emphasis on the avoidance of stereotyping, and there is also avoidance of spiritual matters. Eagletail works with a selection of individuals who have something to offer to tourists: dancers, caterers, owners of tipis or horses and manufacturers of arts and crafts. A major factor in overcoming community opposition to his venture is without doubt the fact that Eagletail attempts to spread the benefits as widely as possible. Another important characteristic of his tourism venture is that all tours are guided, and no groups trespass onto reserve lands unaccompanied. Hal Eagletail works with approximately 20 tour operators who include his tours into their package of tour offerings. They include large bus tour companies such as *Brewster* and smaller specialized tours, exemplified by *Creative Western Adventures*. He also organizes youth camps for domestic and foreign students. Another interesting feature is that *EagleStar Tours* does not restrict itself to using the community as a host, but also acts as a travel agent for na-

Illustration 2.2

Hal Eagletail of Eaglestar Tours recounts the story of his people.

tion members, for example organizing a tour to the Indian Rodeo Finals in Rapid City, South Dakota. Furthermore, they offer cultural training to the local police force, and are hired by Chief and Council to introduce off-reserve partners in economic development to the community. This has contributed considerably to overcoming local stereotypes (Notzke 2004:37).

It is often difficult to pinpoint the reasons for success or failure of economic development on Indian reserves. This is as true for tourism as for other economic activities. Directing the Harvard Project on American Indian Economic Development, Joseph Kalt and Stephen Cornell arrived at some interesting conclusions (Cornell 2002; Kalt 2000; Cornell & Kalt 1990; Cornell & Gil-Swedberg 1995). They started out with an important question, faced by indigenous communities worldwide:

> What are the ingredients that are necessary for a society to improve its economic standard of living with social and political consequences that the members of that society find acceptable? How does a society accomplish a substantive economic transformation without losing control of its own desired character and direction? (Cornell & Kalt 1990:90)

They observed circumstances and socio-economic characteristics on American Indian reservations similar to those described above with regard to Canadian Indian reserves. In both cases there is a heavy dependence on the "transfer" economy: i.e., tribal or federal governmental transfer or other public assistance programs. This must be distinguished from employment in productive enterprises (private *and* public), which add output to tribal economies (Ibid.:94). However, the researchers found considerable diversity within this aggregate picture of Indian poverty, diversity that could not be explained by the communities' endowment with resources, their dependency, and cultural conservatism alone. There were certain characteristics that economically successful tribes had in common. One was **sovereignty**. Economically successful tribes were usually characterized by an aggressive assertion of self-government and independent decision-making over economic development affairs on the reservations. But sovereignty alone is not enough; everything depends on how this sovereignty is used:

> But tribal sovereignty is such that if the central government of the tribe cannot set in place an economic and social and cultural environment in which inside and outside economic actors, investors and others feel safe and secure in making investments in tribal development, the tribal government has the ability to destroy those

The conclusions of the (ongoing) Harvard Project on American Indian Economic Development (www.ksg.harvard.edu/hpaied/) regarding sovereignty, institution building and the creation of a secure and positive environment for human and financial investment have a wide applicability to indigenous people's communities not only in the United States, but also in Canada, and in other parts of the world. They are certainly relevant for northern aboriginal communities, whose economies differ from those on southern reserves and reservations in several important ways.

Northern Mixed Economies

A basic knowledge of how northern communities and economies function and a thorough understanding of the nature of socio-economic change are indispensable for understanding the forces that shape tourism in the North and for assessing the impact of tourism. Peter Douglas Elias has tackled the complex task of constructing a detailed model of how northern communities work: in particular, northern economies. His work is based on decades of personal experience as well as on the collective knowledge contained in the primary literature — that is, empirical research data, collected by 133 authors in 74 communities representing 30 identified cultural populations in Canada, Alaska and Greenland (Elias 1995:4; see Figure 2.1).

One important objective of this exercise was to offer planners and decision-makers a tool to help them determine where development initiatives may have beneficial or harmful effects, and how scarce development resources may be applied in an optimum manner. Some of the more salient findings with relevance for tourism are presented here.

Northern communities are small, seldom numbering more than several hundred inhabitants. Their populations are predominantly aboriginal, as well as young and fast growing. By national standards they possess very modest physical infrastructures. They are geographically remote from non-aboriginal population centres, and are located in relatively pristine natural environments. These communities feature "mixed economies" in which incomes are derived from a mix of domestic production, wage labour, transfers, and enterprise. Due to the high cost of living in the North, life would be problematic in many villages without income from domestic production — hunting, fishing, trapping, and gathering.

Although domestic production makes a very significant contribution to the local economy, little of that contribution is in the

Figure 2.1

Location of communities discussed in primary literature evaluated by P.D. Elias, 1995

Source: Peter Douglas Elias, Northern Aboriginal Communities: Economies and Development (Concord, ON: Captus Press Inc., 1995), p.6. Reprinted with permission of Dr. Peter Douglas Elias and BESS Program, Faculty of Management, University of Lethbridge.

form of cash. Because all needs cannot be satisfied through domestic production, it would be equally difficult to continue life in Northern villages without cash. Cash incomes are earned through sale of labour and commodities, and enterprise. Of these, wage labour is most important, but rarely are there enough jobs for all who want employment, and opportunities usually grow more slowly community (Elias 1995:11). How tourism can be fitted into such an economy, is illustrated by an example from the western Arctic:

> Some of the people who are making the richest contribution to a visitor's northern experience are enabled to do so by the fact that they are not full-time tourism professionals, but are firmly rooted in a way of life that ties them to the land. The tourism part of their mixed economy provides the cash to supply households with consumer goods, and underwrites the cost of their domestic production. The local operators for *Arctic Nature Tours* in Tuktoyaktuk, a married couple, are an excellent example of how this can be accomplished.
>
> These tourist outfitters combine a land-based way of life with tourism and pursue both ecotourism and guiding and outfitting sport hunters. The husband has been involved in tourism for approximately nine years. During the summer of 1995 he was completing his certification process as a whitewater rafting guide. The couple are in the process of setting up their own tourism company, *Ookpik Tours and Adventures*, which is to combine adventure and ecotourism with big game hunt outfitting and guiding (Table 2.1). Presently all their non-sport hunting tourism is booked through *Arctic Nature Tours* in Inuvik; sport hunting clients are allocated by *Beaufort Outfitting and Guiding Services*, a community corporation. As the wife points out, in this manner they are able to spend almost 10 months out on the land. The couple come across as genuinely enjoying what they are doing, and tourists respond to this attitude. They also report considerable interest in land-based tourism on the part of younger people, whenever they are looking for employees (Interview with the operators in July 1995).[2]

The importance of cash in northern economies is likely to increase in the future. For this reason, most households, whether or not they are currently dedicated domestic producers, will welcome any initiative that increases access to cash. Despite this urgency, it is hardly surprising that there is much individual determination and collective political will to safeguard domestic production and its resources from trespass and the competition of cash-producing

---

[2] Reprinted from Claudia Notzke, "Indigenous Tourism Development in the Arctic", *Annals of Tourism Research*, 26(1), p.68. Copyright 1999 with permission from Elsevier.)

Table 2.1   Seasonal Cycle of Community Residents Combining a Land-Based Way of Life with Tourism Activities

Date	Activity
September:	sport hunt for caribou, fishing for subsistence and dogs
Late October–December:	trapping
	Christmas break
January–February:	trapping, preparation for polar bear hunt
March–April:	sport hunt for polar bear, muskox and barren ground grizzly
May:	traditional spring hunt for geese (subsistence only) and icefishing. The operators plan to attract "spring tourists" for the Beluga Jamboree (a spring festival) with dog team rides and visits to the pingos (local landforms)
June:	tourists start arriving
June 20–July 23 (appr.):	river rafting trips
June–August:	whaling, community tours for visitors

Source: From Claudia Notzke, "Indigenous Tourism Development in the Arctic", *Annals of Tourism Research,* 26(1), p.69. Copyright 1999 Reprinted with permission from Elsevier.

activities, be they resource-based or not. This is achieved by the process of co-management of natural resources, which creates an operational environment with this priority in mind.

Co-Management Regimes
Northern Comprehensive Claims Regimes

"Co-management" broadly refers to the sharing of power and responsibility between government and local resource users. This is achieved by various levels of integration of local and state management systems. Co-management ranges from the tokenism of local participation in government research to local communities that retain substantial self-management. Co-management regimes may concentrate on a particular species or include all renewable resources of an area. As a rule, co-management schemes result in the establishment of co-management institutions, such as boards or committees with government and user-group membership.

Co-management regimes by native and non-native parties for renewable resources are being established in all parts of Canada (and increasingly in countries all over the world) under different circumstances and for different purposes (Notzke 1993; 1995c). One of the most important vehicles for the establishment of co-management regimes is the settlement of comprehensive claims. Claim settlements usually involve exclusive or preferential harvesting rights for aboriginal people on Crown lands within their claimed territory and involvement by aboriginal people in the management of resources. The latter is accomplished by schemes that allocate control of resources among competing interests and facilitate the merging of local environmental and Western scientific knowledge.

Case Study: The Inuvialuit Final Agreement

The 1984 *Western Arctic (Inuvialuit) Final Agreement* created a complex co-management scheme, encompassing all aspects of natural resource management, environmental impact assessment and review, and the establishment of new national parks (Notzke 1995a). This agreement constitutes the settlement of the Inuvialuit comprehensive claim, based on traditional use and occupancy, to lands in the western Arctic. More than 3,500 Inuvialuit were represented under the *Inuvialuit Final Agreement*; they are the majority residents of the western Arctic and live in the six Inuvialuit communities of Inuvik, Aklavik, Tuktoyaktuk, Paulatuk, Sachs Harbour, and Holman (see Figure 2.2). In settlement of their comprehensive claim, the *Inuvialuit Final Agreement* granted to the Inuvialuit specific rights, including title to lands in fee simple, US$31.3 million in cash, and rights related to participation in resource development, renewable resource harvesting, and management of renewable and non-renewable resources.

The goals of the Inuvialuit with regard to their comprehensive claim settlement, spelled out in Section 1 of the *Inuvialuit Final Agreement*, are to preserve Inuvialuit cultural identity and values within a changing northern society; to enable Inuvialuit to be equal and meaningful participants in the northern and national economy and society; and to protect and preserve the Arctic wildlife, environment and biological productivity (Government of Canada 1984:1). These goals can be summarized as being related to cultural identity, integration and conservation (Doubleday 1989:211). They may also

Figure 2.2

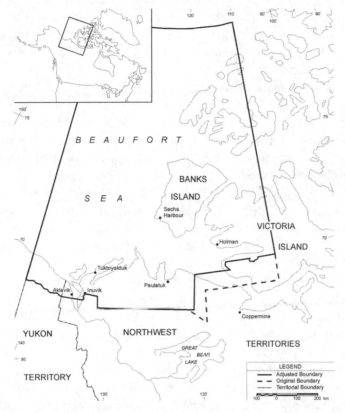

Map of the Inuvialuit Settlement Region

Source: Reprinted from Claudia Notzke, "Indigenous Tourism Development in the Arctic", Annals of Tourism Research, p.57. Copyright 1999 with permission from Elsevier.

be interpreted as containing a dual mandate: development as well as conservation. This apparent dichotomy is mirrored in the two principal management structures created by the agreement, the Inuvialuit Game Council and the Inuvialuit Regional Corporation. It is being addressed by five co-management institutions, the so-called Renewable Resources Committees (Notzke 1995:38). The resultant regime strives to provide a regulatory environment that makes allowance for both traditional and innovative modes of resource utilization. It is a complex regime for any industry, including tourism, to operate in. It endeavours to do justice to Inuvialuit society and economy, and to the nature of socio-economic change and continuity as the

Inuvialuit perceive it. Aboriginal tourism products in this region include guided community tours, visits to fishing and hunting camps, homestay programs, fishing lodges, outfitting for big game hunting, and arts and crafts sales. Many of the non-consumptive visitor activities combine an experience of the Arctic or Subarctic ecosystem with varying degrees of cultural immersion. This reflects the growth of ecotourism in the region (see Chapter Six).

In land claims settlement regions, not only government regulations must be satisfied when it comes to licensing and operation of tourism enterprises. In the case of the western Arctic there are also numerous Inuvialuit and Gwich'in (neighbouring claim region) boards, committees and community organizations, that must be accommodated. These institutions are creations of the claims process and the operational expressions of the resultant co-management regime. For the Inuvialuit and Gwich'in such a management environment can be empowering and constraining at the same time.

The Regional Tourism Manager for Economic Development and Tourism, Government of the Northwest Territories (NWT), felt in the mid-1990s that the licence application and consultation process had become a major roadblock for many prospective tourism entrepreneurs or outfitters (Notzke 1999:65). The Inuvialuit, with the maturing of their management regime after a decade of claim settlement implementation, had come to adopt a slightly more relaxed attitude and sought to streamline some of their procedures. The Gwich'in, on the other hand, were just in the process of establishing their management regime and, understandably, were exercising their management and decision-making power more assiduously. While big game hunting, and guiding and outfitting activities associated with it, fall under the authority of the Government of the NWT Renewable Resources Department, other sub-sectors of the tourism industry are the jurisdictional responsibility of the Department of Economic Development & Tourism (and, where applicable, Parks Canada). The most important piece of legislation in this context is the *Travel and Tourism Act*, with its Regulations for Outfitters and Tourist Establishments. A need to revise this allegedly outdated piece of legislation is often expressed by the industry; to date, no action has been undertaken, however.

The Inuvik office of Economic Development & Tourism provides prospective applicants with a Tourist Outfitter's licence with an information package included in the application process. Part of the package is a licensing checklist of authorities that need to be consulted. They include, at the consultation process level, such institutions as Town, Hamlet or Settlement Council, Gwich'in Tribal Council, Renewable Resource Council (Gwich'in Land), Inuvialuit

Land Administration, Hunters' and Trappers' Committee (Inuvialuit Land), Community Corporations, Environmental Impact Screening Committee, Band Council, and Metis Association. Government agencies on the checklist include the Department of Fisheries and Oceans, the Canadian Coast Guard (for proposed operation on coastal and inland waters), the Department of Renewable Resources, and the Canadian Wildlife Service in Yellowknife (for permits to enter migratory bird sanctuaries). Still other licensing requirements cover registration with Corporate Registries and the Department of Justice, and registration with Workers' Compensation Board of the NWT as well as Public Liability Insurance.

The first part of the list largely consists of institutions created by the claim process. Most outfitters will be concerned either with the Inuvialuit Settlement Region or with neighbouring Gwich'in lands, but there are land use overlaps, and some operators may want to travel in both areas. Tourism proposals — be it river travel, dogsledding, a camp or lodge — within the Inuvialuit Settlement Region, including national and territorial parks, are all considered "developments" by the Environmental Impact Screening Committee (one of the five Inuvialuit Renewable Resource Committees). A tourism proposal will therefore be screened by the committee to determine any potential environmental impact the proposed activity may have. Since the screening process involves consultation with local community organizations, it takes several weeks or even months. Upon completion it is referred to the licensing agencies (Economic Development & Tourism or Renewable Resources) for their approval, or sent for further environmental review and public hearings. Depending upon the complexity of the proposal, the latter process may again take several months.

New applications must be submitted by licence holders, if there is even a slight change in their operations, such as a new stopping point on the river or a new campsite. Until recently, even established tour operators with a track record in Ivvavik National Park needed to go through the approval process on an annual basis in order to run their Firth River rafting trips, which has caused them serious problems. Only lately has this procedure been replaced by a multi-year approval process.

For aspiring Inuvialuit entrepreneurs in the tourism sector the application and approval process in individual cases may take in excess of one year, and a positive outcome is by no means guaranteed. Inuvialuit, who have worked "on the inside" of the system, do not perceive the process as excessively onerous, but concede that an "in-house educational process" may be useful (Interview with Richard Binder, Inuvialuit Joint Secretariat, Inuvik, July 1995).

Candidates less familiar with the requirements may be deterred not only by the multiplicity of agencies, but also by the possibility of being turned down by their own communities. A problem that local aboriginal people find hard to deal with is the "personal nature" of their denial or approval within their community or claim area. It contrasts with the anonymous nature of government dealings and is much harder to accept and to cope with. A negative experience with non-native or external tourism operators may prompt a community to deny an opportunity to one of their own (Interview with Floyd Roland, Chairman of the Inuvik Hunters' and Trappers' Committee, Inuvik, July 21, 1995). Furthermore, politics enter into the decision-making process.

On the other hand, it must be acknowledged that community decision-makers may be faced with very difficult choices. One of the most sensitive issues concerns the admission of visitors into hunting and whaling camps. Many Inuvialuit individuals firmly believe in the educational potential of "cultural immersion" tourism, in educating visitors about the realities of a land-based way of life. But in the wake of the 1980s' demise of the sealing industry and the trapping controversy, the communities were also extremely concerned about the "Greenpeace syndrome" and were reluctant to make harvesting activities publicly accessible. This caution still lingers.

Most of the measures to regulate and control tourism (and other activities) are designed to protect the natural resource base of the Inuvialuit Settlement Region and the integrity of Inuvialuit harvesting activities. It is the Inuvialuit vision that what the land provides will always remain central to Inuvialuit life, modern economic aspirations notwithstanding. For this reason it is very important to examine the relationship between the Inuvialuit land-based economy and the tourism industry. For the Inuvialuit the challenge of embracing tourism is twofold: to protect the integrity of their land-based economy and way of life from trespass and the interference of the tourism industry; and to engage in tourism industry activities in a way that enables tourism to fit into, nurture and benefit community mixed economies to an optimum degree. The latter can be accomplished by optimizing the integration of tourism-related activities into the mixed economy of households and communities (see Table 2.1).

The Inuvialuit have responded to the first challenge in a constructive way by their development of Tourism Guidelines for beluga-related tourism activities. Considering the devastating impact the animal rights movement has had on northern aboriginal peoples' lives and economies (Notzke 1994b:127ff), the Inuvialuit are justified in being extremely wary of granting the public access to harvesting activities. During the summer tourist season whaling is *the* harvesting activity, and consequently the communities' greatest concern. The Tourism Guidelines are designed to prevent physical interference with whaling as well as misrepresentation of the activity. The Beaufort Sea Beluga Management Plan of 1991 points out that whale hunting and tourism are not necessarily compatible activities (Fisheries Joint Management Committee 1991:16); any encounter between the two requires sensitive management. The Guidelines provide the Hunters' and Trappers' Committees of the harvesting communities (mostly Inuvik, Aklavik and Tuktoyaktuk) with the authority to strictly control access and other activities in the harvesting zones, camps and vicinity thereof, and they clearly stipulate that subsistence hunting takes priority over any tourism activities.

The Hunters' and Trappers' Committees designate areas that may be used for the purpose of whale watching within the Inuvialuit Settlement Region, but retain the right to impose every kind of limitations on these activities. As a condition for their licence, tour operators visiting camps need written Agreements with the Hunters' and Trappers' Committees and camp owners in question. No one is allowed to take photographs or video footage of harvesting or related activities without the explicit written consent of the relevant Hunters' and Trapper' Committee(s), the camp owner and hunters involved in the hunt, or the Inuvialuit Game Council. Media involvement is even more strictly controlled. These are only some of the provisions that pertain to harvesters' concerns in particular. Other provisions address marine mammal harassment, artifact removal, garbage disposal and aircraft restrictions.

How effective are these guidelines? In the late 1990s Dressler (1999:109) found that their efficacy was questioned by many. Charter aircraft were still flying over the whaling camps. They were even known to tilt and circle back to allow tourists to take photos of hunters out on the water. Different problems were caused by independent tourists passing by or arriving at coastal or inland whaling camps, or in other hunting territory, by way of charter plane or kayak. This clearly showed that the Tourism Guidelines' requirement of a community consultation process was not adhered to. However, the issue was fairly complex. Many tour operators and visitors felt that the Mackenzie River system and Beaufort Sea were public domain, and that they should thus be treated as common property. There was potential for conflict between the public right to pursue leisure activities and the Inuvialuit right to engage in their traditional lifestyle (Ibid.:110). The intrusive "tourist gaze" was also objected to in communities, particularly in Tuktoyaktuk, where visitors often encroached on residents processing whales, to take photos and ask questions. The popular "Tuk Town Tour" attracted over 2,000 visitors annually (Ibid.:133). As a result many residents felt "on display," while tourism benefits were only enjoyed by those directly involved in the industry. The introduction of mini-vans has improved the manageability of tour groups, but independent travellers are more difficult to control.

Land claims regimes are the operationalized form of aboriginal rights and as such enjoy legal and constitutional protection. Their successful implementation requires constant review and adaptive management practices. They empower in some ways and constrain in others. But they do equip aboriginal people with the means to direct socio-economic change as they see fit, and they do improve the prospects for aboriginal communities of protecting their renewable resource base and the way of life it has nurtured for countless generations. It is increasingly recognized that the right kind of tourism just may be able to assist in both, but its management is likely to remain challenging.

Community-Based Wildlife Management Regimes

Not everywhere are indigenous peoples in a position to negotiate their future and to have their claim to land and resources officially recognized and protected. But innovative land and resource management regimes are being established on different bases, and the trend towards experimentation with community-based natural resource management (CBNRM) in general and community-based wildlife management (CWM) in particular is worldwide. Indigenous people have been particularly important participants in these initiatives, and tourism has played an outstanding role in efforts to make such schemes work.

Until very recently, the classic approach by the authorities to wildlife management, in both developed and developing countries, was "top-down." This was accomplished by the establishment of protected areas (frequently accompanied by displacement of local populations), wildlife legislation enforcement, and the assumption of ownership of wildlife resources by the state. While this protectionist approach, commonly known as the fences-and-fines-approach (Songorwa, Buehrs & Hughey 2000), has sometimes contributed to the survival of species and ecosystems and has promoted foreign exchange earnings in developing countries through international tourism, it has often had a negative impact on the food security, livelihoods and cultures of local people (Roe 2001:1). In many cases this has resulted in a level of conflict that has undermined the purpose of the parks in question. As human populations have grown, demands on remaining resources have increased, leading to environmental degradation and further conflict. This trend has, in turn, reinforced the commonly advocated protectionist argument that local people do not have the knowledge, the will or the training to practise sustainable wildlife management (IIED 1997:5).

Over the past 20 years, there has been a growing realization by resource managers of the importance of understanding the needs and perspectives of local people, of appreciating local wisdom and skills, of interactive and cross-cultural communication, and of strengthening local institutional capacity in decision-making. This has resulted in the worldwide emergence of participatory planning approaches, which, in the case of wildlife management, have helped to engage communities or to use the expertise of local people in finding solutions to problems.

These initiatives have also striven to ensure that local people do not solely pay the price for living in close proximity to wildlife and healthy ecosystems (opportunity cost, damage to crops, personal risk). They have helped communities reap tangible benefits from wildlife and ecosystems, such as direct and indirect financial gains, livelihood diversification, infrastructure, institutional development, empowerment and cultural strengthening. In many cases such benefits arise as a result of tourism, in the form of sport hunting, wildlife viewing and ecotourism. A number of projects and programs based on participatory approaches to wildlife management were initiated in Africa during the 1980s and have provided both models and inspiration for collaborative initiatives that have subsequently been started in other developing countries around the world, many of them with tribal and indigenous peoples.

However, community-based wildlife management is not without its critics, and its track record is anything but conclusive. As Songorwa, Buehrs and Hughey (2000) point out after a critical review of initiatives in Africa, a major weakness of community-based

---

What is CWM?

Community-based wildlife management *is the regulated use of wildlife populations and ecosystems by local "stakeholders"*. Local stakeholders may be a village, or group of villages, an individual, or group of individuals with a shared interest in the resource. The key issue is not how the community is defined, but the fact that stewardship (ownership or secure rights) over wildlife resides at the local rather than the state level.

CWM occurs within, around and outside protected areas. CWM initiatives can be consumptive or non-consumptive, subsistence or commercial, traditional or modern.

Source: Roe 2001:2; emphasis in original

wildlife management on this continent lies in the problematic character of the basic assumptions that underlie all these approaches:

> Four assumptions underlie CBW [CWM]: (1) that the national governments and their wildlife authorities are willing to devolve ownership of, and management responsibilities for, wildlife to rural communities; (2) that the communities are interested to participate in managing wildlife; (3) that the communities have the capability to manage wildlife; and (4) that wildlife conservation and rural economic development are compatible (Songorwa, Buehrs & Hughey 2000:603).

It is beyond the scope of this chapter to provide a detailed discussion of the topic, but in most cases the validity of every single one of these (often implicit) assumptions must be seriously questioned. The problem is compounded by the fact that the assumptions along with the impetus for CWM initiatives in Africa almost without exception originate with international conservation organizations and donor agencies rather than from within the communities:

> Even when participation mechanisms are said to be in place, it is often of a lesser degree than that in which the community, or the most vulnerable of the community, have any real influence in the outcome of the decision to be made. One inherent flaw in the process is that the instigating agency calls together the stakeholders it identifies, *but ironically fails to recognise themselves as one.* It therefore retains control over the agenda throughout the process, to the extent of selection or emphasis of local views .... Training in participatory techniques by agency staff and rural extension agents is not sufficient to achieve participation; institutions themselves must change to reorient their structures and goal-oriented approach, reporting lines, rewards systems and finance management if they are truly able to effect a change. Local institutions must be built on if local livelihoods and natural resources are to survive (Goodman 2002:284f; emphasis added).

Community-based wildlife management programs have the best chances of success in areas where there are sizeable populations of wildlife, large stretches of unsettled and uncultivated land, and relatively small, economically less stratified human populations

(Songorwa, Buehrs & Hughey 2000:640). These conditions seem to apply to an example from Namibia, where the development of ecotourism and community-based tourism is closely tied to new patterns of land tenure and land management. Namibia has the strongest legislation in the region that devolves authority over wildlife and tourism directly to community-level institutions (Ashley & Jones 2001:409).

Case Study: Conservancies, Community-Based Tourism and the Ju'/hoansi[3]

In 1990 Namibia's Ministry of Environment and Tourism embarked on participatory socio-ecological surveys to collect data on local communities' perceptions, needs and aspirations with regard to lands and resources. This process and its results laid the foundation for Community-Based Natural Resource Management in Namibia (Suchet 1998:59). Appropriate legislation was drafted in 1994 and the cabinet approved the Wildlife Management, Utilization and Tourism in Communal Areas policy in 1995. What was aimed for was a system flexible enough to accommodate Namibia's ecological, ethnic and cultural diversity and the evolving needs and outlooks of its communities. The approach chosen was "the establishment of communal area conservancies with rights to use and benefit from wildlife" (Ministry of Environment and Tourism, no year given, quoted by Suchet 1998:60):

> A conservancy consists of a group of commercial farms or areas of communal land on which neighbouring land owners or members have pooled their resources for the purpose of conserving and using wildlife sustainably .... Conservancies therefore promote sustainable environmental management, rural development and improved income and livelihoods for rural families and communities (Ibid.:1).

Commercial farmers (meaning farmers of European descent) had been able to acquire similar rights as early as 1968, when the State devolved limited rights over wildlife to farmers who met certain conditions. This has done much to halt the decline of wildlife on commercial land and has given rise to a burgeoning wildlife indus-

---

3 For more information on the Bushmen or San in Namibia, refer to Gordon 1992a&b, Isaacson 2001, and Van der Post & Taylor 1984.

try (Jones 1995:1). These rights had, however, never been granted to residents of the communal areas of Namibia, home to the majority of the country's population. This is also where a substantial decrease in wildlife was experienced, and where poaching was particularly rife in the 1970s. The significance of this new policy cannot be overstated. Legally constituted conservancies have the right and duty to manage wildlife resources within their areas. This means that communities (self-defining social units) have the right to

- use and benefit from wildlife on their land,
- propose recommendations for quotas for wildlife utilization,
- enter into agreements with private companies and establish tourism facilities,
- have ownership over huntable game,
- conduct trophy hunting and buy and sell game (Suchet 1998:60).

From the beginning tourism was viewed as a major component of the national CBNRM program (Jones 1996:11). Wildlife is one of the cornerstones of the country's tourism industry, which is the third largest sector of Namibia's economy. Ecotourism was considered one of very few economic activities that can be undertaken in remote rural areas by local communities (Jones 1995:2). Thus it is not surprising that 1995 also witnessed the formation of the Namibia Community-Based Tourism Association (NACOBTA), a grassroots membership organization, funded by international governmental and non-governmental organizations. One of its main objectives was to close the gap and improve cooperation between community-based tourism and private sector tourism interests in Namibia. Cooperation is poor and major misconceptions exist on both sides (Schalken 1999:40).

In trying to achieve the objective of integrating the community-based tourism (CBT) subsector into the larger Namibian tourism product, NACOBTA conducted inventories of both its member enterprises and the private tourism sector. It became clear that the destination facilities offered by the community enterprises did not meet the market's requirements. While communities were aware of the link between the conservation of attractions and the economic benefits from visitors, with no "tourism behaviour" in their own society there was limited understanding of the tourism concept or market dynamics (Ibid.). This recognition necessitated a shift in NACOBTA's approach. Initially community-derived benefits were expected to be reaped by community-based tourism enterprises, which were wholly owned and managed by the local community. NACOBTA is now supporting a shift towards community *involvement* as its main objective. Community involvement in tourism aims to optimize one or more of the following benefits: fees (bed-night levy, entrance fees, concession fees), employment (including training), management (joint ventures, land use planning), and enterprise (community camp site, traditional village, craft centre). Realistically, the benefit package for communities is often optimized when an upmarket, private sector lodge is developed that employs and trains community members, lets the community operate its own craft shop and cultural performances, and pays a bed-night levy per visitor (Ibid.:41).

Namibia's first communal area conservancy was Nyae Nyae, or what used to be eastern Bushmanland under the South African apartheid system. The 9,000km² conservancy is inhabited by about 2,000 people spread over 30 villages. This San group, the Ju'/hoansi, pursues a mixed economy, which includes subsistence cattle farming and dryland cultivation. They still derive a large part of their diet from wild plants (veld food), and many of the older men continue to hunt traditionally (Jones 1996:12). They also have adapted their traditional land tenure system to modern circumstances. Their homeland has been a destination for adventure tourism for several years.

Sampling the Hunting and Gathering Life

Old Kwi abandoned the steenbok trail after an hour or two, telling us we were too noisy to ever get close to the shy, swift antelope. Instead, he started pointing out other tracks: an old elephant footprint, an oryx, a roan antelope. Along the way, he found fresh leopard tracks. He showed us where the night stalker had urinated and where it had rested. "It is headed for water," he said. And sure enough, the tracks ended at a small well which provided a nearby village with water.

....

Cilliers, formerly the chief warden of Etosha, Namibia's largest national park, says, "There is nothing I can teach the Jung-kwa about conservation. They understand it completely." "But," he adds, "I can help them learn new ways to earn income from their wildlife through limited ecotourism."

Cilliers works with an elite group of Jung-kwa trackers who helped one of Namibia's top zoologists study Bushmanland's leopard population. He stands back, allowing the trackers to take visitors into their world.

Source: Butler 1996

Mostly Namibian and South African nationals used to visit the area on off-road expeditions, looking for the San, called "the wild ones" by the local tourists. Before the establishment of the conservancy, few benefits accrued to the local population, and they had no control over the invasion of their territory. A few years after the conservancy formation the new management system seemed to be paying off. The Ju'/hoansi were entitled to compensation for the overnight stay of all visitors, and to the entrance fees of commercial tour operators. They also signed a joint venture with a private guest/ hunting farm regarding the harvest of selected big game species on their land. Other benefits accrued to the communities through camp-sites set aside to cater to visitors in all parts of the large area, and payment for cultural activities, such as tracking and traditional food gathering trails. The latter became so important that the gains exceeded those of standard bed-nights (Schalken 1999:42). The way community tourism in Nyae Nyae was organized allowed for total village and family involvement. NACOBTA is still looking for ways to involve in tourism those villages who are not located in the vicinity of campsites in order to achieve an even more equal division of benefits. By the year 2000 the Nyae-Nyae Conservancy had received over N$3 million (appr. US$280,000) in grants from the WWF/LIFE program, as well as additional funds and other assistance from the U.K. Department for International Development, the Nyae-Nyae Development Foundation of Namibia, the Rossing Foundation and the Namibia Community-Based Tourism Association. These funds have been used to construct infrastructure, train community members in skills relevant to tourism and wildlife conservation, employ staff and purchase vehicles (Buckley 2003:34).

Obviously, less than a decade of involvement with community-based wildlife management and tourism is not enough to evaluate the success of such initiatives. The strongly egalitarian ethic characterizing San society and the absence of representative leadership have in the past constituted a major problem when interacting with government which invariably sought some form of traditional leadership structure through which to work (Jones 1996:19). The equitable distribution of benefits from natural resources has constituted a problem in almost all similar initiatives throughout southern Africa. A recent evaluation of community-based wildlife management in that region (including Namibia) seems to indicate that conflict is in the process of shifting from earlier disagreements between authorities and communities to dissent within communities over benefits and power. Intra-community conflict is associated with the emergence of a new elite who receive a disproportional amount of the benefits (*Newsletter of the Evaluating Eden Project* April 1999:6f). In an egalitarian society such as the San, this could be particularly damaging.

Other problems arise from a lack of control over access, since the villages cannot be contacted in advance by prospective visitors. Problems of stereotyping and overblown expectations at the prospect of an encounter with the celebrated hunting and gathering culture of the "Bushmen" are almost inevitable (see Chapter Four). There is also disturbing evidence that the push for ecotourism to supplement as well as showcase hunting and gathering may have a stronger backing by development workers (to keep Ju'/hoansi culture more in tune with the conservation mission of their project) than by the Ju'/hoansi themselves, many of whom deplore a lack of support for their small farms (Epler Wood 2003:1f). A recent documentary by veteran filmmaker John Marshall (2002), *Death by Myth* (Part 5 of *A Kalahari Family*), constitutes a devastating indictment of international aid organizations, who are accused of forcing fledgling Ju'/hoansi farmers in search of a better life to fit the image of the "Bushman myth" of people born to hunt and living in unique harmony with nature (*www.der.org/films/a-kalahari-family.html*).

These (potential and actual) problems must be weighed against certain benefits and advantages: economic pay-off, a new element of control, cultural validation and an increased transferral of skills to the younger generation, to name but a few. Furthermore, tourism was already here to stay, with or without San involvement. Considering that the San have for decades been one of the most marginalized groups in southern Africa, the establishment of a framework that gives them at least an element of control over an industry like tourism and an opportunity to derive benefits beyond the subsistence level from the resources of their land, must be viewed as progress. This does not change the fact, however, that tourism can be a double-edged sword, and that cultural stereotyping may dictate outsiders' development agendas. The San continue to be one of the most vulnerable ethnic groups in southern Africa.

Summary

This chapter further refines the stage for indigenous tourism established in Chapter One. It explores two crucial aspects of its operational environment: the paradigm of indigenous economies and communities, and the framework provided by various co-management regimes. Both considerations exert a strong influence on how tourism is conceptualized, approached and managed. While closely interrelated, the former (economies and communities) provides the overall operational environment for tourism in a particular setting, whereas the latter (co-management) focuses on decision-making about use and allocation of natural resources. The topic of indigenous communities and economies calls for a distinction to be made between underdeveloped economies robbed of their traditional economic base and its philosophical underpinnings, on the one hand, and "alternative economic systems" — namely, mixed economies, on the other hand. Canadian Indian reserves (and American reservations) are explored as examples of the former, where "economic displacement" has been complete, and frequently accompanied by social trauma and political disenfranchisement. Such communities usually present a very unsupportive environment for economic development in general and tourism in particular. Nevertheless there are success stories that defy these odds, and that challenge the observer seeking an explanation for this success.

The findings of the Harvard Project on American Indian Economic Development shed some light on this riddle: Evidence suggests that successful aboriginal communities are characterized by an aggressive assertion of jurisdiction over their own affairs, and a government that is culturally legitimate and effective in its endeavour to remain "above board" in dispute resolution and to refrain from political interference in business activity. These principles seem equally applicable in those communities that retain at least a partial involvement in their traditional livelihood. They are exemplified by northern communities who pursue a mixed economy. In such a mixed economy framework, tourism has the potential to play a crucial role in underwriting the costs of land-based activities such as hunting, fishing, trapping or traditional agriculture. However, in order to fulfil this role in a manner that safeguards domestic production and its resource base from trespass and the interference of cash-producing activities, tourism (and other economic activities) must be strategically managed. This is achieved by the process of co-management of natural resources, which creates an operational environment with this goal in mind.

Co-management broadly refers to the sharing of power and responsibility between government and local resource users. It is taking place in many parts of Canada, and increasingly in numerous countries of the developed and developing world. Northern comprehensive claims regimes in Canada, exemplified by the Inuvialuit Final Agreement of the western Arctic, demonstrate how co-management regimes can be empowering and constraining at the same time, when it comes to tourism development. But they do equip aboriginal people with the means to direct socio-economic change as they see fit.

Joint management initiatives also occur, where indigenous people are not given full recognition as land and resource owners. In many parts of the developing world innovative approaches to community-based natural resource management are being experimented with: in particular, community-based wildlife management featuring various forms of wildlife-based tourism. During the 1980s Africa emerged as a leader in this field. The case of Namibia's communal area conservancies and community-based tourism was chosen in this chapter to shed light on the potential and pitfalls of this approach. Namibia has the strongest legislation in the region that devolves authority over wildlife and tourism directly to community-level institutions, and is home to the San or Bushmen, an indigenous population whose stereotypical image has become firmly entrenched in the cultural mythology of different tourism market segments. It becomes clear that under the right circumstances community-based wildlife management and tourism can yield economic benefits and an element of control over resources and industry, and can contribute to cultural validation and skill development. But it is also characterized by the prevalence of dubious assumptions by those who provide the external impetus and financial means for such initiatives, and it can result in dissent over benefits within communities. These dangers are magnified in the case of the San, whose social, economic and political powerlessness is entrenched rather than diminished by the power of an image not of their making, the "Bushman myth."

Introduction

The following three chapters will investigate three closely intertwined elements of indigenous tourism: the stranger, the native and the land. These elements are in fact so closely interconnected that their clear separation is not always possible. The shifting angle of each chapter is an attempt to do justice to the complex reality of aboriginal tourism. A study of the role of "the stranger" in the indigenous tourism equation sends the researcher in pursuit of different themes. An obvious one is a closer look at the market for indigenous tourism, which is anything but a well-known variable. The fact that the assessment of this market is sometimes based on misconceptions makes it seem advisable to explore potential "dead ends": What role do certain European/Euro-American subcultures play in the potential market for indigenous tourism? Finally we must bear in mind that the relationship between an aboriginal product supplier and the consumer of the product is often an indirect one, mediated by travel trade intermediaries, the most important of which are tour operators. As a result, their characteristics, practices and agendas need to be explored.

Before we embark on an investigation of the role of "the stranger" in aboriginal tourism, it is useful to consider some basic facts inherent in the phenomenon of tourism, and consequently, also in the nature of the tourist. Even though tourism consumption patterns and motivations are changing, there are "some fundamental truths about tourism" (McKercher 1993) that set the parameters for the industry and circumscribe its potential and its limitations. The following points illustrate some of these truths as they have been emphasized by tourism scholars over the decades, with a focus on the visitor's perspective and potential impact:

- A tourist may be considered "a temporarily leisured person who voluntarily visits a place away from home for the purpose of experiencing a change" (Smith 1989a:1). There is an inherent paradox in tourism. The tourists' search for novelty and adventure is counterbalanced by a need to retain something familiar, something to remind them of home (Cohen 1972, [1990:198]). Many tourists seek to experience the novelty of the macroenvironment of a strange place from the security of a familiar microenvironment, which may take the form of familiar food, means of transportation, accommodation, infrastructure and a cultural buffer zone.

    Indigenous cultural tourism and cultural ecotourism are at the crux of this classic paradox of tourism, as people seek to relate to a foreign land through an alien culture, but want to do so with a comfort zone that does not leave them with a feeling of alienation. Such a comfort zone can be provided by an "environmental bubble" of the travellers' home environment, through which they view the people, places and culture of the host society, but within which they interact in much the same way as in their own habitat (Ibid.). Almost every tourism experience thus combines a degree of novelty with a measure of familiarity, the security of old habits with the excitement of change and adventure. The extent to which familiarity and novelty is experienced on a particular tour is determined by the preferences of the traveller and by the logistical and organizational setting of the trip in question. There is a continuum of possible combinations of novelty and familiarity that may be considered the prime underlying variable for any sociological typology of tourists. On this basis Cohen (1972) proposes his four types of tourists (the organized mass tourist, the individual mass tourist, the explorer and the drifter), representing a continuum of increasing novelty and an environmental bubble decreasing in size and elaboration.

The same distinction underlies other tourist typologies: Plog's identification of tourist types as psychocentric, midcentric and allocentric (Plog 1974) and Smith's types of tourists as explorer, elite, off-beat, unusual, incipient mass tourist, mass and charter tourist (Smith 1989:4ff). While society, and along with it, the tourism industry, are subject to constant change, which necessitates a rethinking of tourist types from time to time, the underlying principle is of timeless relevancy: The degree to which strangeness or familiarity prevails in any particular journey determines the nature of the tourist's experiences as well as the effect he or she has on the host society. The larger the size of the required "environmental bubble," the more profound the visitor's impact on the host community is likely to be.

- In his discussion of "the motives of the mobile leisureman," Krippendorf (1989) draws our attention to some basic tenets of the phenomenon of tourism that, in his opinion, stand in the way of the development of a "better" and more ethical tourism. He explores the role of travel for recuperation and regeneration, escape, freedom and self-determination, self-realization, and broadening the mind, and arrives at some disturbing conclusions. Two things run like a thread through all studies of tourist motivation. First, travel is motivated by "going away from," rather than "going towards," something or somebody. Shaking off the everyday routine appears to be much more important than the interest in experiencing new places and people. This is closely related to the second point: Travellers' motives and behaviour are markedly self-centred. Egoistic motives, whether we realize it or not, are always first and foremost.

- Two of McKercher's eight "fundamental truths about tourism" (McKercher 1993) address the nature of the tourist: Truth (6) "Tourists are consumers, not anthropologists"; and Truth (7) "Tourism is entertainment." McKercher warns that it would be a grave mistake to assume otherwise. Even ecotourists, who may have strong ethical and environmental motives for travel, are first and foremost consumers when they participate in ecotourism experiences. When on vacation, most people do not want to be burdened with the concerns of the normal world. They expect to be entertained, particularly in "cultural" and "environmental" tourism situations. In order to be successful and, therefore, commercially viable, the tourism product must be manipulated, packaged and modified in such a way that it can be easily consumed by the public (Ibid.:12).

The past two decades have witnessed profound social changes that have spilled over into the tourism industry. Environmental concerns, a new sense of social justice and human rights and a stronger preoccupation with healthier lifestyles coupled with the never ending quest for "something new" lie behind the growth of new types of "alternative tourism" and a search for more sustainable options. Whether these aspirations are just a fad, a myth or, indeed, a new reality is subject to considerable debate. Poon (1993), for example, argues that the emergence of a new kind of traveller is indeed a mass phenomenon, made possible by information technology. The new production principle is flexibility which allows for an unprecedented level of market segmentation, "where travel and leisure services will increasingly cater to specific lifestyle characteristics of the new consumers. Marketing will be focused on the individual consumers, rather than on groups of undefined tourists" (Ibid.:48).

The new trend is mass customization. New consumers and technologies are driving the new tourism, while new management techniques and production practices facilitate the development of the new services. The fundamental guiding force of the new tourism is change in consumer behaviour and values. Changing values are also creating a demand for a more environmentally conscious and nature-oriented holiday. Furthermore, the motivation of the new tourists is different from that of the old. For the old tourist, travel was a novelty. For the new tourist a vacation is an extension of life, a journey of discovery (Ibid.:51) According to Poon, new consumers are characterized by six key attributes:

- they are more experienced;
- they have changed values;
- they have changed lifestyles;

- they are products of changed demographics;
- they are flexible; and
- they are independent-minded (Ibid.:53).

But does this really change any of the "fundamental truths about tourism" or Krippendorf's observations about tourists' egoistic motives? What are the implications for tourism's sustainability? Is the problem of unsustainable tourism one of volume, or is it intrinsic to tourism as such? The latter is the stand taken by Wheeler (1991), in whose view even responsible tourism is "a micro solution to what is essentially a macro problem" (Ibid.:62). He poses many valid questions, for example about the idealistic notion of educating the tourist, and the role of the "sensitive traveller" in spreading tourism. He also calls our attention to the conundrum of size, appropriateness and economic viability of tourist activity — are these conflicting, incompatible objectives?

The jury is still out on many of these questions, but they are important ones to consider for indigenous hosts contemplating how to accommodate "the stranger". Such accommodation and its implications are more complicated than it would seem at first glance, as explained by Jafari (1989). He illustrates that there is more involved than just a cultural encounter between two parties. Figure 3.1 highlights the impacts of different cultures that interact at a tourist destination. The effects of the tourist culture, residual culture, and tourism business culture (transitional companies) are filtered through the state of development, local and national policies, local business environment and quality of natural habitat, and all these combined forces have an impact on the host culture. The severity and quality of tourism's impact are a function of how divergent the extraneous cultures are from the host culture, as well as of the scope and pace of development.

Tourist culture is a product of the industry and based on the activities tourists pursue at their destination. Depending on whether leisure activities (of the sun, sand, sea and sex variety), adventure or knowledge acquisition predominate, tourist cultures differ widely. According to Jafari (1989), tourists exist in a non-ordinary world at the destination, while host societies remain in their own ordinary world. This is often one of the core reasons for a clash of cultures. Tourist culture results from a sense of freedom from the constraints of ordinary life and usually exhibits a strong play component. When host societies are unable or unwilling to become a part of the tourist culture or to influence or control the course it takes, negative cultural impacts and social reactions easily result.

Tourists who adopt a tourist culture by observing other tourists at the destination are still constrained from total abandonment of

Figure 3.1

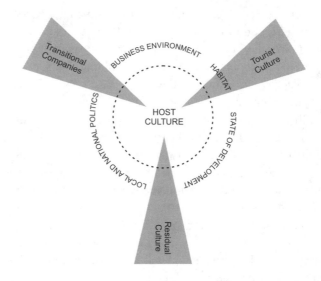

Compounded Cultural and Operational Forces in Tourism

Source: Jafar Jafari, "Tourism as a Factor of Change: An English Language Litera-ture Review", in Julian Bystrzanowski, (ed.), *Tourism as a Factor of Change: A Sociocultural Study,* (Vienna: European Coordination Centre for Research and Documentation in Social Sciences, 1989). Reproduced with permission of Jafar Jafari and International Social Science Council (ISSC).

their own ordinary life by the extent to which a residual culture remains (Gartner 1996:163). A residual culture consists of the norms and standards of conduct that determine a tourist's ordinary behaviour, which may not be completely rejected upon a traveller's immersion in tourist culture. Certain tourist activities or attitudes may be rejected as immoral or unethical by new initiates to the culture. Responsible behaviour guidelines expounded by nature tourism operators and indigenous authorities are an attempt to instil travel ethics in the residual culture of tourists. They are designed to reduce the psychological distance between the travel-ler's non-ordinary life and the host culture's ordinary circumstances. While the tourist culture can act as a unifying or "blending" force for different residual cultures, it is also true that tourist cultures emerging from different geographical and cultural areas vary widely in their service expectations, sense of adventure and tolerance of novelty. The different "travel cultures" of Europe, North America and Asia are a good example.

Companies that direct the flow of tourists to an area constitute yet a different culture that impacts the host society. The majority of these "transitional companies" (Jafari 1989), such as tour operators and tour wholesalers, are located outside the destination and tend to promote and encourage the tourist culture. Transitional companies may also be in the business of hosting tourists: for example destination resorts. Such companies are instrumental in generating images and perceptions of destinations and tourism products through their advertising, which may or may not be compatible with the preferences of members of the host communities. As host societies become more empowered, however, they are in a position to influence the business culture of transitional companies. Innovative tour operators and wholesalers in niche markets can indeed serve as very helpful partners and allies for indigenous tourism product providers and host communities.

The Elusive Market for Indigenous Tourism

In many ways, the greatest unknown in the equation of indigenous tourism development is the market. There even seems to be lack of clarity as to how much we actually know about this market. Market demand for Canadian aboriginal tourism products is deemed to be strong by product suppliers and tourism organizations, but tour operators and wholesalers and other industry insiders tend to be much more cautious in their assessment of this market. There are pronounced differences between international markets and the domestic market, which, after all, provides the lion's share of visitations in most destinations. It appears that aboriginal product suppliers and the promoters of their products are focusing their efforts and expectations more strongly on the international markets than on domestic travellers.

The question of what determines domestic demand (or lack thereof) for aboriginal tourism products is under-researched. This makes Ryan's (2002) and Ryan's and Pike's (2003) investigation for New Zealand a particularly valuable contribution. Ryan (2002) argues that even though there is a common cultural antecedence between *pakeha* (non-Maori New Zealander) and European culture, the lack of spatial distance between Maori and domestic tourists means that New Zealanders of European origin are not drawn to

then of imagery of defiant masculinity within a politically charged atmosphere of resentment on the part of both extremes of the debate about land settlements? Immink (2000) suggests that Maori warrior images and the *haka* actually inhibit a number of Asians from visiting New Zealand when they are encountered at overseas tourism trade fairs. It can be contended that this might apply to some within *pakeha* culture (Ryan 2002:965).

Ryan and Pike (2003:318) suggest that current representations of Maori in tourism do little to disperse stereotypes. Similar to indigenous representations in other countries, tourism packaging in New Zealand seems oblivious to the achievements and popularity of Maori music and dance in modern pop culture. Somehow, contemporary forms of cultural expression fail to be viewed as "authentic" and, hence, desirable for tourist entertainment. This may be another reason domestic audiences, who are used to the *haka,* choose to bypass cultural performances at well established tourist attractions with strong indigenous association, such as Rotorua:

> In short, perhaps Rotorua and Tourism New Zealand require a Maori equivalent to Michael Flatley's "River Dance." Such a product would reposition any stereotyped view of Maori culture, and is quite consistent with the notion that tourism is part of the entertainment industry and is, in fact, fun (Ibid.).

The implications of these findings and questions clearly go beyond the context of Maori tourism and New Zealand. It is a truism that tourism does not exist in isolation from society. Tourism reflects and impacts pre-existing tensions and conflicts. Imagery, rituals and associated political symbolism in tourism products — which may or may not be reflective of stereotyping, and which may or may not be initiated by and/or have the support of, indigenous groups — are likely to have a differential attraction for domestic and international market segments. The "distance breeds enchantment" theme will probably remain an important factor in attracting visitors for a long time to come, even in this age of globalization (see Chapter Eight). It is particularly relevant in juxtaposing domestic and international markets, but is also operational *within* large countries of continental proportions, like Canada, the United States and Australia, which exhibit considerable diversity in natural landscapes and socio-cultural conditions of both their indigenous and immigrant populations.

All countries with indigenous populations have to contend with controversial issues of status, rights, land and resources, and cultural expression, which are likely to affect any discourse, including the touristic one, between aboriginal people and other nationals. This is also true for developing or newly industrialized countries, where both domestic tourism and the acknowledgement of indigenous peoples' rights are just emerging.

Over the past decade, there have been a number of market analyses for aboriginal tourism (for Canada: Hart, Steadman & Wood 1996; PricewaterhouseCoopers 2000; Williams & Dossa 1996, 1999; Williams & Stewart 1997), and there is ongoing market reconnaissance, gauging long-haul and domestic travellers' potential interest in aboriginal culture. Most of these studies present impressive numbers in terms of potential gains of an aboriginal tourism industry, but they contain only very generalized ideas as to travellers' potential predisposition to seek out an aboriginal tourism experience. Most anticipated demand is linked to some specific European markets. According to the latest study by PricewaterhouseCoopers (2000:55), the Italian, U.K. and German markets hold the strongest potential for attracting aboriginal culture travellers to Canada, with a potential ability of accounting for 8.3 million aboriginal product visitors over a five-year period. For all three of these top markets the consultants recommended further study through focus groups, as well as in-depth interviews with the travel trade, to obtain insights into appropriate product development and marketing strategies.

Research also suggests that rather than constituting a stand alone product, aboriginal tourism experiences are best marketed as part of a regional theme linked to mainstream tourism experiences. This is reflected in a recent shift of the Canadian Tourism Commission's marketing strategy for aboriginal tourism products. There is need for market realism. The fact remains that we still know too little about what kind of aboriginal experience travellers may actually seek. The following two case studies from southern Alberta and Canada's western Arctic and some observations in Australia and New Zealand only begin to provide some answers to this question.

Case Study: Aboriginal Tourism Product Interest among Visitors to Southern Alberta[1]

During the summer of 1998, 130 tourists in southern Alberta filled out a questionnaire sharing their ideas and experiences concerning aboriginal tourism. Based on the author's acquaintance with several

---

1   This section summarizes part of an article published in *Journal of Sustainable Tourism* (Notzke 2004: 40–46)

local aboriginal product suppliers and their voiced expectations, the survey was anticipated to catch a sizeable proportion of tourists who had sampled "experiential" cultural tourism products. However, the actual presence in the marketplace of aboriginal tourism products, in terms of market-readiness, availability upon request and knowledge about them, turned out to be much more limited than expected. Consequently the survey results are more interesting for what they reveal about people's preferences and viewpoints pertaining to aboriginal tourism products than for people's reaction to "indepth" experiences, though these are not completely lacking. Obviously, an opportunistic sample does not provide a representative cross-section of southern Alberta's travelling public. The self-administered questionnaires were subject to a self-selection process that is reflected in the character of the sample. It is skewed toward high educational achievement and high income, with an amazing 36 percent reporting a graduate degree and a further 45 percent having completed post-secondary education.

This can most likely be explained by a stronger interest in and more "sympathetic" disposition toward, university-based research (a letter attached to the questionnaires identified this project as such) by those voluntary respondents who have had more exposure to it. It is also likely to be prompted by a certain level of interest in the subject of the research. The same explanations are likely to account for the large non-Canadian proportion of the sample: 20 percent were visiting from overseas, 25 percent from the United States, 30 percent from other parts of Canada, and 25 percent were from Alberta. This compares to 78.6 percent of person trips in Alberta originating in Alberta (accounting for 51.2 percent of visitor spending), 12.7 percent from the rest of Canada (19.6 percent of visitor spending), 5.0 percent from the United States (15.4 percent of spending) and 3.6 percent overseas visitors (13.8 percent of spending) (1998 *Statistics Canada* data quoted by Travel Alberta: www.tourismtogether.com).

The general socio-economic characteristics of the sample do, however, bear strong resemblance to those associated with the market segments that have been identified by market analysts as the native interest travel market (with some geographical variation). They also partially overlap with ecotourism market segment descriptions discovered elsewhere: baby boomers and slightly older travellers, who tend to be well-off and well educated (Hart, Steadman & Woods 1996; Williams & Dossa 1996, 1999; PricewaterhouseCoopers 2000). This becomes even more evident when we consider the respondents' travel preferences: The vast majority (regardless of nationality) are well-travelled, seek vacations that offer natural as well as cultural ex-

Figure 3.2

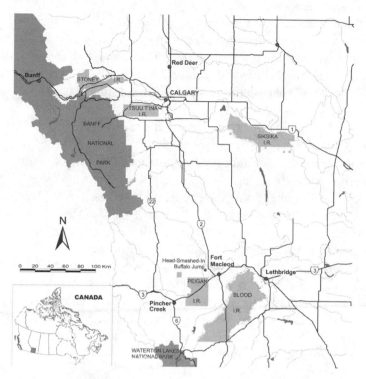

Map of Southern Alberta

Source: Notzke 2004:30

periences and are educational at the same time, and they enjoy the encounter with different cultures. Thus the fact that this sample can be assumed to represent the potential aboriginal interest travel market makes the expressed ideas all the more interesting.

The sample was constituted mostly of independent travellers, with only 7 percent belonging to a tour group. Those travelling independently did so for various reasons, such as visiting family and friends, autotouring, and outdoor adventure. The vast majority professed to be very interested or interested in aboriginal people and their lifestyle, with only 8 percent expressing no particular interest. It is not surprising that an aboriginal tourism experience constituted only one element of many in people's travel plans. Only for a small percentage, mostly those on an "aboriginal tour," did an encounter with aboriginal people and culture constitute the key element of their journey.

The questionnaire also inquired about people's particular interest in terms of an aboriginal tourism experience, and Table 3.1 lists their preferences in descending order.

Other selected specified interests (not on the list) included religion, beadwork, interaction with government, education and a three to four day cultural immersion experience in a tipi camp. Overall, these results, while reflecting a broad interest on the part of travellers, suggest a somewhat detached focus of this interest: a prevalence of a historical perspective over a current perspective; and a stronger concentration on material culture than on human interaction. This is particularly interesting0 because it sharply contrasts with the results of a similar survey conducted by the author in the western Arctic where it was found that there was an overwhelming interest in learning from the people themselves about their everyday life (see next section of this chapter). Considering the different contents and context of aboriginal tourism experiences in southern and northern Canada, this is not really surprising.

Turning to the southern Alberta travellers' actual exposure to aboriginal experiences, we find that almost three quarters encountered aboriginal people on their journey, usually in a tourism context. It is equally telling, however, that 22 percent commented that their experience did not include such encounters, but that this was for lack of opportunity, not lack of interest:

In the past when I have gone travelling it has always been my wish to learn about traditional aspects of the

---

Table 3.1 Focus of Travellers' Interest in Aboriginal Tourism Experience in Southern Alberta

(Respondents were encouraged to name multiple items from a list of options)

History	68%
Arts and crafts	40%
Observing native culture	38%
People's everyday life	37%
Learning about current issues	28%
Festivals	23%
Learning from native people about the environment	22%
Experiencing and participating in native culture	20%
Personal contact with native people	16%
Native cuisine	9%

Source: Notzke 2004:41

Illustration 3.1

Illustration 3.2

Illustration 3.3

(Illustrations 3.1, 3.2 and 3.3) Head-Smashed-In Buffalo Jump Interpretive Centre. In pre-contact days buffalo were stampeded over a cliff by aboriginal hunters. This site is considered the world's oldest, largest and best preserved buffalo jump. An elaborate interpretive centre was opened here in 1987, showcasing the history and prehistory of northern plains bison hunters. Tourists have the opportunity to sample living in a tipi. Strict cultural protocol was observed in the transferral of these painted lodges from the Peigan to Head-Smashed-In.

Aboriginal culture. I enjoy going to the powwows etc., but would find the experience much more enjoyable to be able to speak more with Native people. I found many non-Natives in my travels (a visitor from Ontario).

I would like to have more contact to [sic] natives but didn't see the possibility (a visitor from Germany).

Only 4 percent stated that their lack of contact with aboriginal people was by choice. Almost half of the respondents (49 percent) visited the World Heritage Site of Head-Smashed-In Buffalo Jump

Interpretive Centre. This site features aboriginal cultural exhibits and programs under Alberta provincial control and management, with extensive native employment and input into programming and design of exhibits. Many visitors enlist aboriginal guides to acquaint them with this impressive site. Approximately eight percent visited powwows organized either by one of the reserve communities or by Head-Smashed-In. The same number of travellers underwent intensive aboriginal-focused travel experiences. The remainder sampled aboriginal tourism products on the Stoney Reserve (restaurant, lodge) or the Indian Tipi Village at the Calgary Stampede, or visited other sites, where their "aboriginal tourism experience" was more indirect, such as historic forts or other historic sites. The overall degree of satisfaction with aboriginal tourism products was high.

Approximately 45 percent of the sample provided a highlight of their aboriginal tourism experience. Of these, the majority mentioned some aspect or detail of what they learned at Head-Smashed-In about historic and prehistoric bison hunters or the architecture of the complex. Of those who did comment, more than 37 percent mentioned aspects of their experience featuring hands-on/interactive/personal encounter characteristics:

> The more down to earth, real and authentic the event, the better. At HSI [Head-Smashed-In] I enjoyed being able to handle the tools and look closely at them in one room (a visitor from Montana).

> Seeing the displays and observing the First Nations People running quite a bit of the centre. Seeing how kind and gentle they are with their children was great also (a visitor from British Columbia).

> My native friend telling me the history of the last battle and reading the monument at Bull Trail, and as I walked down into the coulee I could feel the anticipation of such an event: the honour and insanity of war — my heart broke by the thought of the blood loss which fertilized the soil. The sadness of distinct tribes being senselessly obliterated (a visitor from Alberta).

> Perhaps it will be at the powwow as they might want to listen to me as an Elder of the Mandandaryi Aboriginal Tribe from Australia (an Aboriginal visitor from Queensland, Australia).

The degree of visitor dissatisfaction with their experience was very low. Selected criticisms focused on details of Head-Smashed-In exhibits and management; the absence of live bison; lack of friendliness of Stoney staff at Nakoda Lodge and lack of maintenance of trails in its vicinity; and, most significant, the desire for more personal contact with and guidance by aboriginal staff at Head-Smashed-In. There were also negative comments on the occasional encounter with intoxicated individuals in communities adjacent to reserves such as Fort Macleod.

Finally, travellers indicated what they found most important in an aboriginal tourism experience (Table 3.2).

Other features mentioned (not on the list) were: the relationship with the environment; quality of the product; a concern that tourism should not exploit or encourage self-exploitation and cultural degradation; learning about political issues; learning about spirituality; and meeting people. Most travellers did not have abundant experience or knowledge on which to base their expressed opinion, and the "gut reaction" character of their response is particularly telling. Travellers want their experience to be grounded in reality, to be authentic, and they want a connection with today's representatives of a culture they have come to sample:

> In my experience, many people visiting here from Europe are genuinely and sympathetically interested in the predicaments and achievements of the native peoples. I have been fortunate enough to go to the pow-wow at Head-Smashed-In Buffalo Jump and the Indian Village at the Calgary Stampede, and although these events are colour-

---

Table 3.2 Most Important Characteristics of an Aboriginal Tourism Experience in Southern Alberta

(Respondents were encouraged to name multiple characteristics from a list of options)

Authenticity	64%
Learning something about people's current lifestyle	45%
Native owned and operated	38%
Price	17%
Entertainment	12%

Source: Notzke 2004:44

ful and attractive, and are events tourists may well see, they are tantalisingly uninformative for those of us who want to see more.

....

The museums, such as Glenbow and Head-Smashed-In Buffalo Jump, are excellent, but still they do not quite convince us, the unenlightened visitors, that there still exists a living and vibrant native society .... In Oahu, Hawaii, the Polynesian Cultural Center is an outstanding example of a tourist centre where diverse groups of peoples present many varying aspects of their own cultures for visitors .... It provides a place of contact with native peoples which most visitors otherwise would never have. In a country the size of Canada, would not a central point, serving more than one group of native people, attract and educate many who have limited time to learn? It is so interesting and varied and colourful a culture, with such a fascinating history, that it seems a great pity those people briefly visiting Canada often have little chance to do more than just "scratch the surface" of such an important part of its heritage. Surely there is great potential in bringing the native culture closer to Canada's tourists... (a visitor from Alberta and recent immigrant from England)

This being our first visit and contact with Indians, we opted for attending a powwow at Head-Smashed-In. Next time, we would avoid this and rather choose to visit Stand-Off [administrative centre of Blood Indian Reserve]. Interpretive centres such as Head-Smashed-In are indispensable as a source of information for tourists, but the encounter with Indians is regrettably superficial (a visitor from Germany; translated from German).

I feel it is very easy for "Tourism" like this to become circus-like and this is something I feel uneasy about. It is imperative that any events/exhibits etc. are either run directly by Aboriginal people or are organized in very close consultation with them (a visitor from Ireland).

The quest for authenticity, however, does not provide a simple recipe for product development, as authenticity has proven to be a very elusive concept. This will be further explored in Chapter Four. The author's personal encounters with travellers in North America and Australia and discussions with tourism students (that is, actual and potential travellers) have yielded abundant evidence of a certain "rainbow quality" of authenticity. Based on their different perceptions of reality, different tourists have divergent ideas of what constitutes authenticity. They may measure their experience against an exotic or romanticized image; they may base their expectations on a static notion of culture; or they may have a realistic appreciation of a living culture. Travel trade intermediaries play an important role in shaping their clients' expectations (Silver 1993). Aboriginal hosts must decide what kind of expectations they are willing and able to cater to. They may have to show generosity of spirit by being willing to engage with naïve expectations on the part of visitors; they may choose not only to cater to a market, but also to educate this market.

The respondents' strong sense that their experience, limited though it may have been, taught them something about aboriginal people, indicates that this may be a worthwhile effort: 61 percent of the sample confirmed such learning experiences, which in many cases was not confined to some technical or historical detail, but was, quite simply, a lesson in humanity. Thirty-eight percent of the respondents provided further thoughtful comments, which, in many cases, reflected great personal concern about the future of aboriginal communities and tourism's impact upon it and, surprisingly enough, a strong endorsement of this research:

> I hope that the results of this survey become public. It is of grave importance that people begin to understand and **respect** the Native history and present cultures. I would like to see more museums with as good presentations as the ones I have seen in Canada (Emphasis in original; a visitor from Arizona).

> I think the negative impacts of cultural tourism will far outweigh any positive ones. I feel this has been the case with current trends in ecotourism. People need to approach their experiences of the natural world and other cultures with an open and sincere heart. Anything less is just another 'quick fix' and trendy vacation experience. The increased interest will soon result in much corruptive greed on the part of the experience providers. Cultural degradation will follow and any authenticity that survives will be that which goes back underground. To promote or encourage cultural tourism is, in my mind, a big mistake. Such experiences are already available to

those who sincerely seek them out; anything more will lead to trouble (a visitor from Montana).

I hope your research experiences and results will contribute to integration of Canadian society by developing Aboriginal tourism (a visitor from Germany).

Case Study: Aboriginal Tourism Product Interest among Visitors to Canada's Western Arctic[2]

In the summer of 1995 the author conducted a questionnaire survey among tourists in Inuvik (see map — Figure 2.2 on p.53) to gain an impression of their "aboriginal tourism experience." Seventy completed questionnaires were collected. The sample bore much resemblance to visitor characteristics reported by other studies conducted by or on behalf of the Government of the Northwest Territories (Government of the NWT 1995; Bufo Incorporated 1992a&b). Like the previously described sample for southern Alberta, and for the same reasons, this sample, too, appeared slightly skewed towards high educational achievement. Commensurate with other studies, most travellers sampled here appeared to be well off. The majority, over 60 percent, were Canadians; almost 25 percent were Americans, and 15 percent came from other countries, such as Australia, Germany, Mexico, Japan and Poland.

The majority of the travellers had visited the Canadian North before, but only 11 percent knew Inuvik from a previous visit. The largest percentage, 44 percent, identified their travel as "auto-touring" (although 56 percent had arrived in Inuvik by vehicle); 27 percent had come for "outdoor adventure"; 25 percent were visiting family or friends, or their travel was partly work-related; and 4 percent wanted to go fishing. Most of the visitors, 79 percent, were travelling independently. Except for those who were visiting friends or family, most travellers spent very little time in Inuvik, most commonly between one and four days.

Statistics sometimes fail to do justice to the variety of the human element among travellers. There was

...the "stay at home Mom" from Alberta;

---

2   This section summarizes part of an article published in *Annals of Tourism Research* (Notzke 1999: 70–73).

...the physical therapist from California, leading a Sierra Club trip;

...the college student from Calgary visiting her Inuvialuk boyfriend;

...two retired teachers from Virginia and New York State, having the time of their life;

...the professor from Poland;

...the German writer, driving his red van from Alaska to Tierra del Fuego;

...another professor from Japan, and

...the graduate student from Illinois, who was "loathe" to identify himself as a "tourist."

What united all these people was their great interest in aboriginal northerners and their lifestyle. Seventy-one percent of the respondents claimed to be very interested in native people, 28 percent were interested, and only one respondent said that he was not particularly interested. For 16 percent of the travellers an encounter with northern native people constituted the most important part of their trip. Asked what they were particularly interested in regarding aboriginal people, by far the largest percentage, 77 percent, named people's everyday life; arts and crafts were mentioned by 69 percent; traditional land-based activities by 50 percent; learning from native people about the environment by 47 percent, and country food by 44 percent. (People were encouraged to name multiple items.)

Almost all of the travellers reported encounters with aboriginal people (94 percent), many of them informal in nature or privately arranged, but the majority of visitors took advantage of the two Inuvik tour companies. People reported a high degree of satisfaction with the tourism product. Asked about the highlight of their experience, 54 percent considered it to be their "personal encounter with native people"; the next most frequent response, with 29 percent, referred to their "native guide's performance", and 20 percent particularly enjoyed the country food.

The strong emphasis placed by visitors on their personal encounter with aboriginal people and on their native guide's ability to communicate his/her culture to the traveller is extremely important. It corresponds closely with the response given by most tourists when asked what they were particularly interested in: 77 percent wanted to

Illustration 3.4

Lena and Geddes Wolke of Sachs Harbour on Banks Island have hosted numerous visitors in their western Arctic homeland.

find out more about people's everyday life. Learning about people's daily lives from the people themselves seems to constitute an important measure of the quality of a visitor's aboriginal tourism experience. This sounds very simple, but is anything but simple. Putting on a paid performance for a visiting public is much easier than sharing one's life in a genuine manner. Many (though not all) tourists in the western Arctic may be given credit to be able to tell the difference. Among those who (in the questionnaire) claim to have enjoyed themselves "very much," there actually is a wide spectrum of satisfaction, illustrating once again the importance of personalities and individuals at this stage of tourism development in the region. Depending on their community guide, people may proclaim that they had "the experience of a lifetime," or that "it was nice." Taking into account the importance of "word of mouth" advertising, this is not to be taken lightly. The following is just one example of a comment:

> I enjoyed spending time with Maureen and James in their home, partaking of "lunch" with them. They shared their food, lifestyle and culture with us. We learnt about the wonderful way they live on the land, preserving food, making clothing and yet live in town.

Having established that people report a high degree of satisfaction with their aboriginal tourism experience, it is equally important to investigate potential areas of complaint. Among the 70 respondents, 14 put forward complaints or suggestions for improvement. Six of those concern the two tour operators in Inuvik. Among the points raised were false advertising, inefficiency, disorganization and poor salesmanship:

> Both tour companies in Inuvik have advertising that mis-represents them. Although many tours are listed for both companies, they in fact only have <u>4 or 5</u> readily available when you arrive — and then you never know till the last minute if it will leave. If they had better management they could prosper. The bookers are very "unsalesman-like" and don't seem really informed or to care about booking more than one trip per person. These tours should be set up to rotate days so people could do 3 or 4 trips. They do too many to same [sic] site — dumb.

Comments like this reflect two things:

1. A very real sense of frustration on the part of many tourists with what they perceive as the difference between myth and reality of advertising. Considering that the majority of visitors are in Inuvik for less than four days, it must be acknowledged that only a handful of the tours are available on a daily basis (or every other day), and that many tours are conducted only occasionally or every other season, unless an individual or couple is prepared to pay a group charter price (which is unrealistic). This differentiation is not reflected in the advertising of either tour company.

2. A lack of education of the visitors about the conditions that northern tour operators have to contend with. Most northern visitors come to their destination for an authentic northern experience. It will not do them any harm to experience first hand the factors that control northern tourism: the weather, indigenous northern culture, and the role of tourism within northern land-based economies. Travellers must be made to understand that in the North these factors do not exist solely on paper (in fine print...), but are very real indeed. This, in itself, may be turned into a "tourism experience." Honesty is at a premium.

The issue of educating the traveller appears to be a recurrent theme. Some of the most motivated and successful aboriginal tourism product providers are driven by a desire to educate visitors about the realities of northern land-based economies. Educating the tourist is also part and parcel of honest advertising. It is encouraging to note that this lesson is not lost on northern travellers. Seventy percent of questionnaire respondents replied to the question "Did this experience teach you anything about aboriginal people?" by sharing some of their lessons. These lessons covered many different topics, such as the role of hunting and whaling in northern people's lives, political and social issues, human nature and social norms. The expressed opinions reflected a wide spectrum of experiences and perceptions. For the most part they did not appear reflective of stereotypes or pre-conceived ideas. The same is true for a variety of other comments volunteered by 47 percent of survey respondents. To the degree that northern aboriginal hosts are interested in getting their point across to southern or foreign guests, by and large, they are meeting with a receptive audience.

Observations from Australia

Australia has much in common with Canada with regard to recent developments in indigenous tourism. Both countries have in the past used indigenous images to enhance their attractiveness as a tourism destination in the international marketplace. Throughout the 1990s the governments of both countries undertook various initiatives to further tourism ventures by indigenous people in the interest of the national tourism industries as well as to ameliorate the dismal socio-economic situation of their aboriginal populations. In Australia as well as in Canada, there is a lack of concrete information with respect to current supply and demand. While on the one hand there seems to be a mismatch of supply and demand in the sense that there is a lack of market-ready aboriginal tourism product to satisfy visitor interest, on the other hand there also appears to be a tendency to overestimate the market for indigenous tourism experiences. Ryan and Huyton (2000b:15ff) point out an example of such discrepancy in market perception. In 1994 the Australian Commonwealth Department of Tourism published a booklet entitled *A Talent for Tourism — Stories about Indigenous People in Tourism* (Commonwealth Department of Tourism 1994). This publication showcased a number of enterprises throughout Australia, mostly in Aboriginal ownership, that feature indigenous culture and art as a tourist product. It noted that "International and domestic tourists are crying out for information about Australia's indigenous culture and the demand will only get stronger" (Jerry Pratley, citing Mick Roe, Manager of

Kurrawang Emu Farm). The significance of this quote is that it is reproduced in bold, large font on the page. As the authors point out, "This theme of a growing demand and interest for things Aboriginal by the tourist market is repeated almost as a mantra in a series of reports published by Australian governmental and tourist bodies" (Ryan & Huyton 2000b:15). On the other hand, a more cautious attitude is expressed in the *Tourism Industry Strategy* of the Aboriginal and Torres Strait Islander Commission (ATSIC 1997) and the *Masterplan* of the Northern Territory Tourist Commission (Ibid.). The conclusion reached by the *Aboriginal Tourism Strategy* of the Northern Territory Tourist Commission in 1996 still appears to have validity:

> Data on tourist demand for Aboriginal cultural product has been at best inconclusive and at worst inaccurate. Either way it has never been timely, appropriate, or continuous enough to be of practical value.
>
> Surveys have been carried out by a range of departments and agencies over the past 15 years or so, but differing methodologies limit the value of much of this research. In addition, there has been little focus on longitudinal data (i.e., taken over a period of time) for trend monitoring.
>
> The industry cannot with any confidence answer questions regarding the strength of Aboriginality as a factor in the choice of holiday destination, preferred activities and market segments likely to be attracted to certain Aboriginal cultural activities.
>
> Price, placement, access and satisfaction levels of those who have participated in an Aboriginal tour product need to be monitored (NTTC and the Office of Aboriginal Development 1996:8).

Inconclusive as it is, research indicates a desire on the part of many visitors for access to Aboriginal culture (Northern Territory Tourist Commission and the Northern Territory Office of Aboriginal Development 1994:10). Qualitative research commissioned by the Northern Territory Tourist Commission indicated that people preferred to experience Aboriginal culture first hand rather than through static displays. However, museums were seen as useful information sources, and closer investigation revealed that the experiential travel opportunity was sought only by a relatively small segment of the market. Focus group sessions indicated that Aboriginal cultural tourism was not a prime objective in the travellers' mind; although, when prompted, many travellers did claim a higher degree of satisfaction with places that offered Aboriginal interpretation. Generally, dissatisfaction was expressed with unmet expectations of "face to face" contact (Ibid.:11).

Shortage of data notwithstanding, more research on tourist preferences in indigenous tourism has been done in Australia than in other locations. The following paragraphs present four examples of academic research in this field.

In 1989 Moscardo and Pearce presented some results of their research on "The Tourists' Perspective" (Moscardo & Pearce 1989) in ethnic tourism, based on travellers' experiences with one of the longest-standing Aboriginal tourism products in Australia, *Tiwi Tours* in the Northern Territory. Founded in 1981, Tiwi Tours, which features a visit of the Tiwi community and homeland on Bathurst Island (off the northern coast near Darwin) by plane, is still going strong more than two decades later. The data from the researchers' survey of participants suggest that three key ingredients are necessary for a successful ethnic tourist product in Aboriginal communities: direct contact with Aborigines, an effective guide to explain and present Aboriginal culture and an interesting environment (Ibid.:390). These results closely correspond with those of this author in Canada's western Arctic. They also attest to the close link between ethnic tourism and environmental/nature-based tourism, which continues to be documented by other studies of tourist motivations.

Another interesting observation by Moscardo and Pearce in the late 1980s concerns the fact that, not infrequently, there is a discrepancy between what tour operators take tourist demand to be, and what tourists themselves actually desire in an ethnic tourist product. Based on Balinese or South Pacific cultural presentations and dance performances, operators tended to underestimate the appeal of Australian Aboriginal cultures exhibiting less flamboyance. Tourists, on the other hand, were primarily interested in direct personal contact and the current lifestyle of Aboriginal people.

A decade later, Moscardo and Pearce published another study that focused on "Understanding Ethnic Tourists" (Moscardo & Pearce 1999). It was based on experiences with another celebrated Australian Aboriginal tourism product, *Tjapukai Aboriginal Cultural Park*, near Cairns, Queensland. This cultural park evolved from the world famous *Tjapukai Dance Theatre* and offers a variety of performances and activities for visitors. It is the kind of attraction that people interested in Aboriginal culture would visit, but also has a reputation that makes it a "must see" stopping point for visitors with a more generalized interest. Based on a cluster analysis of visitor survey data, the researchers arrive at a typology of tourists according to the kind of ethnic tourism experiences preferred:

In short, this study provided detailed information about the nature of ethnic tourists, with two core points emerging from the data. The first is that tourists do differ in terms of the experience they seek in ethnic tourism situations. There does appear to be a post-industrial group concerned with their own impacts and disinterested in the commercial aspects of the experience, the Passive Cultural Learning group. There also appear to be two types of postmodern ethnic tourists: one group enthusiastically embracing all aspects of cross-cultural contact (the Ethnic Tourist Connection group) and one interested in fun and activities but reluctant to directly contact ethnic people (the Ethnic Products and Activities group). The second important point is that the study provided evidence that some visitors may see direct ethnic contact as difficult or uncomfortable. The Passive Cultural Learning group, for example, was clearly composed of regular ethnic tourism participants and expressed high levels of interest in learning about ethnic cultures but had less enthusiasm for direct contact. The Low Ethnic Tourism and the Ethnic Products and Activities groups were also less interested in direct contact than in other features of the experience (Moscardo & Pearce 1999:431).[3]

In an analysis of the degree of interest in Aboriginal culture on the part of 471 domestic and international visitors to Katherine, Northern Territory, Ryan and Huyton (2000a&b) found that 40 percent of tourists expressed such an interest. As a result of their cluster analysis the researchers warned, however, of the perception of these tourists as "amateur anthropologists," since their interest in Aboriginal culture was coupled with an equally strong interest in experiencing the natural environment and engaging in adventure activities. Therefore, the vast majority of interested tourists should not be expected to seek a detailed and in-depth understanding of Aboriginal culture. From a practical marketing perspective it also meant that Aboriginal tourism products were competing with the other products; thus had to be as professional as these others and, in all likelihood, were not in a position to command a pricing pre-

---

3 Zeppel (2002:98f) documents a very similar profile for cultural tourism experiences based on her visitor study at Cowichan Native Village in Duncan, British Columbia, Canada. Besides a strong visual component focused on native artwork and cultural icons such as totem poles, a pronounced interest in history, and interaction with native staff, visitors also expressed an interest in contemporary culture.

mium (Ryan & Huyton 2000b:20). Demand for arts and crafts was high, as shown by levels of expenditure; but for as many as 60 percent of visitors to the Northern Territory, interest in Aboriginal culture was rated low (Ibid.:25). A second important finding of this research project was a confirmation that the overseas markets most interested in Aboriginal tourism products were those of northern Europe and North America, not the ASEAN new markets experiencing the strongest growth (Ryan & Huyton 2000a:82).

Ryan and Huyton (2002) replicated this research project at another location in the Northern Territory, Alice Springs and Uluru-Kata Tjuta National Park Visitor Centre. These places are synonymous with the heart of the Australian Outback. Survey results closely mirrored the researchers' previous conclusions. Overall interest in Aboriginal tourism experiences and products appeared to be low; and where present — i.e., with between 18–29 percent of the travellers (depending on the tourism product; Ryan & Huyton 2002:642f) — it constituted but one aspect of the overall conceptualization of "The Outback" (Ibid.:638). The highest level of interest was documented for British, German and North American travellers:

> But if the interest of tourists is less than previously thought, does this matter? From one perspective, it may mean that if Aboriginal communities are unsure about tourism, and wish to solely maintain a presence through the sale of artifacts and Aboriginal art, such actions may be appropriate .... It certainly means that Aboriginal people can provide a souvenir market without having tourists intrude upon their communities. The findings also raise the need to avoid too many new businesses coming onto the market, as such businesses may adversely affect the financial viability of those that currently exist (Ibid.:642).

...and New Zealand

The most recent study of tourists' perception of indigenous tourism products comes from New Zealand. McIntosh (2004) makes a point of confirming many of the findings of the above mentioned studies by Moscardo and Pearce, Notzke (1999), and Ryan and Huyton. What makes her investigation of international tourists' appreciation of Maori culture particularly interesting is the fact that her study did not target visitors at indigenous attractions or sites, but was carried out at Christchurch International Airport. Here semi-structured face-to-face interviews were conducted with a range of nationalities and different types of international tourists arriving and departing. Thus, visitor perspectives on Maori culture could be attained by measuring tourists' perceptions and experiences both immediately before and after a visit to New Zealand (McIntosh 2004:4). Even though her sample was small, the results constitute an important first step and lay the groundwork for a more extended quantitative study. Some of the highlights of McIntosh's findings are listed in point form:

- Tourists were generally unaware of the contemporary nature of indigenous cultures. Even the departure surveys confirmed visitors' traditional and stereotypical views of Maori people. The majority of respondents did not feel that their impression of Maori culture had changed as a result of their visit to New Zealand, which may be explained at least in part by the nature of the existing tourism product (Ibid.:6).

- Maori culture was not a major motivation for visiting New Zealand. Less than half of the arrivals had any intention to seek out an experience of Maori culture. For those who did, Maori culture constituted a point of "difference" in their total New Zealand experience (Ibid.:7).

- Despite being a subordinate influence on their decision to visit New Zealand, the majority of travellers interviewed in the departure survey (32 of 46) reported that they had experienced Maori culture during their visit. An indigenous tourism experience appears to be an integral part of the standard tourism consumption pattern in New Zealand. Most of the experiences gained of Maori culture were in Rotorua or Waitangi, areas notable for their association with Maori history. The most common tourism products included visits to museums, dance performances, visiting a Maori village, social interaction with Maori, visiting the Treaty house, watching a *haka* or observing a demonstration of Maori carving (Ibid.:8).

- Considering tourist preferences for experiencing Maori culture, it was found that tourists were interested in visiting Maori communities and learning about their culture from the indigenous people themselves, albeit in a superficial manner (Ibid.:12). Informal personal contacts appeared preferable to staged cultural events. This contrasts with the character of existing Maori tourism products, as well as with current public policy priorities for future indigenous product development.

McIntosh warns, however, that despite tourists' expressed preference for genuine interaction with indigenous people, the brief and superficial nature, as well as the generalist context of the encounter, must be taken into account:

> As such, this study shares Ryan and Huyton's [2000b] concern that it would be a mistake to regard tourists as amateur anthropologists seeking a detailed understanding of indigenous peoples and their culture. Findings from the present study did provide some evidence that tourists did reportedly gain an increased understanding and appreciation for Maori culture from their visit, although the level of learning was shallow. However, an increasing number of studies have concluded that indigenous culture is consumed somewhat superficially as a unique "point of difference," or as an object of the tourist gaze. As such, there is increasing concern that experiences of indigenous culture are consumed out of the desire for a "romanticised" version of the culture and may constitute desirable but not essential aspects of a trip itinerary, or alternatively, constitute "one-off" experiences.
>
> ....
>
> However, delivering cultural information as an added-value product to tourism experiences may serve as an appropriate development option that meets tourists' desires for meaningful and sincere encounters whilst ensuring heightened appreciation of indigenous culture.... As such, less formally structured or less staged cultural experiences that allow both tourist and host to communicate and interact in a meaningful manner, in what may be termed an "exchange of sincerity," may constitute the most appropriate development option for indigenous tourism, thus effecting the ability of tourism encounters to be mutually beneficial for host and tourist alike (McIntosh 2004:12f).

These findings from three countries have important implications for product development, which will be discussed in the following chapter. The overall importance of market realism in aboriginal tourism development worldwide cannot be overemphasized. It is unconscionable and irresponsible for government officials, industry representatives or community leaders to encourage indigenous people to develop tourism products on the assumption that all visitors have a strong interest in their culture. Particularly in view of the potential role of tourism in furthering cultural pride and revitalizing cultural traditions, wrong assumptions about a potential market for indigenous tourism products can be extremely damaging not only for socio-economic sustainability, but also for cultural sustainability. On the other hand, it is worthwhile for all stakeholders to further explore visitor preferences to enable aboriginal people to match visitor demand in a fashion that nurtures their culture, society and economy.

European Subcultures and their Implications for Indigenous Tourism

Indianism or Indian Hobbyism

One of the reasons for overly optimistic expectations regarding the European and particularly the German market for North American indigenous tourism is the phenomenon of Indianism or Indian hobbyism. In Germany, Indianism finds its expression in an estimated 100 separate Indian clubs, where members organize camps, powwows and other festivals, don Indian dress, paint and headdresses and live the Native American world as they imagine it. Most of these "Hobby Indianer" have never visited North America, and have no detailed knowledge of the historical or current reality of Native Americans or First Nations, nor are they aware of their cultural variety and complexity, adhering mostly to the Plains tipi and feathers prototype. Others, however, own extensive artifact collections, wear hand-sewn costumes patterned after museum exhibits or textbook illustrations, and have deeply immersed themselves in studying a (historical) native culture of their choice. Some individuals have designed a whole way of life around this "hobby" and feel enriched by the experience (*Globe and Mail*, April 16 and September 3, 1996).

Germany's infatuation with North American Indians is nothing new. Throughout the 20th century the first Indian that many Germans came to love was Winnetou, legendary chief of the Mescalero Apaches and noblest of all Indian warriors. This "noble savage" prototype and his bloodbrother Old Shatterhand (so-called because he could kill a man with a blow of his fist), a German immigrant, were both creations of the imagination of Karl May (1842–1912), a hugely popular turn-of-the-century German adventure writer. Almost unknown to readers in North America, May wrote more than 60 books, the most celebrated of which were his tales about the American West. Initially aimed at a juvenile market, Karl May's stories began appearing in the late 1870s. His writings were quickly adopted by a wider reading public, and he became

Illustration 3.5

Winnetou and Old Shatterhand, as depicted in the 1964 Film *Winnetou II*. This film and its companions introduced the Karl May phenomenon to the 1960s generation of Germans.

Source: www.karl-may-archiv.de. Reproduced from Michael Petzel, "Der Weg zum Silbersee" (Schwarzkopf & Schwarzkopf Verlag 2001). Illustration #20 of the Winnetou II section. Reprinted here with permission of Michael Petzel.

more famous throughout Europe than any other writer on the subject, including American writers.

Ironically, when he wrote his books, the author had never set foot on American soil, and he largely researched his material in German prison libraries while serving time for, among other things, fraud and impersonation. Nevertheless, his books continue to be hugely popular. They have sold more than 100 million copies in 30 languages worldwide, far more than any other single German author, including Goethe, Hesse and Mann (Langley 1997:10). Karl May's history and ethnology are far from accurate, but, a voracious reader himself, he had a vivid style, was a wonderful storyteller, and all his tales showed a strong humanitarian and pacifist undercurrent. Above all they are characterized by a positive and sympathetic portrayal of the American Indian (and other oppressed groups, such as the Kurds in his Middle Eastern tales). The Winnetou tales in particular experienced a strong revival during the 1960s, with the German production of a number of films loosely based on May's writings. They were produced at spectacular locations in Croatia, with Pierre Brice, a French actor, providing the ideal incarnation of Winnetou. They introduced the main characters to a whole new generation. Being a German child of the sixties herself, this writer can attest from personal experience to the near cult status of these films. An unprecedented marketing campaign, with collector postcards, pictures and figures, went hand in hand with these productions.

The 1990s witnessed a revival of these films and the production of a new film in 1998, with Winnetou returning from the dead! Annual open air productions of May's works are another time-honoured tradition in Germany. Though not all Hobby Indians credit Karl May as a motivating force, he has had an important impact on the German psyche vis-a-vis the North American Indian.

Germans and other Europeans of the late 19th and early 20th century, however, were not only exposed to fictional Indians. In 1887, "Buffalo Bill's Wild West" embarked on its first European tour, starting in London. After visiting France, Spain and Italy on a second tour, it finally reached Germany in 1890. Ninety-Seven Native Americans, most of them Lakota from North and South Dakota, as well as Arapaho and Cheyenne, accompanied Buffalo Bill's show (Bolz 1989:480). Buffalo Bill and his entourage spent extended periods of time in Germany, performing in countless cities. In the present age of mass media the impact of such exhibits is difficult to fathom. As described by Bolz (Ibid.:481), long before the show opened it was advertised on large posters and in newspaper advertisements, drawing huge crowds to the train stations to witness its arrival. A Dortmund newspaper of May 13, 1891, describes the spectacle as follows:

> "Hundreds of people have gathered to watch the strange spectacle. This jumble of Indians, horses, and buffalos that finally fell into formation and slowly marched towards the Fredenbaum [festival grounds in Dortmund] was quite a sight indeed. First came the buffalos, surrounded by mounted drivers, and then the Indians on their horses, trailed by a strange vehicle, obviously a former stage coach from the Wild West pulled by four mules. Especially the Indians attracted attention with their

copper-coloured faces that were sometimes painted, their fantastically bright-colored costumes, and their strange headdresses." (quoted in Klotzbach 1982:37)

Bolz (1989) gives us a fitting assessment of the likely impact of such an experience in Germany:

> At a time when people did not get to view the wide world each evening through television, this mass concentration of figures coming from a far away land and bygone days must have made an impression that can hardly be comprehended today. The after-effects, however, can still be traced up to the present. The characters appearing in the works of Karl May and other authors were mere products of the imagination and either so noble or so evil that their deeds could hardly be identified with nor were worth striving after. With Buffalo Bill it was another matter. Here real live people appeared before the public to offer at least a glimpse of their true life experiences as well as exotic costumes. Garments, feathered headdresses, dances, camp life, etc. were concrete things for Germans, which they could copy and through which they could transform fantasies that had been stimulated by literature into active deeds.
>
> Other authors who have studied the after-effect of the Wild West also trace the development of Wild West clubs in Germany back to Buffalo Bill: "Large crowds of Germans thronged to Buffalo Bill's shows — and they didn't lose their enthusiasm for the Wild West after the troupe had departed again. For years they had kept track of the fantasy deeds of Old Shatterhand, the frontier hero of German author Karl May. Now they founded associations in order to act out their frontier fantasies. Wild West clubs were born in almost every German city." (O'Neill 1981:78) (Bolz 1989:482)

Buffalo Bill had a number of emulators, none of whom matched his success. There were other types of shows that also brought Indian people to Europe, among them Colonel Frederic T. Cummins "Ethnological Congress of Red Men," which toured Europe, including Germany, between 1907 and 1912. Lakota were also featured in human exhibits by Carl Hagenbeck's Zoological Garden near Hamburg in 1910 and by circus director Sarrasani in 1912 (Bolz 1989:483). Considering the frequent appearance of Lakota in Germany between

1890 and 1914, it is hardly surprising that their culture is better known and more frequently emulated by hobbyists than any other, including Karl May's noble Apache. There can be little doubt, that the emergence of Indian hobbyism or Indianism in Germany can be traced to the appearance of Lakota and other Plains Indians prior to World War I (Ibid.:484). Many of these early clubs and associations were revived after both World Wars and continue their activities to the present day.

The perceived German affinity for North American Indians is the most intensely studied and publicised case, and also the most frequently invoked one in tourism circles. As documented by Feest (2002), there is abundant evidence, however, that the desire to identify with Indian people is indeed a widespread European trait, rather than just a German aberration. The same is true for the phenomenon of Indianism, which not only has a tradition throughout Europe (Taylor 1988), but also in the United States (Powers 1988). The roots for this fascination with another culture and the forces shaping it vary from place to place and over time. Its origins in the United States are closely tied to the Boy Scouts movement, but Indian Hobbyism evolved from there to become imitative of pan-Indianism (Ibid.:560).

An important factor elsewhere was escapism from technological society, as well as from contemporary political realities, the latter particularly in eastern Europe prior to the fall of the iron curtain. Three articles in a 1993 issue of the *European Review of Native American Studies* illustrate this phenomenon for France, Hungary and the former East Germany (Dubois 1993; Turski 1993; N.N.1993), and Nowicka (1989) presents an interesting account on the "Polish Movement of Friends of the American Indian." Particularly in former socialist countries, activities in Indianist groups reflected a 'drop-out' position and represented a certain potential for political opposition. Such groups were also frequently joined by young people, who were primarily interested in ecological alternatives, and who saw no other outlet for alternative lifestyles under their state's restrictive practices. Indianist groups are also found in Russia, Great Britain, Bulgaria, Denmark, Sweden, Belgium, the Netherlands, Italy and even Japan. Some have made contact with Native Americans and First Nations. The following is an excerpt of a letter from Bulgaria that was received in 1994 by the publishers of *Spirit Talk*, a Blackfoot journal in Montana:

"You Can Recognize a Red Indian by His Way of Life, Not by His Blood Percentage." Chief Lame Deer (Lakota)

....

The Red Indian Way, which we, the people from the Eagle's Circle have adopted, is good and powerful. Native Americans had, in their life, achieved a harmonious balance between their inner being and the outer world. Then the White Man came; he robbed and destroyed that world, thus committing a heavy sin. Perhaps the Great Spirit's wish is that we, descendants of white folk, but bearing Red Indian hearts, should add our effort to restore the broken balance. We ardently believe that is so, because we are steadily following our Way. It all started back in the years of our childhood and adolescence, with the "Red Indian" novels and films, which later inspired an unquenchable thirst for authentic information on Red Indian history, culture, and spirit, so scarce to find in Bulgaria. Our knowledge gradually expanded, our feelings and thoughts matured, and although there is still a lot to learn, we are well aware which our way is, as well as how and why we are following it. We have the sincere and whole-hearted support of our friends from Russia, Germany, Belgium and other countries. We have also established connections with some Native Americans, representing the people of Black-feet, Lakota, Apache, Navajo, and Mohawk; the Omaha people sent the Eagle's Circle a Sacred Pipe, which is the symbol of Red Indian faith.

Our society includes a number of groups: Lakota, Cheyenne, Blackfeet, Crow, Pawnee, Comanche, Navajo, Ojibwa. The members of each group study "their" people's culture and traditions in great depth; they have a sense of belonging to this people and its spirit; they treat it as their second native home!

You can find us in the libraries, where we spend our time researching on the spiritual and material culture of the native Americans. You can also find us at our camps, on our powwows, where we dance, sing and exchange opinions in the traditional Red Indian style. Bulgarian mountains, river valleys and lake shores are a beautiful and everlasting source of energy and inspiration (*Spirit Talk* 1(1):9).

Indian people in North America have reacted to this phenomenon with puzzlement as well as a great generosity of spirit. In 1995 a Canadian film team followed three aboriginal people from Manitoba (two Cree and an Ojibwa) as they travelled to the former Czechoslovakia to meet several hundred Czechs and Slovaks who had set up a remarkable "Indian" community. The resultant film by John Paskievich, with the title "If Only I were an Indian...", introduces a group of people who do more than just set up tipi camps and wear Indian clothing. To a remarkable extent they have embraced elements of traditional Cheyenne society, including food preparation, play and recreation, as well as child rearing and conflict resolution, religion and philosophy. This moving film also documents the conceptual journey of the three Canadian Indians, who, after initial shock and alienation, came to accept this "European tribe" with a sense of brotherhood and humanity.

While the Indian Hobbyist or Indianist movement reflects an important cultural phenomenon in Europe (and North America) and certainly attests to a strong feeling of affinity with North American Indians within certain segments of the population, its positive implications for aboriginal tourism are vastly overrated. This socio-cultural phenomenon varies considerably from country to country, but none of the sources detailing Indianist activities and interests makes any mention of travel and tourism. This is not really surprising, since Indian hobbyism and recreational travel serve essentially the same function: escape from the daily routine and immersion in a different reality. Indianists accomplish this without leaving their home environment; they create and manufacture their parallel universe in their own backyard, often investing substantial time and financial resources that otherwise might be used for travel. As a result, people active in such organizations do not necessarily have the means or inclination to travel, and those few who do may have very specific and unrealistic goals, such as participating in a sundance (see next chapter). Empirical research on this interesting issue is still outstanding:

> Another fact that is frequently overlooked is the relatively minor scope of this kind of cultural transvestism. Even if the number of organized Indian hobbyists in Germany is in the range of between 10,000 and 20,000, this may seem much when compared to the residential population of most Indian reservations, but then this number is widely scattered across the country and amounts at best to as little as a quarter of one tenth of a percent of the total population (Feest 2002:33).

New Age Travel

Like Indianism, the New Age movement is a socio-cultural phenomenon in Western society with important implications for indigenous people. Unlike Indianism, for most indigenous hosts this is not a market to be courted, but rather one to be cautious of. It can be described as a broad-based amalgam of diverse spiritual, social and political elements with the common goal of transforming individuals and society through spiritual awareness (Microsoft Encarta 1998). The movement introduced feminist, ecological, spiritual and human-potential concerns into the mainstream in the 1980s, and has created a huge market in the United States and Europe for books, magazines, workshops, retreats, and expositions on the subject, as well as for natural foods, crystals, meditation and healing aids. Drawing on several sociological studies, Kyle (1995) profiles New Agers as follows:

> The New Age is an international phenomenon... yet its greatest strength is in North America, especially the United States. Within the U.S., New Age representation varies according to geographical region .... New Agers are most likely to live on the Pacific coast, the Rocky Mountain region, and the South Atlantic area, especially Florida .... New Agers tend to live in clusters. Authorities outside the movement [contend that now] the movement attracts middle-aged people — primarily women (about 70 percent) who are in most cases financially able to maintain a comfortable lifestyle .... New Agers usually possess a better-than-average education and are urban, middle class, upwardly mobile, and not particularly alienated from society. New Age religion .... has a special relationship with the baby boomers (those born between 1946 and 1964) .... and was a response to the social situation of the counterculture. [They] have incubated/transmitted New Age religion to other parts of American society (Kyle 1995:10f).

Often viewed as resurgent paganism, the modern movement has more recent roots in 19th century spiritualism and in the 1960s counterculture, which rejected materialism in favour of Eastern mysticism, and which preferred direct spiritual experience to organized religion. The New Age movement is extremely multi-directional, embracing eastern philosophies, extrasensory perception, alchemy, the occult, divination, shamanism, psychic healing and numerous other elements in a seemingly arbitrary fashion. It is not a focused reorientation towards indigenous European roots, such as Celtic or Germanic beliefs and practices, but in many ways constitutes a spiritual quest of a spiritually disconnected culture. One may even go so far as identifying it as yet another aspect of cultural and social globalization, despite its counterculture orientation.

In view of the modern America of consumer-driven culture and comparison shopping, Creedon (1998, quoted in Attix 2002:51) describes it as a "smorgasbord, a cafeteria approach to spirituality."

The New Age phenomenon has created a whole new segment in the travel market. Unlike Indian hobbyists, New Agers are prolific travellers. A 1985 audit of magazine subscribers revealed that 50 percent of *New Age Magazine* readers went on foreign trips, compared to a 14 percent average among 85 other magazines covered by the audit. Also, 40 percent more *New Age Journal* subscribers travelled domestically than other readers (Attix 2002:53). A study of New Age tour operators showed a preoccupation with travel to so-called power sites, sacred sites and energy vortices (for example around Sedona, Arizona, the capital of U.S. New Age tourism) and engagement with their unique qualities. Related interests were focused on the practice of indigenous or earth-centred rituals, such as Native American sweat lodges and the exploration of self for wellness and personal development through yoga retreats and other Eastern practices (Ibid.):

> In compiling results from the survey of New Age tour operators, it became apparent that each of the six tour topic segments [power sites; eco-spirit; shamanism; vision quests; health/wellness; other] may represent a type of orientation paralleling psychographic market segmentation typologies developed since the late 1970s: first, inwards (towards the process of self-improvement); second, outwards (towards an identification with the earth and related nature spiritualities — often site-specific); or third, an integration of both (combining process-driven practices with the use of certain special places, as is usually the case with most indigenous religious traditions). These are termed here "inner," "outer," and "both." Clearly, *the largest interests in topics among these operators and their clientele were in the area of indigenous practices (e.g., shamanism)* and versions of vision questing, within the "both" category. Secondary interest, at least in terms of survival rate of small business over the past five years, lies within tours focusing on power-sites and eco-spirit, which can be considered "outer" directed categories. Finally, the tours or workshops that focus on health/wellness, inner retreat centres and other New Age travel services (tailoring themselves to the visitor/group), have had mixed results over the past five years, at least in this sample. They now appear (2002) to be among the fastest growing.

A contrast worth noting is that while many tour clients had cited personal rites/testing as their reason for touring, they seem to be gravitating to those operators who offer a strong emphasis on Place in their programming. *The goal for these travellers is not merely an internal quest, yet they also show little indication of awareness about how they may be externally impacting host populations and religious sensibilities* (Attix 2002:56, emphasis added).

A characteristic of the New Age paradigm is the belief that there are no boundaries to an individual's potential and, thus, no clear demarcations between cultural and religious traditions (Ibid.:53). This is in sharp contrast to indigenous people's belief in the connectivity between people, place and spirituality and the sense of belonging to a particular place. New Agers tend to deconstruct traditionally observed protocols of behaviour and respect; they do not recognize an exclusive relationship between a sacred place and its traditional stewards or between sacred rituals and their rightful "owners." Krippendorf's (1989) observation of travellers' motives being primarily self-centred and egoistic seems to be validated here to a remarkable degree. On the other hand, New Age tour operators cite concern for the environment as their primary reason for entering into the travel business (Attix 2002:55). It is significant that hardly any of the New Age guidebooks offer their readers any directives as to appropriate protocols of behaviour or etiquette in the practice of pseudo-traditional ceremonies or at culturally sensitive sites, let alone point out that such attempts at replication are not welcome and have, indeed, been banned by indigenous authorities in recent years (Ibid.).

For many indigenous people New Agers commit cultural appropriation and cultural theft of the worst kind. They object to Westerners attending workshops on indigenous spirituality or even undergoing apprenticeships with indigenous shamans in such diverse environments as the Ecuadorean Andes, the Amazon, Guatemala, South Africa and Siberia. Charlotte Black Elk, a spiritual and cultural leader of the Lakota, expresses her view of New Age spiritual "wannabes" as follows:

> As for New Agers, you have people who are on a genuine search for fulfilment, but they don't want to take the time to learn their own traditions, or they're totally fascinated with Native American religion. They're seeking power now, like the weight loss pills.

I'm Charlotte Black Elk. People come up to me all the time and say, "I read your grandfather's book, *Black Elk Speaks*." They want to be part of something poetic. Well, I tell them, I'm not my grandfather.

One of the dividing lines has been when I tell the New Age practitioners, "Go prepare for seven years." Most of them want a hodgepodge of things without embracing the total culture. Those people treat Native American ceremonies like they would a diving vacation to the Bahamas...

In white America, they're able to buy their place in society. They can't understand why they can't buy a place in a Native American community (*High Country News,* May 26, 1997:9).

Other concerns focus on the invasion of sacred places by outsiders (see Chapter Five). Invariably such undertakings are facilitated and marketed by external organizations or institutions. The Internet is abuzz with opportunities to "explore ancient shamanic knowledge." Despite widespread protests from indigenous people, there are willing hosts within aboriginal communities, and there seems to be little critical discourse about the implications of this kind of cross-cultural encounter.

Travel Trade Intermediaries

Tourism is about partnerships, and nowhere is this more relevant than for newcomers to the industry like aboriginal tourism product suppliers targeting a niche market. Among the various representatives of the travel trade, tour operators are by far the most important for local product providers to consider as potential conduits for accessing the international market and part of the domestic market. Having their product incorporated in a package designed by an inbound or overseas outbound tour operator not only provides the critical mass of products to attract clients but also gives the local operator access to a marketing network and marketing expertise, that would otherwise be missing. Such a partnership, however, is not easily developed. The need to protect themselves (EU consumer protection legislation) and their reputation means that tour operators are generally reluctant to work with product suppliers who have not proven themselves for at least two years.

Many tour operators express the opinion that there is considerable demand for aboriginal tourism experiences, but that they do not know enough about what is available and whether it is up to standards. There is a perceived lack of reliability and consistency with regard to product delivery, particularly in view of the need for advance planning and long term supplier commitment. The following are examples of travel trade intermediaries, who feature aboriginal tourism experiences in their packages. They exhibit considerable variety in terms of size, ownership, location and degree of specialization.

Creative Western Adventures is a Canadian inbound tour operator based in Calgary, Alberta, offering adventure, cultural and ecotourism experiences in western and northwestern Canada. Switzerland, Germany and Belgium constitute close to 90 percent of this operator's market. *Creative Western Adventures* offers pre-packaged, customized and self-guided tours, and sells directly as well as through European wholesalers. The company works with selected Aboriginal tourism product suppliers, such as *EagleStar Tours* on the Tsuu T'ina Reserve, and two others in northern Alberta and British Columbia, respectively. President Susanne Eugster emphasizes the importance of quality control and of hand-picked partnerships with product suppliers that evolve and are cultivated over years. Reliability and trustworthiness are key ingredients in such relationships. She also stresses how important it is to realize that the market for aboriginal tourism is a niche market. She cautions against overestimating the interest of the overseas market in native tourism products, based on the phenomenon of so-called "Hobby-Indianer" and Indian clubs in Germany and other European countries. *Creative Western Adventures'* experience seems to bear out the importance of developing "themes" in tour packages. Aboriginal elements can easily be fitted into a "Western" theme, be it culture- or adventure-oriented. "Footsteps of Athapascan Tribes in Alberta" (11 days) is a rare example of an exclusively aboriginal themed tour, and also one of those packages rarely filled to capacity.

Coming to terms with a rather limited market demand was also a problem for *The Talking Bridge*, an outbound operator in Germany. This company, which operated from 1994 to 1999, concentrated exclusively on aboriginal destinations and experiences, primarily in Canada and Montana. In order to make their tours affordable, they tried to work directly with local suppliers, without using inbound tour operators. This created difficult logistical and communication issues. Tour participants tended to be well-off, well educated and genuinely interested in aboriginal people and their culture. The main problem was limited demand: group sizes between two and six participants simply did not permit economic viability for the company.

A third example of a travel trade intermediary dealing in aboriginal tourism experiences is *Trail of the Great Bear*. The *Trail of the Great Bear* is an international tour traversing 2,085 miles of the Rocky Mountains in Canada and the United States. It derives its name from the grizzly bear of the Rocky Mountains. Travelling existing roadways, the Trail links the world's first national park, Yellowstone, to Canada's first national parks, Banff-Jasper. It is a unique example of an ecosystem-based approach to tourism destination management, focused on creating awareness of the region's natural and cultural heritage. The *Trail of the Great Bear* also functions as a private sector tour operator (with offices in Alberta and Montana), offering a variety of programs and services, such as tour reservations, customized packages, fully escorted group tours and personalized itineraries and trip planning. Its major marketing focus is long-haul U.S. travellers.

The aboriginal element is an important one for the *Trail of the Great Bear*. However, success with this type of experience has been mixed. For approximately five years the organization experimented with cultural immersion home-stay programs and a Blackfeet Country Tour (for a British wholesaler), but with limited results. President Beth Russell-Towe feels that this may in part be due to not finding the right wholesalers, but it is more likely that the market for such experiences is extremely limited. She, too, thinks that it is more realistic to include aboriginal tourism as just one component in a broader tourism experience, and reiterates the importance of partnerships between tour operators and local product owners.

Nevertheless, there are other specialty operators, exclusively focusing on the encounter with indigenous peoples. True to its name, *Journeys Into American Indian Territory* (based in New York State) offers an immersion in Native American cultures in various parts of the United States. Its founder and director, Robert Vetter, is a non-native anthropologist who builds on his established relationships with select Native American groups to conduct three- to seven-day-long immersion programs. On an international scale, *Turtle Tours,* based in Arizona (www.turtletours.com), has been in operation since 1988 and specializes in small group travel, to meet with indigenous groups such as tribal communities in India, the Bayaka Pygmies in the Central African Republic and the Tuareg of Niger. This enterprise, too, owes its existence to the initiative and special interest of an individual, in this case Irma Turtle. Her focus is on Africa, and her personal contacts yield possibilities for unique journeys. Visitation by her groups seems to be viewed as a positive influence by host communities, as great care is taken to avoid negative impacts, while trip members bring along such items as aspirin, antibiotics and small practical gifts (Ginsberg 1994:92). The company accommodates 80 to 100 people per year who are willing to make do with a minimum "environmental bubble."

Considering the role of such transitional companies in shaping the tourism business culture and in generating tourist perceptions and expectations (see Jafari 1989 and beginning of this chapter), it is important that indigenous people are not only in a position to influence such companies, but that they also gain control and ownership of them. This is increasingly happening in many parts of the world. In Canada's western Arctic, for example, the two principal inbound tour companies based in Inuvik (packaging and combining products offered by local operators in Inuvik and other locations), *Arctic Nature Tours* and *Arctic Tour Company,* are both aboriginal owned.

In Australia, Aboriginal Development Corporations are increasingly entering the tourism business by either establishing their own companies or by acquiring majority shares of existing ones. *Mamabulanjin Aboriginal Tours* in Broome, Western Australia, is an example for the first option. It is one of several enterprises owned by Mamabulanjin Aboriginal Corporation along with a construction company, and business incubation and security services. This diversification enables employees of the seasonal tourism business to find employment in other branches of the corporation. The tour company is fully Aboriginal owned and operated and offers visitors day tours in Broome and surroundings for an introduction into the Aboriginal lifestyle. Currently there are plans to coordinate the activities of various outlying Aboriginal communities of the Dampier Peninsula, some of whom have already started tourism initiatives of their own (Interview notes of October 19, 2001, Broome).

Kimberley Wilderness Adventures, also based in Broome, had been in existence for a decade when in 2000 the Wunan Foundation acquired 70 percent of its shares. The Wunan Foundation is an Economic Development Corporation owned by Aboriginal groups of the East Kimberley Region. While the tour company receives direction from an Aboriginal board, its day to day business continues under non-Aboriginal management. The change in ownership has not effected any fundamental changes in *Kimberley Wilderness Adventures'* practices, since there was already a strong orientation towards Aboriginal community involvement, and there had been ongoing negotiations with Land Councils for establishing camps on Aboriginal lands. At times half of the company's 10 guides (respon-

Illustration 3.6

Travelling with *Kimberley Wilderness Adventures*: Guide Ros Consoli explains Aboriginal rock art to a spellbound audience (Manaro Site, Western Australia).

sible for tours and vehicles) have been Aboriginal, but there is a high turnover. The guides on these extended tours in very remote country are the key to tourist behaviour and "tourist culture." This writer had the opportunity to participate in a 10-day tour with this company, which took a small group of seven through little visited parts of the Kimberley region of northwestern Australia. Our guide was a young non-Aboriginal woman, who was deeply immersed in, and quite knowledgeable about, Aboriginal culture.

With the explicit permission of the traditional owners (of the "country" in question) we visited not only rock art sites usually open to the public, but also more sensitive places, such as strongly spiritual sites and burial grounds. In each case prohibition of access to certain parts, prohibition of photography and symbolic purification were strictly and respectfully observed by everyone. Visitation of such sites is, however, a sensitive subject, and there have been cases, where spiritual sites have been abandoned by traditional practitioners due to too many visitors trespassing. *Kimberley Wilderness Adventures* can probably be regarded as a "best practices" case, not only in terms of shaping visitor behaviour, but also with regard to environmental practices in its seasonal camps set up on Aboriginal lands. There are further plans for increasing on-site guiding by Aboriginal people and for more involvement of traditional owners in the camps, each of which seems a better fit for Aboriginal participation than full-time employment as guides. There are also plans for expanding the innovative concept of "Bush University," which will be discussed in the next chapter.

Indigenous people's motivation for getting involved in the tourism industry is often focused on more than economic benefits, and includes social and cultural well-being. For this reason the ethical nature of tourism operators is a valid concern for indigenous product owners when faced with a choice of a joint venture partner or with a prospective operator to include their product in a tour package. While ethical practices in a business context in general have attracted considerable attention by practitioners and researchers in recent years, the investigation of the ethical aspects of tourism is at a relatively early stage (Fennell & Malloy 1999:940). Fennell and Malloy set out to explore the ethical nature and standards of conduct of tourism operators in various fields of the industry, namely ecotourism, adventure tourism, fishing, golf and cruiseline operations in the western United States and Canada. Operators were asked to respond to tourism-specific scenarios, illustrating economic, social and ecological dilemmas.

The findings of this study gave a strong indication that operators in the tourism industry can by no means be considered homogeneous in terms of their ethical orientation. Specifically, the results suggest that ecotourism operators have a more heightened sense of ethical conduct than do their peers in other ventures. The authors speculate that three variables may be responsible for such heightened ethical orientation (Ibid.:938f). First, the education level of the ecotourism operators was significantly higher than that of other cohorts in the tourism industry. There is evidence of a positive correlation between the level of education and the ability to make more cognitively complex moral decisions. A second rationale for this finding is the fact that ecotour operators reported the use of codes of ethics in their business practices to a much greater degree (95 percent) than other tourism operators. Hence they can be expected to have a heightened awareness of acceptable conduct and a consistent ethical approach throughout their business operation. A third rationale concerns organizational size. There is evidence that the larger the organization, the more difficult it becomes to maintain a consistent ethical approach as a result of physical and psychological distance from the central leadership. In this study the cruiseline/golf operators were the largest in terms of organization size as compared to ecotour, adventure, and fishing operators. They were also the least ethical of the four cohorts. At the turn of the millennium, few industry associations or political jurisdictions employed the use of ethical standards in the evaluation of tourism operations. This is gradually changing with current efforts being concentrated on an alliance between GREEN GLOBE and the Australian Nature and Ecotourism Accreditation Program (NEAP) to develop and establish an international ecotourism standard. Such efforts need not be confined to the field of ecotourism alone.

There is a need for the various stakeholders and players in the tourism industry to learn more about the Aboriginal tourism product and its environment. The operators briefly portrayed above are exceptional in that they are knowledgeable and culturally sensitive. Tour operators and wholesalers operate in a high pressure, competitive and volatile environment, and it is not easy for them to take a leap of faith with a new product or a new partner. This may explain the rather cautious reaction on the part of European wholesalers and travel agencies to the Canadian Tourism Commission's exorbitantly expensive *Live the Legacy* initiative, a glossy brochure showcasing Canada's aboriginal tourism products, aimed at overseas buyers. In Germany the latter expressed concerns about liability and quality standards and the special requirements of niche products. In some cases inbound receptive tour operators, such as *Creative Western Adventures* or *Trail of the Great Bear,* who are intimately familiar with local conditions and cultural protocol, may serve to alleviate such concerns.

Summary

This chapter critically engages with the first of the three key elements of indigenous tourism, "the stranger." It starts out with a discussion of some cautionary assumptions about tourists in general and the implications of social change for their validity. Conclusive evidence as to how "different" modern tourists really are is hard to come by. It would be wise for aboriginal hosts to bear in mind that tourist motives can be egocentric and escapist. Such caution is particularly important in view of the complexity of the tourist encounter. Not only does the host meet the guest, but the host culture is exposed to a "tourist culture" (a product of the industry and varying according to tourism activities), a residual culture dependent on the traveller's ethics, and the business culture of transitional companies such as resorts, tour operators and wholesalers. The degree to which these external cultural forces can be influenced by the host community depends on its empowerment.

The market for indigenous tourism remains surprisingly elusive. Product development and planning tend to be strongly focused on international markets, even though in most destinations domestic travellers predominate. For aboriginal hosts it is important to realize that there are substantial differences between foreign and domestic market demand regarding quality and quantity of aboriginal tourism products. Not only is there the notion of "distance breeds enchantment" versus "familiarity breeds contempt" that affects interest in indigenous tourism; domestic tourism is embedded in the broader discourse between aboriginal people and other nationals. Conflict between these parties over land, resources, and political emancipation is likely to impact domestic interest in aboriginal tourism products negatively. This is particularly the case if indigenous people choose to incorporate their struggle in a "tourism message."

Overall, we still know too little about what kind of indigenous tourism experience travellers actually seek. Selected case studies from Canada, Australia and New Zealand only begin to scratch the surface of this problem. Differences between these studies in research design, sampling method and overall context make it difficult to draw general conclusions from them. Nevertheless, preliminary lessons can be gleaned from their examination. The research findings do not suggest that indigenous tourism should be viewed as a stand-alone product for a larger market, but that its potential lies in being combined with other themes, such as nature-based tourism, adventure tourism or even other cultural themes. On the other hand, there are also indications that there is a more limited market for in-depth, interactive ethnic experiences. Among those visitors who are interested in interacting with indigenous hosts and immersing themselves in aboriginal culture, a broad spectrum is present ranging from a desire for relatively superficial encounters to an interest in more cultural intimacy than may be acceptable to hosts.

Market realism is of paramount importance. North American stakeholders in aboriginal tourism often have anecdotal knowledge of Indianism or Indian Hobbyism in Germany and other European countries, and automatically conclude that there is a huge market for aboriginal tourism products in these locations. A closer investigation of this socio-cultural phenomenon in different countries reveals considerable complexity as to its roots and expressions. To date no empirical research on the relationship between Indianism and tourism has been conducted, but there is every indication that overblown expectations of these groups as a potential market for indigenous tourism are misplaced. The New Age movement is another socio-cultural phenomenon in Western society with important implications for indigenous people. New Agers are prolific travellers, but present numerous challenges for aboriginal hosts, many of whom regard their interest in aboriginal spirituality and sacred places as inappropriate and intrusive.

The chapter concludes with a discussion of travel trade intermediaries. These are organizations such as tour operators and wholesalers that mediate between aboriginal product suppliers and visitors who consume this product. They may be aboriginal or non-aboriginal, and play a very important role in determining how a product is presented to potential consumers and how the consumer approaches the product and the host community. Strictly speaking, they are fully part of neither "the stranger" nor "the native," but may belong to both and are crucial players in the industry. A number of different tour operators who feature indigenous tourism products are introduced. Tour operators and wholesalers must function in a very competitive and volatile environment and understandably place much value on reliability and consistency of product delivery. aboriginal product suppliers must overcome potential buyers' concerns about liability and quality standards.

4

...the Native...

Introduction

The last chapter has shown how challenging it can be to understand the complexity of "the stranger" as a factor in indigenous tourism. Part of the challenge is a realistic assessment of the market for indigenous tourism products. On the one hand, it appears most feasible to combine aboriginal tourism products with other themes such as nayure-based or adventure tourism. On the other hand there is a more limited market for specialized and interactive ethnic tourism products on a stand alone basis. These two approaches to product development and packaging are not mutually exclusive, and they each carry their own inherent risks and pitfalls. As pointed out by Ryan and Huyton (2000a:82f), a recommendation to offer aboriginal culture as an "added value" to mainstream tourism products should be explored with considerable caution. One of the main pitfalls is a risk of simplification, commodification and loss of control by indigenous people.

Where there is, on the other hand, a genuine interest on the part of the visitor to learn more about and penetrate deeper into indigenous culture, it should be made clear that such demand does not itself convey rights. It is indigenous people's prerogative to refuse participation in this kind of tourism and/or to establish boundaries as they see fit. The use of social space and the assignment of certain roles to tourists by indigenous hosts play an important part in their management strategies. These management strategies provide the main focus for this chapter. It investigates how different indigenous groups accommodate large and small numbers of tourists, some of them content with staged presentations "at arm's length," others intent on penetrating into the host culture's inner sanctum. Furthermore, wherever cultural representation is involved in tourism, we encounter the issue of authenticity, which is also explored in this chapter.

Not all tourism impacts on host communities can be explored here in detail. The potential for socio-cultural impacts such as the demonstration effect, "marginal men (or women)," a rise in prostitution and crime, and a lack of control over a change in values is counterbalanced by possible socio-cultural benefits, such as positive cultural exchange, validation of cultural identity and education. Tourism is an equally double-edged sword with regard to economic and environmental impacts. The quality and severity of such impacts are determined by several variables:

• The type of tourism pursued and the resultant nature of the relationship between hosts and guests;

- The length of the period during which tourism development occurs, and the speed of this development;
- The relationship between the number of tourists and the social and environmental carrying capacity of the community/facility/region (adapted from Tsartas 1992:531).

The factor of control is a crucial one in determining the extent to which these variables come into play. In their Indigenous Tourism Matrix (Figure 4.1), Hinch and Butler (1996:9f) illustrate the interplay of two key aspects of indigenous tourism: control and indigenous culture content.

In this matrix, the horizontal axis represents the degree of control that indigenous people have over a given tourism product. At the left end of the continuum aboriginal groups have no control at all, whereas on the right end they are fully in control, including ownership and management. Between these extremes there are different levels of control, including the influence of indigenous people in a variety of roles such as employees, advisory board members, and formal partners in development. The vertical axis represents the degree to which the tourist attraction is based on an indigenous

Figure 4.1

		Indigenous Control	
		Low Degree of Control	*High Degree of Control*
	Indigenous Theme Present	Culture Dispossessed	Controlled Culture
Indigenous Theme			
	Indigenous Theme Absent	Non-Indigenous Tourism	Diversified Indigenous

Indigenous Tourism Matrix

Source: Richard Butler and Thomas Hinch (Eds.), *Tourism and indigenous peoples*, 1e, edited by , (London and Boston: International Thomson Business Press, 1996), p.10. Reprinted with permission of authors.

theme, which may be anything from totally absent to the primary focus of the product:

> Tourism enterprises which are both controlled by indigenous people and which feature an indigenous attraction theme clearly fall within the scope of the definition of indigenous tourism (Culture controlled). Just as clearly, tourism activity which is neither controlled by indigenous people nor which features an indigenous theme, lies outside of the purview of this book [*Tourism and Indigenous People*] (Non-indigenous Tourism). Tourism enterprises which are controlled by indigenous interests, but which do not feature a central attraction that is based on indigenous culture represent part of the middle ground between the two extremes just noted (Diversified indigenous). Examples of this type of activity include the trend towards native-owned casinos in the United States. Similarly, there is a substantial level of tourism activity that is developed around indigenous attraction themes but in which indigenous people themselves have little or no controlling interest (Culture dispossessed) (Hinch & Butler 1996:10).

Depending on where in this matrix indigenous hosts find themselves, the challenges encountered and the options to address them will vary considerably. An interesting process regarding the level of involvement in tourism and control by the host community was illustrated by Zeppel (1998) for the case of the Iban in Sarawak, Borneo. It involved the transition **from entertainers to entrepreneurs, from "culture providers" to "culture managers."** Three different Iban longhouse communities represented a continuum of different levels of Iban involvement in tourism. They ranged from the community acting as a service supplier to one tour operator in one village, a partnership with an ecotourism company in a second community, to community control of tourism and guesthouse facilities in a third case (Ibid.:43).

A qualitative change in the tourism experience seemed to go hand in hand with this transition. In the first case, where the Iban acted as mere "culture providers," tours tended to be object-oriented and focused on "cultural sightseeing" and "staged authenticity." With increased community involvement in the case of the ecotourism partnership, and particularly with full community control in the third case, there was a stronger emphasis on a meet-the-people aspect, personal interaction between visitors and interested members of the community, and overall spontaneity and personal involvement. There was every indication that tourists appreciated the genuine experience, while being less preoccupied with photographs and souvenirs (Ibid.:42).

It was previously mentioned that indigenous hosts can effectively use **social space** as a control mechanism in tourism. The tourist experience of culture can be conceptualized as taking place in **frontstage and backstage regions** (MacCannell 1973, 1976). There is a connectivity between cultural experience and spatial elements for many indigenous cultures. Indigenous hosts may protect and insulate their culture by dividing their lives into "backstage areas," where they continue valued traditions away from the gaze of visitors, and "frontstage areas," where a limited range of activities are performed for tourist consumption within a framework of "staged authenticity." A community keen on preserving its privacy may permit cultural tourism activities in frontstage areas and present them to the outsider as backstage. Alternatively, a host community may permit visitors into the backstage, but create protective mechanisms of a physical nature or other prohibitive means to protect the inner sanctum of their culture.

Furthermore, where there is interaction or even cultural immersion, the **host may ascribe different roles to "the stranger."** As Ryan (1999:272) suggests with regard to Maori use of cultural symbolism, Maori may view the tourist as a child (ignorant of, and not yet ready for, knowledge), as a **novice** (certain types of knowledge may be revealed) or as an **outsider** (with whom knowledge may not be shared). For other cultures, there may be different roles. Conflict arises when there is a discrepancy between the roles ascribed by the host and those envisaged for themselves by visitors or tour operators.

The crucial role of indigenous guides was already highlighted in the last chapter. Based on their research in Mutawintji National Park in New South Wales, Australia, Howard, Thwaites and Smith (2001) point out important differences in the requirements and functions of tour guides in different types of tourism. **In indigenous tourism a critical role of the indigenous guide is that of a gatekeeper to both the site and the society** (Howard, Thwaites & Smith 2001:37). A guide may act as a conduit for information as well as a buffer between tourists and the host society. At Mutawintji, Aboriginal guides saw their roles not just as guides but as representatives of Paakintji (their tribe), the NSW National Parks and Wildlife Service, and of all Aboriginal people in Australia (Ibid.:34). The personal encounter with a representative of the local culture immediately placed the visitor into the context of the site, because the guide was part of the fabric of the experience (Ibid.:38). Indigenous guides played a central role in controlling the impact of tourism because

Illustration 4.1

Illustration 4.2

(Illustrations 4.1 and 4.2) Encountering "the Other": be it in Algeria or Australia, the tourism setting complicates human interactions by turning them into commercial transactions.

they regulated access to aboriginal culture in a physical sense as well as a conceptual sense. They made decisions on the depth of cultural knowledge to be communicated to visitors. Furthermore,

> ...Aboriginal guides attempt to remove pre-conceived notions that the site and society is [sic] a part of history and replace it with an understanding of the site and society in a contemporary context. The ecotour guide often creates a conservation ethic by simply stating the types of behaviours appropriate for long-term conservation .... By contrast, indigenous tour guides create long-term understanding, attitudes and behaviours towards Aboriginal culture by challenging stereotypes or misconceptions through talking to participants and emphasising the contemporary nature of their society. Should a non-indigenous tour guide try to interpret the site the same way, the experience and message would not be the same and perhaps less effective. This suggests the Paakintji see authentic and worthwhile cultural exchange with the tourist also as a critical part of the tour experience (Ibid.:37f).

Encountering "The Other": Business + Social Contract

There are many different ways for indigenous groups to host outsiders, and for outsiders to gain access to another culture. The issue, however, is a complicated one. By its very nature, tourism commodifies the encounter and the experience. A commercial transaction takes place, but the purchased goods are intangible. For the transaction to be satisfactory for all parties, there needs to be a social contract whereby explicit or implicit agreement is reached on the degree of access that the visitor gains to the host's culture in terms of physical space as well as social and spiritual dimensions. The greater the degree of cultural immersion "physically and mentally" the more complicated the scenario becomes.

Model Cultures

Model cultures are living museums, featuring reconstructions of a historic past or an ethnographic model or, frequently, a combination of both. As emphasized by Smith (1989a:11), model cultures have the great advantage of directing tourist visits to a site away from the daily lives of ordinary people, to a space specifically reserved for tourism. One of the best known examples of model cultures is the **Polynesian Cultural Center** in the community of Laie, Oahu, Hawaii (Stanton 1989). This extremely popular visitor attraction is privately owned and operated by the Church of Jesus Christ of Latter-day Saints. It was established in 1963 by Brigham Young University with a three-fold purpose: (1) to preserve the culture of different Polynesian groups; (2) to provide employment and work-scholarship support for the students attending the Brigham Young University-Hawaii Campus; and (3) to provide direct financial aid to the university (Ibid.:248). In the late 1980s the centre employed three hundred full-time staff as well as five hundred student-workers, while catering to between 1,500 and 2,500 visitors daily. The exhibits focused on material culture (houses, canoes, artifacts) and the performing arts:

> In fact, one central theme pervading most of the presentations at the PCC is that this is *not* what typically exists today in the various Polynesian Island groups. The Center is basically an attempt to reconstruct lifestyles that are vanishing or have disappeared in the wake of the vast flood of technological gadgetry of the twentieth century. The model caters to ethnic tourism, providing to the tourist an opportunity to see in one afternoon what many of the indigenous residents of the various Polynesian societies themselves rarely, if ever, see. The visitor is, through the model-culture experience, able to gain a brief insight into a selective array of Polynesian cultures without the necessity of travelling throughout the Polynesian Triangle. Another PCC purpose is to keep alive (or even revive) traditional art forms and practices, giving the guest a chance to view some limited historical aspects of a life-style as it once was (Stanton 1989.:252).

Obviously, an important question is: Who constructs the model culture? In the case of the Polynesian Cultural Center input has been sought from scholars as well as respected representatives from Polynesian cultures. Nevertheless, several concerns with regard to the model culture approach to ethnic tourism become evident from Stanton's case study:

• Projection of ethnic reality
• Superficial portrayal
• Attempt to meet visitors' expectations

- Failure to address controversial issues
- Risk of producing a "fake culture"; staging of the exotic
- Pressure to fulfil naive or uninformed tourist expectations
- Difficulty of choosing cultural era to represent
- Emphasis on material culture and performing arts
- Danger of partial image becoming the cultural reality of the host
- Incomplete cultural education for employees
- Lack of appreciation of a "living culture" concept

Based on the same source, these risks are counterbalanced by considerations of the positive effects:

- Superficial portrayal better than none at all
- Employment opportunities
- Economic benefits for workers and their home communities
- Preservation or revival of traditional art forms and practices
- Training and education
- Pride in cultural heritage
- Reinforcement of cultural identity
- Intercultural exchange between workers
- No disruption of local lifestyle

These positive impacts have made the Polynesian Cultural Center a successful undertaking within the social context of Laie. Indeed, as Stanton emphasizes, the frequent outpouring of anti-tourist sentiment encountered in so many other communities of Hawaii is conspicuously absent among the permanent, long-term residents of Laie (Ibid.:259). The location of the centre on the periphery of Laie rather than in the middle of the community, ensures much less interference with people's daily lives than in similar "model cultures" such as Leavenworth, Washington (modelling a Bavarian village), or Rothenburg-ob-der-Tauber (a "picture book romantic" town) in Germany. The Polynesian Cultural Center is located on an island that is one of the busiest tourist centres of the world. Stanton expresses doubt that it could be as successful anywhere but in Oahu in the State of Hawaii. Even here it is usually visited *after the fact*, because visitors are already there (Ibid.:262). This is also true for other model cultures such as Rotorua in New Zealand, Orchid Island in Fiji, or Tjapukai Aboriginal Cultural Park in Queensland, Australia.

Tjapukai Aboriginal Cultural Park was already introduced in the last chapter, illustrating visitor attitudes. In the late 1990s Dyer, Aberdeen and Schuler (2003) investigated tourism impacts of this enterprise on the Djabugay Aboriginal community, whose culture is being portrayed by this tourism venture. Even though the relevant fieldwork was undertaken in 1997, only one year after Tjapukai Aboriginal Cultural Park had evolved from the Tjapukai Dance

Theatre, it reveals some potential pitfalls that indigenous people interested in getting involved in such ventures would be well advised to take notice of. The Tjapukai Park is a fundamentally different undertaking from the Polynesian Cultural Centre in that it is not a multicultural park. It features Djabugai culture and is located on land to which they "belong", and which traditionally "belonged" to them (Ibid.:83). The Djabugay community is an equity partner in the Park. They negotiated an agreement and signed a deed with the other shareholders in the enterprise, who included other Aboriginal and non-Aboriginal private parties as well as government authorities (Ibid.:87).

The researchers encountered considerable confusion about the substance of the agreement and the extent of the equity owned by the Djabugay. What became clear, however, was that the Djabugay were minority shareholders (with poor prospects of acquiring a majority of shares), with minimal power, control and voting rights relating to Park business. The management team was entirely non-Aboriginal, and there was general agreement amongst managers and the Djabugay people themselves that it was very doubtful that the Djabugay would become sufficiently skilled to manage the venture within a decade, the timeframe suggested as reasonable for the realization of full Djabugay ownership of the Park. Another disturbing finding was the fact that the Park managers were unable to identify who were in fact Djabugay employees, i.e., custodians of Djabugay culture. The latter, in fact, constituted a minority among Park employees (Ibid.:88). Even though Djabugay culture provided the *raison d'être* for the Park, the Djabugay were not in control of how their culture was represented. Many employees, indeed, felt that the Park's portrayal of their culture was inauthentic, as they were periodically forced to adjust their dancing style in response to tourist surveys to suit tourists' perception of what constitutes Aboriginal culture.

Another complaint concerned the use of the didgeridoo in the Park, a musical instrument that does not belong to this part of the country. These complaints notwithstanding, the Djabugay expressed pleasure and pride in being able to showcase a culture that had been repressed for so long. Djabugay participation in Tjapukai Aboriginal Park, however, forecloses other opportunities to embark on their own ethnic tourism ventures. The Deed of Partnership between the Djabugay and the Park prohibits any cultural initiatives that may be viewed as competing with the Park (Ibid.:92). This had created some resentment, particularly in view of the fact that the Djabugay Elders and community members had yet to receive financial benefits to which their agreement with the Park entitled them, nor were there any other positive spin-off effects. Their lack of experience with advocacy had prevented the Djabugay from channelling their frustration into a more proactive stance (Ibid.:94):

> Because of the range and complexities of tourism impacts, the gap between capitalist corporate culture and traditional indigenous culture needs to be addressed openly and honestly. Reciprocity, timelines and contingencies should be in place so that cultural and intellectual property remains in the hands and control of the rightful owners.
>
> Ultimately, it is in the interest of the corporate owners and managers to nurture the culture that they promote for commercial gain. This entails an awareness and understanding of how the historical, geographical and political antecedents shape the Djabugay community. Currently, the community does not operate as an equal participant in the Park and therefore does not control or benefit fully from the presentation of its culture for tourist consumption. The issue of identity is complex and particularly problematic for both Park management and the Djabugay community in this context. Anyone involved in cross-cultural tourist ventures needs to be mindful of this issue and its implications which demand a genuine commitment to ongoing negotiations and consultation that recognises different attitudes to time and decision making processes (Ibid.:94).

In 2001 the Indian Affairs Minister in Alberta, Canada, envisioned the establishment of elaborate First Nations "theme parks," Indian villages recreating traditional lifestyles of Alberta's diverse aboriginal cultures (*Calgary Herald*, April 21, 2001). These villages would also contain other attractions such as casinos. Provided there is a market for such product, there is no reason why First Nations could not be successful in such approach to indigenous tourism development as long as they enter into such venture without misconceptions about its pros and cons. On the one hand model cultures constitute a "safe" approach, where visitors do not venture into aboriginal communities, let alone gain access to backstage aspects of a culture. They are labour intensive and create opportunities for people who are willing to be active in the frontline in face to face contact with visitors as well as for those who prefer to stay in the background and be only indirectly involved by creating material culture items or participating in other capacities.

On the other hand, model culture facilities require a high initial capital outlay as well as considerable operating expenses for relatively long periods of time as they become known in the marketplace. For indigenous peoples, working with investors is bound to raise questions of control over the venture, including the central question of who constructs the model culture. A model culture may be viewed as a "living museum," but typically fails to represent a living culture. One aspect of a living culture is the likelihood that even amongst bearers of this culture there may be disagreement as to how a culture is best represented and what constitutes authenticity. If these issues are honestly addressed (mindful of the Djabugay experience), model cultures can make a positive contribution to the lives of hosts and guests. Model cultures may also be complemented by opportunities for visitors to participate in the living culture of their hosts, as reported for the Ainu in Hokkaido, Japan, by Yasumura (1996:121).

Zeppel's study of cultural tourism at the Cowichan Native Village in Duncan, British Columbia, Canada, found that a majority of tourists wanted to learn about both traditional and contemporary Cowichan culture (Zeppel 2002:98). While Aboriginal guides and other staff can help to provide a modern context for model cultures, there are always tourists, on whom the fact is lost that staff without traditional "costume" are indeed "real Indians." Zeppel (1998a:33) reports similar observations for Australia. This suggests that in cases where the attraction is indeed owned and operated by indigenous people, like the Cowichan Native Village, this fact needs to be explicitly promoted as a key attraction (Zeppel 2002:99). Then it is up to the aboriginal hosts to decide whether their cultural representations remain confined to a model culture, or whether visitors will be allowed to sample the living culture of their hosts.

The Golden Hordes

Model cultures have been advocated as effective means to accommodate mass tourism, the Polynesian Cultural Center being a prime example. Mass tourism has elicited extremely bitter reactions on the part of indigenous people, as shown by the following example from Hawai'i, arguably the place that "suffers the greatest number of tourists per square mile of any place on earth" (Trask 1993:184):

> This fictional Hawai'i [of tourists' expectations] comes out of the depths of Western sexual sickness which demands a dark, sin-free Native for instant gratification

between imperialist wars. The attraction of Hawai'i is stimulated by slick Hollywood movies, saccharine Andy Williams music, and the constant psychological deprivations of maniacal American life. Tourists flock to my Native land for escape, but they are escaping into a state of mind while participating in the destruction of a host people in a Native place.

To Hawaiians, daily life is neither soft nor kind. In fact, the political, economic, and cultural reality for most Hawaiians is hard, ugly, and cruel.

In Hawai'i, the destruction of our land and the prostitution of our culture is planned and executed by multi-national corporations (both foreign-based and Hawai'i-based), by huge landowners (like the missionary-descended Castle and Cook — of Dole Pineapple fame — and others) and by collaborationist state and county governments. The ideological gloss that claims tourism to be our economic savior and the "natural" result of Hawaiian culture is manufactured by ad agencies (like the state supported Hawai'i Visitors' Bureau) and tour companies (many of which are owned by airlines), and spewed out to the public through complicitous cultural engines like film, television and radio, and the daily newspapers. As for the local labor unions, both rank and file and management clamor for more tourists while the construction industry lobbies incessantly for larger resorts (Ibid.:180f).

Of course, many Hawaiians do not see tourism as part of their colonization. Thus tourism is viewed as providing jobs, not as a form of cultural prostitution. Even those who have some glimmer of critical consciousness don't generally agree that the tourist industry prostitutes Hawaiian culture. To me, this is a measure of the depth of our mental oppression: we can't understand our own cultural degradation because we are living it (Ibid.:195).

These are bitter words, reflective of a situation, where an indigenous culture and indigenous lands have been usurped by an immigrant society and tourism industry interests, whereas the original representatives of this culture are economically and politically disenfranchised. As illustrated by Altman (1989) for Australia's Northern Territory, it makes a crucial difference for indigenous tourism scenarios whether tourism is imposed or invited. In the majority of cases, where indigenous communities are faced with mass tourism, tourism is imposed rather than invited. Aboriginal parties may or

Illustration 4.3

Illustration 4.4

(Illustrations 4.3 and 4.4) Taos Pueblo, New Mexico, is the oldest continuously inhabited site in North America and a prime tourist attraction.

ity of Taos Pueblo Indians to safeguard their traditions while taking advantage of the economic benefits of the tourist trade:

- The pueblo had a strong cultural and religious foundation prior to the influx of tourists.

- The pueblo residents have maintained control over the regulation of tourism at the pueblo.
- They have learned how to protect their religion from outside interference (Ibid.:117).

This is not to say that the coexistence between hosts and guests is idyllic. Many pueblo residents do feel on exhibit under the constant tourist gaze. Chiago Lujan (1993) suggests that Taos Pueblo may actually be experiencing the last two stages of attitudinal change according to Doxey's "irridex": irritation and antagonism towards visitors (Doxey 1976). But the fact remains that the pueblo government strives to optimize rather than maximize the economic benefit of tourism by imposing strict limitations on visitor access to the pueblo in space as well as in time. While pueblo residents may occasionally feel annoyed or irritated by visitors, they do not feel culturally threatened. When we compare Taos Pueblo to other pueblos who do not admit tourists, we find that tourism does not act as an agent of change, since Taos Pueblo operates from a position of cultural strength, which is reinforced rather than weakened by involvement in tourism. As observed by Chiago Lujan (1993:118), Taos Pueblo's accommodation of visitors is characterized by a high degree of tolerance combined with a minimal level of acceptance. This philosophical attitude has been honed by centuries of coping with invaders, starting in pre-contact times with nomadic tribes such as the Navajo and Apache and with Spain's colonization of northern New Mexico in 1598. Taos Pueblo was a key player in the Pueblo Revolt of 1680, and it remains a key player in preserving Pueblo cultural identity:

> When every effort was made to wipe out our culture and religion, we made adjustments to insure that there was an outward showing of compliance. We managed to keep our religion and culture going (underground, as it were) so we were able to survive the Spaniards. So too are we able to survive the tourists and culture they represent (Taos Pueblo member quoted by Chiago Lujan 1993:101, 114).

The use of **secrecy and concealment** as a means of cultural preservation is a common trait of Pueblo culture. Another means of control is **strict regulation**. Sweet (1990, 1991) documents such strategies for several pueblos, particularly the villages of Acoma, Santo Domingo, San Ildefonso, and San Juan. Unlike in Taos Pueblo, mass tourism is not yet common in most pueblos, but large numbers of visitors are encountered on certain occasions, and the issues and strategies used are the same. Their historical experience and legal and political status render pueblos particularly well equipped to effectively control their visitors. Pueblo officials have the right to exclude visitors and to set rules for acceptable behaviour. They may close the village to outsiders at any time. They also have the right to police their reservation and enforce their regulations, and there is abundant evidence that regulations are being enforced.

In short, the pueblos can determine what tourists may see or do while on the reservation and whether or not tourism will be encouraged, simply tolerated, or discouraged (Sweet 1991:62). Pueblo secrecy is used to protect privacy as well as what is considered sacred space. Sections of villages may be closed to visitors permanently or temporarily, and kivas — Pueblo sacred ceremonial chambers — are always off-limits to tourists. There are also days when an entire village is closed, with Pueblo men guarding the entrances and turning away any would-be visitors (Ibid.:63). Visitor inquisitiveness into Pueblo cultural meanings — even on the part of "Anglo friends" — is actively discouraged and internal social control ensures compliance by all members. Sweet points out an interesting implication of this practice. The generally assumed inequality inherent in the host/guest relationship acquires new meaning: In terms of economic power, the native host often holds an inferior position to that of the tourist; however, the native host has the advantage in terms of local knowledge.

By withholding information, Pueblo people control something that ethnic tourists want — exotic cultural knowledge and experiences — and thus gain an edge in the interaction (Ibid.:65). This is further ensured by subjecting visitors to **strict regulations.** The newly developed (annually appearing) *Visitors Guide for the Eight Northern Indian Pueblos* features a Pueblo Etiquette on one of the introductory pages (preceded by a paragraph discouraging visitors from inquiring into the meanings of dances and rituals). Every pueblo has its own way of communicating its code of conduct and regulations. When entering a village, tourists may be confronted by a crudely painted sign simply stating restrictions on photography, sketching, notetaking, driving speeds and a curfew for visitors, or more sophisticated and professionally printed messages such as the sign at the entrance of the Acoma Reservation which reads:

PUEBLO OF ACOMA OFFICIAL NOTICE

You are entering the Pueblo of Acoma. All lands herein are governed by statutes enacted and/or adopted by the Acoma Tribal Council. Continued entrance beyond this point constitutes a knowing and voluntary consent on your behalf to abide by the laws of Acoma and to be

held accountable to the Acoma judicial system for any
violation of Acoma law (Sweet 1991:67).

Furthermore, when admitted to public dances and ceremonies, tourists should be prepared to be "herded" and segregated, on occasion, to minimize interference with participants and residents. Village officials define the nature of the contact and, in case of non-compliance, visitors may be escorted out of the village, fined or have their notebook or camera confiscated (Ibid.70). Rather than objecting to such treatment, many ethnic tourists feel that by co-operating they are participating in Pueblo culture, and they appreciate being admitted into a "backstage" area for an "authentic" experience.

Sweet (1989) describes yet another Pueblo practice which serves to incorporate the visiting "other" into the Pueblo world view while at the same time putting strangers in their place by humiliating and making fun of them. Tourists, in their paradoxical social position of being appreciated as well as despised, make an ideal target for the **burlesque** by Pueblo comics and ritual clowns. As a peripheral occurrence during regular village dance events, visitors are sometimes singled out to be poked fun at or embarrassed. It all makes sense when we remember that Pueblo clowns serve as agents of social control (Ibid.:71) and contribute to the definition of self of the Pueblo.

The Pueblo villages stand out in having developed a highly formalized response to tourist visitation that is equally effective in dealing with large or smaller numbers of tourists. They set clear limits to the experiences and activities of visitors and make it plain that when setting foot on a Pueblo reservation, visitors must accept a new set of rules and obligations. Secrecy and a reluctance to share cultural information are more than a quirk of Pueblo culture. These traits are deeply rooted in history, and are integral part of how the Pueblo communities define themselves and how they choose to safeguard their culture and collective identity. Tourists are generously admitted to public dances and ceremonies and are graciously hosted on feast days, but the fact remains that they are accommodated rather than embraced. Individual longtime repeat visitors may eventually come to be viewed as friends by Pueblo families, but the very nature of Pueblo culture prohibits the development of a tourism product that emphasizes cultural immersion.

Other indigenous groups have also been faced with mass tourism, feeling equally ambivalent about this type of tourism, but less well equipped by their culture to deal with it. **The Aboriginal owners of Kakadu and Uluru-Kata Tjuta National Parks in Australia's Northern Territory** are an example of such a scenario. Having accepted national park status for their ancestral land, they were ill

Illustration 4.5

Staged presentations at the Indian Pueblo Cultural Centre in Albuquerque, New Mexico, give visitors a glimpse of Pueblo Indian culture without admitting them to "backstage" areas.

prepared for the onslaught of visitors that ensued as a result of the World Heritage status of Kakadu and Uluru and the development of extensive infrastructure. Altman found that many Aboriginal people were reluctant to participate in forms of direct tourism (necessitating a physical interface between hosts and guests), which they felt would be intrusive and negative, and were not always interested in participating in the formal tourism labour market (Altman 1989:469ff; Altman & Finlayson 1993:40). They clearly placed socio-cultural values ahead of commercial considerations. What the Aboriginal owners lacked in cultural preparation they tried to make up for by negotiating co-management structures for the national parks, thus gaining limited leverage in managing the influx of visitors. The outcome of these efforts will be discussed in the next chapter.

Cultural Immersion

Cultural immersion of visitors in indigenous lifestyles is exactly what most Pueblo tribes and many Australian Aboriginal people (but by no means all) want to avoid. Cultural immersion relies on face-to-face contact between host and guest, and is experiential, interactive and direct. Cultural immersion and mass tourism are mutually exclusive. The former gives individuals and small groups the opportunity to share in the lifestyle and glimpse the world view of their hosts, minimizing the "environmental bubble." Such experiences vary in depth and duration. They may last no longer than a few hours or a day. For example, *Mamabulanjin Aboriginal Tours* in Broome, Western **Australia**, emphasizes that it is "100% Aboriginal owned, operated and interpreted," and invites visitors to

> Spend a day with the local Aboriginal people of this region as they show you their country. Learn to see Broome through "Aboriginal Eyes." This is an opportunity for you to learn about "who we are." A chance for you to understand a little about our traditional lifestyles, historical changes and the impact of change and the contemporary issues facing our people.
>
> Come and spend a day with a specialist guide and Aboriginal people who will take you on a journey into the lifestyle and beliefs of traditional Aboriginal people as they have lived for thousands of years.
>
> When visiting the Aboriginal bush you will be able to participate in boomerang and spear throwing, learn about fishing in an Aboriginal way and learn of their traditional hunting techniques and bush survival skills.
>
> Try some bush tucker (*Mamabulanjin Aboriginal Tours* brochure).

There are numerous such opportunities in all parts of Australia (including Kakadu and Uluru National Parks), with bush tucker (bush food) tours, cultural safaris, and cross-cultural ecotours. Most offer only brief experiences, but some, like *Desert Tracks* in the Northern Territory, offer eight-day cross-cultural educational ecotours. In most of these cases, Aboriginal people are truly "culture managers" and entrepreneurs, setting the boundaries of what knowledge is shared with visitors and where they are allowed to go. Other examples of cultural immersion experiences are the previously mentioned Iban longhouse visits on Borneo and weeklong *Marae* stays in New Zealand (Ryan & Crotts 1997:912). A very special experience is offered to visitors of **southern Alberta, Canada**, by *Eaglespeaker Interpretive Services*, a family business on the Blood Indian Reserve:

> [Ken Eaglespeaker] has aligned himself with a small number of specialist tour operators from Germany, Montana

and Alberta catering to small groups. Ken Eaglespeaker believes in a personalized and flexible approach in his cultural tourism venture. He offers his guests a cultural immersion experience with his family and friends. After much soul-searching and consultation with Elders, he decided to incorporate spiritual elements in his hosting activities such as a sweat lodge ceremony, and in some cases, admission to a sundance. Guests are accommodated in tipis in proximity of the Eaglespeakers' home with full board and personalized service. They are made to feel part of the family and given a candid insight in family and community life. Other elements of their visit include tours of the reserve and visits to other attractions in proximity of the reserve (Notzke 2004:37f).

Obviously, it is in situations such as this, in a homestay setting, that the most intense contact between hosts and guests occurs, with a maximum potential for mutual impact. An extension of the bed-and-breakfast concept, **homestays** are becoming increasingly popular and may last from days to weeks. They are available all over the world, including in indigenous communities located in such regions as northern Thailand, Malaysia, Indonesia and North America (Bopp 1999). With contact so close there is much potential for unexpected impacts. While there is the opportunity for genuine cultural exchange and the broadening of horizons, there is also a risk of breakdown of broader socio-cultural concepts within the host society, as illustrated by Wall and Long (1996) for **Bali (Indonesia)**. Drawn by Bali's unique Hindu ritual culture and performing arts, tourists make a major contribution to the provincial gross domestic product. Tourism used to be concentrated in resort enclaves in the south of the island, but a more recent trend has resulted in a proliferation of homestay opportunities in villages in the island's interior.

Homestay operations are generally family-owned and operated and provide supplementary income. The rapidly growing participation in this industry has been facilitated, in part, by the structure of the Balinese housing compound, which (as it features a lot of open space) has proven to be readily adaptable to changing circumstances: e.g., visitor accommodation. However, this has happened at the expense of associated cultural meaning and the environment (Ibid.:28). In Bali, the layout of individual homesteads, entire villages and, indeed, the whole island has considerable cultural and religious significance, reflecting a distinct cosmology (Ibid.:42). The extended family's enclosure contains a family temple and is subdivided with a specific cosmological orientation, delimiting space for different family members and activities, for the sacred and the profane. In some villages, compounds have been modified to house workers, to construct restaurants and build shops, and to accommodate visitors.

Such modifications can easily result in a breakdown of the Balinese architectural cosmology (Ibid.:43) and associated beliefs and practices. In view of the prevalence of mass tourism on the island of Bali, the very fact that the number of homestay accommodations has grown so rapidly constitutes a threat to the quality of the visitor's experience and, thus, to the market niche. In addition to an overburdened infrastructure and environmental stress, Wall and Long observed unhealthy competition within communities and an increased workload for some family members, with consequences for religious and social life. Seizing the opportunity to accommodate visitors in their home has enabled villagers to enter the tourism industry as entrepreneurs rather than employees and to reduce leakage; but it has also become clear that even small-scale, locally-owned tourism developments may be a mixed blessing. This is particularly true before a backdrop of mass tourism. Based on this Bali example, we can identify the following potential drawbacks of homestay tourism:

- Possible cultural disruption of the host society
- Too much growth spoiling the experience, threatening the market niche
- Implications for family life
- Intrusiveness of visitors
- Impact on economic and religious life
- Competition for business
- Breakdown of architectural cosmology
- Environmental impacts

These drawbacks are counterbalanced by beneficial effects:

- Economic benefits for hosts
- Involvement in the industry as entrepreneurs rather than as employees
- Cultural exchange and mutual education
- Genuine cultural experience and interaction
- Opportunity for small-scale development
- Low budget opportunities for guests
- Promotion of pride in heritage
- Motivation of host for cultural learning
- Mobilization of cooperative forces in host community

The quality of a visitor's cultural immersion experience, as well as its impact on the host's society, are strongly determined by the **host's conceptualization of tourism**, which is often influenced by the host society's traditions pertaining to hospitality. In the **Polynesian culture area** in particular, some interesting observations have been made. Like other indigenous cultures, Polynesian peoples traditionally lack any concept of tourism, but since time immemorial they have been master navigators and marine travellers. As a result traditions of hospitality contribute a crucial element to Polynesian societies' sense of identity. Ryan (1997:259) emphasizes how the social contract of *manaakitanga* (hospitality) was serious business for the Maori, and was not always conducted between friendly parties. Maori notions of hospitality implied that visitors were accorded a warm welcome.

However, this gift of hospitality was conditional upon the use made of it by the recipient, and the giver required the recipient's respect. Today it should also be considered a gift that comes with a complex set of associations born of a history of past denial of Maori language and loss of land and threatened identity (Ibid.:273). Nevertheless, the genuine warmth of Maori traditional hospitality seems to have carried over into modern tourism to a point, where Maori hosts are cautioned to curb their tendency to extend hospitality too far if they wish to make money from such new ventures (Barnett 2001:85).

The issue of separating traditions of hospitality from the modern business of tourism can be a real concern for Polynesian societies entering the industry, as observed by Berno (1999) in the Cook Islands:

> When a visitor to a Pacific island is not differentiated as a tourist and is seen as a "guest," cultural obligation dictates that generosity be extended to the visitor. This in itself is not problematic. But generosity in a traditional Polynesian context is about investment in human relationships, it is about establishing an obligation which will be reciprocated in the future. In a tourism context this is seldom understood, or reciprocated by the tourist. Tourists may unwittingly convert this system of social exchange into "unwilling altruism" by stepping in and out of the community without fulfilling expected reciprocal obligations. This has led to the exploitation of the *aroa* [love, kindness, generosity towards strangers] concept ("institutionalized *aroa*"), which could potentially cut deeply into the traditions of Pacific Islanders which are vital to the

psychological well-being and group coherence of island societies (Berno 1999:658).

Particularly outside of Rarotonga, which receives the majority of visitors, there was minimal understanding or appreciation of the consumer nature of tourism (Ibid.). This could result in problems and awkwardness for both hosts and guests, whenever the expectations of the host did not match the intentions of the tourist. Negative consequences need not result from such different understandings if tourists can be attracted who are genuinely interested in island culture, and who are prepared to adapt and respond in culturally appropriate ways. One of the most notable effects of tourism in such environments is that certain social and human relationships are brought into the economic sphere and become an integral part of earning a livelihood, thus commercializing interpersonal relationships (Ibid.:671). A value system based on moral values is potentially replaced by one based on money. Nevertheless, evidence from these islands also suggests that one should never underestimate indigenous societies' capability to cope with the impacts of tourism.

The Spiritual Quest

The risks inherent in the cultural immersion approach to ethnic tourism are multiplied when this immersion process penetrates into the inner sanctum of the host's culture: i.e., the spiritual and religious realm. As shown by the Bali example, when this happens is not always easily determined. In many indigenous cultures the secret, the sacred and the secular are not neatly compartmentalized and clearly separated, as they are in most Western societies. Spiritually sanctioned rules of behaviour or codes of ethics often transcend daily life. When outside visitors enter this conceptual backstage of their hosts' culture, conflicts may occur, regardless of whether they are invited or trespassing into forbidden territory. It is not surprising that host and guest attitudes vary widely regarding this complex issue.

The unequivocal stance of Pueblo Indian Nations has been described. They discourage any cultural inquisitiveness on the part of their visitors. As Laxson (1991:373) points out, members of the majority culture tend to be socialized to value intellectual curiosity and to ask questions, but the Pueblo people feel that when outsiders learn their religious secrets, the spiritual power of the ceremonies is lost. Laxson (Ibid.:388) also suggests that members of "fast-food" societies are accustomed to instant gratification and feel entitled to immediately know all about another culture, because this knowledge is a commodity. But it is not only this "fast-food mentality" that puzzles and irritates Pueblo people and others. Another type of tourist often singled out for criticism by indigenous tourism critics and some tourism planners alike is the New Age tourist who wishes to "go native" and learn cultural practices (Guyette 1998:37; Young 1997). The Hopi in Arizona are particularly popular with this group. With New Age tourists the problem of visitor intrusiveness is compounded by a pronounced lack of respect for cultural boundaries and protocol.

Spiritual learning is also an integral part of cultural tours conducted by reputable educational tour operators. *Far Horizons* (based in Albuquerque, New Mexico), for example, specializes in archaeological and cultural trips accompanied by research scientists. One of their tours takes travellers "On the Trail of the Shaman," and promises a "journey into remote areas untouched by tourism in the highlands of Guatemala, [to] witness shamanistic rites at sacred shrines of today's Maya" (*Far Horizons* Newsletter, Summer 2001). Spiritual and religious tourism represents one of the oldest kinds of travel, as exemplified by pilgrimages to Mecca or shrines in Lourdes, Fatima, and Jerusalem.

Increasingly, tourists are departing from this standard religious tourism variety to seek new spiritual ways to self-discovery, and tour operators and wholesalers are responding to this demand. Many focus on Tai Chi, meditation and Yoga. Elements of spiritual tourism are becoming increasingly integrated in the spa vacation business (Plaine 2000). There certainly is potential for aboriginal people to capitalize on this trend, especially in view of the fact that among many visitors to North America there is a tendency to stereotype aboriginal people as almost mystical, spiritual beings. Whenever this subject is broached with Canada's First Nations, they remain very guarded towards this possibility. In Ontario, Trina Mather of the *Turtle Island Tourism Company* was instructed by her Elders to share only culture, not spirituality (Conference Notes, National Aboriginal Tourism Conference, Saskatoon, April 2000).

This is obviously problematic, since there is a very fine line between culture and spirituality. Aboriginal hosts who incorporate cultural elements in their tourist product are constantly faced with the challenge of sharing their culture without compromising its integrity. As a video produced under the direction of the Canadian National Aboriginal Tourism Association (CNATA 1994b) puts it, "[t]here can be no sustainable product without a sustainable culture." In practice, this often presents individuals and communities with difficult decisions and potential dissent. For example, the ques-

tion of the appropriateness of including tourists in sweat lodge ceremonies remains a contentious issue in many circles. Grossly
oversimplified, a "sweat" constitutes spiritual as well as physical
cleansing. However, its religious significance, spirituality and social
aspects vary widely from tribe to tribe, from community to community and from spiritual practitioner to practitioner. In 1998 the
author was invited to a gathering of aboriginal Elders and tourism
representatives from Alberta that was convened at the Nakoda
Lodge on the Stoney Reserve to discuss this very issue. The
message received from the Elders was unequivocal: Aboriginal spirituality is not for sale, and there is no place for spiritual ceremonies
in tourism products.

Nevertheless, there are initiatives, driven by indigenous people,
to admit strangers into the very heart of a people's spiritual culture. By and large, Australian Aborigenes share the concerns
of Canada's First Nations about communicating aspects of spiritual culture to foreigners (Moscardo & Pearce 1989:391; Altman
1989:467; Dodson & Bauman 2001:123). In some communities,
however, there is a deep-seated desire to educate both non-Aboriginal Australians and international visitors not only about their culture, but about "the law of their country." What sets Australian
Aboriginal beliefs apart is the fact that they are one and the same.
Indigenous cultures the world over, varied as they may be, share
important common features. Foremost among these features is the
intimate connection within a social universe between culture and
what most Westerners would call (animate and inanimate) nature.
This is one of the reasons indigenous people at international gatherings usually do not encounter problems in communicating with
each other. In Australia, its huge Aboriginal cultural diversity notwithstanding, this connection between people and their "country" is
unparalleled in its intricacy and near-incomprehensibility to outsiders:

> Just as there were hundreds of different languages spoken
> across Australia, there were also hundreds of different
> Aboriginal cultures and spiritual beliefs. However, all Ab-
> original people have a common belief in the creation or
> the Dreaming, which is a time when the ancestral beings
> travelled across the country creating the natural world and
> making the laws and customs for Aboriginal people to live
> by. The Dreaming ancestors take the form of humans, ani-
> mals or natural features in the landscape.
>
> Law and spirituality are one and the same thing; our
> laws are also our spiritual beliefs. Spirituality and the

land are also one entity, for our spirituality comes from the Dreaming ancestors whose spirits are alive in the land. The land is us, for we are in the land, as is the spirit of creation in all things. All is one, one is all (Watson 2001:106).

For Australian Aborigines this is not esoteric knowledge, but essential to "caring for country." Neglect of the spiritual and cultural obligations implied by this custodianship brings about disharmony for the country and community. Hence it is important to teach even outsiders the rules of this custodianship, or, at the very least, to convince them not to interfere.

This is the rationale behind *Bush University*, an initiative driven by the vision of the Ngarinyin people of the Kimberley region in northwestern Australia. It is fully owned and operated by them in conjunction with the tour company *Kimberley Wilderness Adventures* (see p.114 of this book). The *Bush University* programs last seven days and provide opportunities for small groups of visitors to live with the Ngarinyin in their cool season camp. Visitors are taken to rock art galleries by the custodians of the sites and have the opportunity for close interaction with their Aboriginal hosts, while learning about Ngarinyin law, spirituality, medicines and bush foods, language and early history, ceremony and songs. Before embarking on this journey, visitors are extensively briefed about protocol and behaviour

Bush University

The following is an excerpt of an interview of the Ngarinyin Elder Mowaljarlai by Jutta Malnic:

M: This European lot came over here. They settled down in Australia. They put down all their rules, British rules. We are holding them now, in Canberra, everywhere, in Sydney ....
There's the imprint now. British Wunggud [creation spirit; living energy of creation etc.] is here and up in space. And Australian Wunggud is also up in space. "You need the Wunggud belong to this country," we're telling them now. We are telling this feller, "Now you listen to me about my Wunggud belong to this country. You have to understand." We're telling them now, the English (descended) mob: "You were born here, but you don't know the rules, the spirit belong to this country. You have to listen to us." Like we had to listen to him. This bush school and all those things are like that, not just in your head, but in your powers.
That's what we Ngarinyin are talking about now. And Worrorra and Wunambal too. That's a gift now, a gift from us, a gift for wider Australia.

J: Do these people at Bush University understand this now?

M: Well, we teach them the beginning, the beginning.

Source: Mowaljarlai & Malnic 2001:210

guidelines, and readings are suggested. The program is essentially unstructured and of an ad hoc nature.

Major challenges are still being encountered in packaging and executing these experiences, whose very nature defies commodification.

The Question of Authenticity: Holy Grail or In the Eye of the Beholder?

...[T]here are at least as many definitions of authenticity as there are those who write about it. This, however, should come as no surprise, especially upon consideration of the persuasive force that the notion of authenticity wields in Western ideological discourse, and the many uses to which it may be put therein. Authenticity has become the philosopher's stone for an industry that generally seeks to procure other peoples' "realities." In tourism, authenticity poses as objectivism. It holds the special powers both of distance and of "truth." These are vital components in the production of touristic value. Fundamental to the authenticity concept is a dialectic between object and subject, there and here, then and now (Taylor 2001:8).

Authenticity of a visitor's experience of an indigenous tourism product appears to rank equally high for hosts and guests. In the author's case study of travellers in southern Alberta, Canada, authenticity far outranked all other factors in their considerations of what mostly mattered to them in an aboriginal tourism experience (see Chapter Three).[2] Similarly, in the 1997 Alberta Meeting of the Aboriginal Tourism Product Identification Project (jointly undertaken by the Canadian National Aboriginal Tourism Association and the Conference Board of Canada), authenticity was one of the central concerns of aboriginal tourism product suppliers. They felt that myths, misconceptions and unrealistic expectations on the part of outsiders would be perpetuated unless product authenticity could be realized. It seems reasonable to assume that a similar endorsement of the concept holds true in many other locations. Such ap-

---

2 That generalizations can be risky, however, is shown by the Australian findings of Ryan and Huyton (2002:643), who contend that authenticity and "reality" matter little to tourists in Queensland, who mostly pursue hedonistic goals.

Cultural commoditization and staged authenticity can have far reaching impacts on people's sense of identity, and can generate totally new cultural configurations, as described by Kroshus Medina (2003) for a Maya community in Belize. The author contrasts two schools of thought before introducing a third scenario. One frequently held opinion in tourism studies contends that the commoditization of culture for consumption renders the resulting practices inauthentic. This point of view distinguishes between traditions surviving in relative isolation from market forces and practices elaborated specifically for the tourism market. A contrasting view is held by scholars who assert that such transactions between hosts and guests can generate new cultural configurations that are both meaningful and authentic to all participants (Ibid.:353f). This school of thought conceptualizes culture as dynamic and emergent. It is advanced the farthest by Cohen (1988), who proposes that not only does tourist validation contribute to cultural salvage and revival, but such "emergent authenticity" can be indicative of a situation where cultural expressions designed for the tourist market may actually evolve to become perceived as manifestations of local culture by the host community itself (Ibid.:380).

Kroshus Medina introduces a third alternative into this debate: the possibility that the commoditization of culture for tourism may involve the utilization of *new channels* to access cultural traditions of *great antiquity* (Kroshus Medina 2003:354). Her research focused on San Jose Succotz, a village of some 1,400 people in western Belize, in close proximity to the ruins of an ancient Maya city, Xunantunich, which had become a popular tourist attraction. During the 2000 national census, about 83 percent of the village population self-identified as Mestizo (a Spanish term, implying mixed European and indigenous ancestry) and only 10 percent as Maya (down from 38 percent in 1991) (Ibid.:358f). While migration may have contributed to this shift to Mestizo identities, a survey of village households suggested additional forces at work; the number of people who identified their parents as Maya was more than twice the number who claimed this identity for themselves.

Closer investigation revealed considerable ambiguity about the issue of self-identification and cultural affiliation in this village. Two factors were at work to produce this ambivalence: judgement of the relative value of Maya versus Mestizo identities, and questions about the validity and legitimacy of individuals' claims to Maya identity. Regarding the latter, Succotzenos invoked three key dimensions that define Mayaness: ancestry, language, and ritual or cosmological knowledge. Maya parentage did not automatically impart Maya status, if language skills were not passed on and if ritual knowledge was not conferred by a local healer or *curandero*. With

Maya language skills falling into disuse, and the last *curandero* having died without training an apprentice, the essentials of the Maya cosmological world view were rapidly fading from memory and practice in Succotz (Ibid.:361).

The situation was further complicated by individuals' perception of the relative prestige conferred by Maya versus Mestizo identities, an enduring legacy of colonialism. Kroshus Medina's research reveals how tourism intersects with both of these factors and may, indeed, present new opportunities for villagers to claim or reclaim Maya identity and culture. The extensive work of archaeologists, which had made Xunantunich accessible for tourists, and tourist visitation of the site, combined with both parties' enthusiasm for "things Mayan" certainly provided validation for Mayan traditions and in turn increased respect for the knowledge of the ancient Maya on the part of Succotzenos, especially those employed in excavations.

It quickly became evident that tourists had very little interest in Mestizo identities and culture, which effectively served to invert the local hierarchy that tended to rank Mestizo over Maya. Guides working in the industry were increasingly motivated to educate themselves about Maya culture. Unable to access this knowledge through the traditional channels of language and ritual practice as their parents and grandparents had, they availed themselves of new channels provided by Mayanist academics, such as archaeologists, ethnographers, and epigraphers. The role of the *curandero* was replaced by workshops and books on ancient Maya culture and cosmology, either purchased or received as gifts from tourists or archaeologists. The same avenues were used to revive ancient skills such as ceramics and stone carving. A pottery workshop was funded by a Canadian agency and taught by Canadians. In 1980 the Xunantunich Organization was formed to preserve Maya culture and to generate income for its members. It quickly attracted financial support from international development agencies and transnational indigenous rights organizations, which in turn further contributed to the revalorization of Maya identity and culture in Belize.

It remains unclear, however, to what degree this rediscovery of a Mayan identity was purely utilitarian in nature within a tourism context, or whether it affected deeper levels of individuals' and the community's sense of self:

> Thus tourism has revalued, in certain contexts, traditional Maya knowledge that most young Succotzenos lack. Unable to access this knowledge by "traditional" methods, tourism workers have turned to the writings of essentialist Mayanist scholars as an alternative means for acquir-

ing such "essential" cultural information. Fortunately, for guides and artisans in Succotz, the conceptualization of Maya embodied in these texts accords with tourists' expectations of a generalizable culture that can be packaged and purchased through transactions such as tours and the sale of artisanal products (Ibid.:364).

Thus, in this case tourist servicing is not generating a new, "emergent" culture, per se. Nor is tourism generating a commoditized culture that is distinct from an authentic or traditional culture. Rather, servicing tourism has prompted Succotzenos to utilize *new channels* to access traditions that may have persisted across centuries. As Cohen (1988) argued, the commoditization of culture for tourism may help to preserve cultural traditions by generating demand for or attributing value to them; in this case, however, this knowledge can no longer be accessed through traditional means (Ibid.:364f, emphasis in original).

Overall, interviews with tourism workers in Succotz suggest that, although they seek knowledge about the central tenets of Maya culture their elders revere, most do so not as Maya but rather as tour guides or artists. Many tourism workers remain ambivalent about the relative prestige of Maya versus Mestizo identities, weighing the positive charge imparted to Maya identities by such forces as tourism and transnational indigenous organizing against the negative charge imposed by colonialism that endures into the present. Succotzenos who do not work in tourism must weigh these same forces in deciding their identity commitments, without the incentive of receiving remuneration for their cultural expertise (Ibid.:366).

Taylor (2001) explores the concept of authenticity in the tourism setting of the Maori in New Zealand and contrasts it with the notion of "sincerity," which, in his view, represents a more meaningful and communicative form of indigenous tourism experience. He, too, views authenticity as a projection of a nostalgic Western psyche, as a reproduction of a mystical past. He asks an important question: ".... [W]ho should hold the power to define the authenticity of a cultural experience? .... In the final argument, if the concept of authenticity is to have any legitimate place in discussions of culture, its definition must rest with the individuals who "make up" that culture." (Taylor 2001:13f) During the past two decades a growing number of Maori operators have emerged who provide tourists with an increasing variety of cultural experiences. Different variations of the theme of MacCannell's "staged authenticity" (MacCannell 1973, 1976) are employed by local Maori communities and larger Maori tourism operators, who tend to view the growing tourist interest in the "genuine" and the "authentic" as positive interest. By taking control of the commodification of their own culture, many Maori purposely undermine the "authenticities" provided by the mainstream *Pakeha* (white New Zealanders)-dominated industry by presenting their own (Taylor 2001:15f). On one end of the spectrum dance, theatre and elaborate staging are used to transport the visitor back in time to experience the essence of Maori-ness, somehow suspended in time and space.

Taylor hastens to emphasize that such images of authenticity (bearing characteristics of "brand images" and serving in market "positioning") are by no means an entirely non-Maori construct. The boundary between negative stereotype and lived identity can be a very thin one, and is largely dependent upon the context of the performance (Ibid.:21). In contrast to such performances, tourists have the option to participate in genuine cultural interaction, in "sincere" cultural experiences, where hosts and guests meet halfway, and redefine authenticity in terms of values that are relevant to both parties. Such exercises in "sincerity" usually take the form of *marae* (traditional Maori meeting place) visits, which still feature the staging of authenticity, while at the same time striving to produce sincere encounters; for example, by involving visitors in a re-enactment of a treaty ceremony:

> Through entering into a symbolic contractual agreement
> based on principles of equality, tourists are encouraged
> to recognize their own position as consumers of culture.
> By employing the notion of sincerity above authenticity,
> operators may blur the boundary between who is on
> display and who is consuming the event. As such, they
> may move away from the objectificatory mode of more
> overtly "staged" events. The emphasis on communication
> also encourages tourists to reveal themselves. The gaze is
> returned (Taylor 2001:24).

This author recalls memorable examples of both overtly staged events and more "sincere" experiences from a visit to Australia in 2001. An example for the former was a *corroborree* (festival or gathering for spiritual or ceremonial reasons) presented by local Aborigines at the camp of the Point Stuart Wilderness Lodge in the Northern Territory. The key performer, Kevin (we never learnt his last name or Aboriginal name, nor his tribal affiliation), was employed by the Darwin-based *Northern Territory Adventure Tours* tour company, and had taken some of us on a bushwalk during the afternoon. The evening *corroborree* featured dancing and *didjeridu* music (a *didjeridu* is a wind instrument made of a branch hollowed out by termites, traditionally only used by communities in the Top End of the Northern Territory). Kevin's overall approach was that of an "animator," actively involving the group by having people re- peat Aboriginal language expressions and having us try to use a spear thrower. During the *corroborree* all of us, men and women alike, were encouraged to give the *didjeridu* a try: this in overt con- travention of Aboriginal cultural law since it is not only considered inappropriate but extremely offensive to see a woman even at- tempting to play a *didjeridu* (Lee 2001). The performance was clearly intended as a crowd pleaser (and met with mixed reactions), aiming at having people not only witness but participate in an "au- thentic" experience, even at the expense of breaking cultural rules.

This author's "sincere" indigenous tourism experience was some- what harrowing in nature. It occurred during participation in the 9th National Conference of the Ecotourism Association of Australia on Rottnest Island (near Perth), Western Australia. The entire sojourn on this island had a peculiar quality to it and produced mixed emo- tions among those of us familiar with Aboriginal circumstances, and even more amongst the few Aboriginal participants. This was due to the fact, that Rottnest Island is not only a popular resort and nature reserve, but was a prison island for Aboriginal men from all over Western Australia from 1838–1903. As a rule these "criminals" were jailed for petty theft, "hunting" livestock, or simply for occupying lands wanted by immigrants. Prison conditions were extremely harsh, and hundreds died in cells now converted to hotel rooms, or were publicly hanged within the hotel complex on a spot occupied today by a picturesque gazebo. Australian consciousness of these circum- stances seemed extremely limited.

On our last day on the island, some of us were taken on an in- digenous tour by two Aborigines, Robert Bropho, a local Elder, and Iva Hayward Jackson, a land and cultural worker for various Aborig- inal organizations. This was only the second tour they had con- ducted. It was only after almost a decade's struggle that they were allowed to tell their story. What they made us listen to showed only too clearly just how raw feelings still were in the Aboriginal commu- nity. While our Aboriginal guides were gracious hosts, it was a very glum and pensive group, that departed from this experience. To speak with Taylor (Ibid.), the gaze had, indeed, been returned.

Such "sincere" engagement with the notion of authenticity in terms of values shared by both parties offers great potential to indigenous people who want to pursue tourism ventures with economic and socio-cultural sustainability, while at the same time communicating meaningful messages about themselves to their guests. There are numerous examples where this is already happening: Infian reserve and northern community tours in Canada, where visitors are acquainted with the cultural heritage as well as modern accomplishments of their hosts; various cultural immersion experiences in Aboriginal Australia, including *Bush University*; an increasing number of indigenous ecotourism ventures (see Chapter Six) and many other experiences involving genuine human encounters wherever they occur. It was mentioned before that aboriginal hosts may have to show generosity of spirit to their guests, meaning that "positive stereotypes" can be used to attract visitors, who may then be educated about the living culture of their hosts, if so desired.

Tourism can be employed to present "the other side" — that is the indigenous perspective of historical events and historical icons; examples such as the Battle of the Little Bighorn in Montana (Buchholtz 1998; Welch 1994), the Frog Lake Massacre and the Riel Rebellion in Saskatchewan and Manitoba, come to mind. Tourists can serve as "witnesses" for their aboriginal hosts' struggle and aspirations to protect land and culture, as has been realized by some Indian nations in South America.

This "rainbow quality" of authenticity, which continues to defy definition, should not necessarily be seen as a liability by indigenous people, but can be capitalized upon as an asset. For this to occur, however, it is of paramount importance that indigenous hosts gain or maintain control over the negotiation of the concept. The approach suggested by the Aboriginal Tourism Team Canada (directed at aboriginal tourism entrepreneurs) constitutes a good starting point:

> The most important aspect of Aboriginal cultural tourism is authenticity. To be culturally authentic, your business needs to satisfy the following five requirements:
>
> 1. Aboriginal people must own and participate in the business.
> 2. Traditional and current Aboriginal techniques or methods must be used.
> 3. Local customs and culture must be accurately portrayed.
> 4. The local community must be involved.

Illustration 4.6

An exercise in "sincerity" (Rottnest Island, Western Australia): Aboriginal Elder Robert Bropho introduces conference participants to the Aboriginal history of their conference venue.

5. The natural environment and its creatures must be treated with respect (Aboriginal Tourism Team Canada, no date a:8).

Such guidelines provide a sufficiently broad scope to make allowance for historical accuracy, the concept of a living culture, and socio-cultural and environmental sustainability:

> It would be difficult to offer a truly authentic Aboriginal cultural campout today and still maintain environmental sustainability. For example, we bring along modern conveniences, if we didn't .... all the trees would be bare. Sometimes we have to find a balance between cultural authenticity and environmental sustainability (First Nation Elder, quoted in Aboriginal Tourism Team Canada, no date b:4).

Summary

This chapter focuses on challenges encountered and approaches adopted by aboriginal people who host large and small numbers of visitors with different levels of interest in indigenous culture. It starts out with a discussion of general principles regarding socio-cultural impact management, commenting on aboriginal people's role as culture providers and culture managers, the use of social space and the assignment of roles to tourists to control physical and mental access to the host's culture, and the employment of indigenous guides to act as "gatekeepers" to societies as well as sites. The encounter between hosts and guests involves a commercial transaction of intangible goods. For this transaction to be satisfactory for both parties, there needs to be a social contract whereby explicit or implicit agreement is reached on the degree of access that the visitor gains to the host's culture in terms of physical space as well as social and spiritual dimensions. The substance of this social contract will vary depending on number and characteristics of visitors as well as the hosting preferences of the aboriginal people involved. Different approaches are examined.

Model cultures may be seen as living museums, but generally fail to communicate the essence of a living culture to the visitor. On the other hand, they enable aboriginal hosts to accommodate large visitor numbers (including visitors lacking in cultural awareness and sensitivity) without disruption of their lifestyle and communities. Such disruption is a common occurrence when indigenous people are faced with mass tourism. This may not only happen as a result of aboriginal tourism products being offered, but often occurs uninvited. Hawaii is an example of a place where the indigenous culture has been usurped and distorted to lend an identity to a tourist destination that attracts hordes of visitors. Pueblo nations of the southwestern U.S. have developed distinctive, culturally-based coping mechanism to deal with large visitor numbers and to benefit from visitation, without actually embracing tourism and without necessarily developing tourism products.

In contrast, cultural immersion brings hosts and guests into close contact. Cultural immersion is experiential and interactive. Examples from Australia, Canada and Bali are explored. Especially in cases where such experience is prolonged, as exemplified by homestays, impacts on the host's culture can be unpredictable and difficult to control. On the other hand, such encounters broaden the horizon of both, host and guest. The quality of cultural immersion experiences and their impact on host cultures is strongly influenced by the host's conceptualization of tourism, which in turn is likely to be determined by the host society's traditions pertaining to hospitality. Polynesian cultural groups offer interesting examples of traditional hospitality enriching modern tourism products, while grave risks are associated with a replacement of moral value systems by commercial ones.

The risks inherent in the cultural immersion approach to ethnic tourism are intensified when spiritual and religious matters are exposed to tourism. In recent years visitor interest in spiritual tourism has grown exponentially. In general, aboriginal hosts remain very guarded vis-à-vis this potential opportunity, and reluctant to allow visitors access to the inner sanctum of their cultures. On the other hand there are indigenous individuals who, for their own reasons, are willing to guide visitors in their quest for spiritual cultural knowledge, as exemplified by *Bush University* in Australia.

A theme that runs like a thread through different approaches to indigenous tourism is the concept of authenticity. It constitutes a characteristic of a tourism product desirable for both hosts and guests, but has proven to be an extremely elusive concept. Aboriginal product suppliers and communities, visitors and the travel trade may have very different ideas as to what constitutes authenticity, and academics have not been very helpful either in clarifying its meaning. Just how multi-faceted the impact of the notion of cultural authenticity can be in a tourism setting is shown by an interesting case from Belize. Descendants of the original representatives of Maya culture access ancient cultural information via modern means and interpret a newfound cultural identity within a complex framework influenced by colonialism and a re-evaluation of Maya relative to Mestizo identity. Finally, drawing on indigenous tourism initiatives in New Zealand, the concept of authenticity is compared to the notion of sincerity. It is suggested, that genuine cultural interactions between hosts and guests, drawing on common values, create "sincere" cultural experiences for tourists. This contrasts with tourism ventures featuring "staged authenticities", which are employed for their own purposes by Maori and *pakeha* alike.

Rather than constituting a liability, the "rainbow quality" of authenticity may be capitalized upon by indigenous people as an asset. This can only happen, however, if aboriginal hosts gain or maintain control over the negotiation of the concept, regardless of whether they encounter "the stranger" in masses or one on one, at a distance or up close and personal.

5

...and the Land

Introduction

The significance of "the land" for indigenous tourism can hardly be overstated. Land is one of the most important (if not the most important) source(s) of self-identification for aboriginal people. It is also the prime attribute for their identification by other parties (Notzke 1994:174). These facts have not been lost on the tourism industry. As previously stated, it is invariably a communal identity on a defined land base that accounts for tourist interest in indigenous groups. This has also been highlighted by Valene Smith's Four Hs of indigenous tourism (see Chapter One). Aboriginal people's ancestral connection with the environment is frequently seen as constituting an important aspect of authenticity in indigenous tourism (Barnett 2001:83). On the other hand, interpretation and image creation in tourism are characterized by a constant tension between what is portrayed as nature or natural, and what is in fact cultural landscape shaped by human intervention (Taylor 1999:69).

The real and perceived connection between indigenous peoples and their ancestral homelands can result in surprising developments, as illustrated by the following headline: "Nez Perce Indians invited to reclaim traditional land." (*The Globe & Mail,* July 23, 1996:A13) The subtitle summarizes what was extensively reported on in the European and North American press: "More than a century ago, they were chased from their homes. Today they are being asked to return as a tourist attraction." (Ibid.) The story of the Nez Perce Indians of the Pacific Northwest (who had been crucial to the survival of the Lewis and Clark expedition in 1805/1806) and their celebrated leader (Young) Chief Joseph is as tragic as it is well known.

As part of what constituted one of the last major Indian wars in North America, this peaceful tribe was driven from its homeland in Oregon and scattered on reservations across the continent, some as far flung as Oklahoma and Kansas. This dispersal occurred in 1877 after the tribe's epic 2,500km flight through the modern states of Oregon, Idaho and Montana, when Chief Joseph's starving and freezing band was forced to capitulate to the U.S. Army just short of the Canadian border, where they had hoped to escape to freedom. Some 250 Nez Perce warriors, joined by 500 women, children and old people, had fought with about 2,000 soldiers in 20 battles and skirmishes. It was, General William Tecumseh Sherman later said, "the most extraordinary of Indian wars." (Ibid.) Chief Joseph's capitulation speech — "From where the sun now stands I will fight no more forever" (Brown 1970:312) — was to become one of the most famous documents of United States Native American history. After the diaspora of the Nez Perce tribe, and countless attempts to reunite his people on a reservation in their ancestral lands, Chief Joseph died in 1904, reputedly of a broken heart.

Despite their historical standing, for over a century the Nez Perce were not allowed to return to their home in the Wallowa Valley in northeastern Oregon. In the early 1900s there were six petitions by Wallowa County settlers in opposition to the establishment of Indian reservations (*Die Welt*, July 25, 1996). All that was left of the valley's original inhabitants was a small Nez Perce cemetery on Wallowa Lake, including the burial site of Old Chief Joseph. But it was this small cemetery, with the aura of the Nez Perce and Chief Joseph, that developed into a major tourist attraction, drawing travellers from all over the world. Towards the end of the millennium things were coming full circle. Wallowa County encountered economic hardship, and its residents believed that bringing back the Nez Perce would help replace the dying logging and ranching economies that were originally created as a justification for removing the Indians. In a turn of events that can only be described as utterly ironic, county residents went about securing funds to purchase land in the Wallowa Valley to be turned over to the Nez Perce and, furthermore, to raise funds for the establishment of a Nez Perce cultural and interpretive centre. Reaction from the Nez Perce, many of whom live on the Colville Indian Reservation in neighbouring Washington State, has been cautiously optimistic. As Soy Redthunder, a descendant of Young Joseph, puts it, "The whites may look at it as an economic plus, but we look at it as homecoming." (*The Globe & Mail*, July 23, 1996:A13).

Indigenous people's homeland — their animate and inanimate environment — thus becomes an integral part of a traveller's experience. This circumstance accounts for much of the unique character of indigenous tourism, but it also engenders important challenges and problems that are likely to occur whenever tourists (who may or may not be interested in an "indigenous tourism experience") set foot on aboriginal people's traditional territory. These challenges include (but are by no means limited to) the management of sacred sites, profound differences in environmental perception and resultant behaviour between hosts and guests, and revisiting the concept of protected areas to accommodate indigenous interests. These topics will be explored in this chapter. It is not surprising that there is much overlap amongst them.

The Sacred and the Profane

"Is a church more holy than a butte?" This rhetorical question was featured in a 1997 special issue of the *High Country News, A Paper*

Illustration 5.1

Sacred places in nature: Chief Mountain, Montana, is a place of great spiritual significance for Alberta's and Montana's Blackfoot people. They call it *Ninastako*, "the mountain that stands apart."

for People who Care about the West (May 26, 1997:12), and presents a very complex problem in a nutshell: the question of what constitutes a sacred site and appropriate behaviour at such site. Sacred sites of the major monotheistic religions are usually easily identified, as they consist of built heritage such as a church, a synagogue, a mosque or a temple. They are usually located in population centres, and "non-believers" may be barred from entry or subjected to strict behaviour rules that are clearly communicated to them and easily enforced. On the other hand, sacred sites of more localized indigenous religions, often animistic in nature (but there are also examples in Buddhism and Hinduism), are less obvious. Many of them are sacred places in nature, such as mountains, caves, natural arches, rivers, lakes, waterfalls, springs, forest groves or individual trees and meadows. Others may feature man-made mounds, rock alignments or effigies, burial grounds, rock art or ruins. Not infrequently, the built heritage of younger religions has been superimposed on sacred sites of older, "earth-based" belief systems. Prehistoric Celtic shrines in Western Europe were incorporated in temples constructed by Roman conquerors and eventually transformed into places of Christian worship. The Spanish conquistadores erected churches on pre-Columbian pyramids.

Commonly, indigenous people's sacred places are remote, unprotected, and not subject to formalized worship, and their sacred character is not generally known or acknowledged. In fact, their location is often purposefully kept a secret from outsiders. As a result, such special places are under considerable threat from resource development and inappropriate visitation, and their legislative protection tends to be either completely lacking or grossly insufficient (Swan 1990; Notzke 1994b:229f). Tourism poses quite specific though diverse threats to indigenous sacred sites all over the world. Documentation is sparse and concentrated on a few examples, but there are certain recurrent themes. In the case of natural sites, particularly mountains or rock formations, tourists seem to want to climb the feature or photograph it, or preferably both, ignoring its special spiritual significance to a local culture. On the other hand, New Age tourists represent a different kind of problem: Without indigenous roots in the land in question, these visitors ascribe special "cosmic" spiritual significance to certain places and wish to worship them in their own way. In most cases, aboriginal peoples find this intrusive as well as inappropriate.

One of the most celebrated examples of a tourism controversy and dilemma is Australia's Uluru (formerly known as Ayers Rock). For many visitors to Australia the world-famous Uluru of the Northern Territory is a must see, and has come to represent the spirit of Australia. It is ranked among the world's greatest natural attractions. This huge monolith towers 348m above the surrounding sandplain in Uluru-Kata Tjuta National Park, which is home to Uluru (Ayers Rock) as well as to Kara Tjuta (The Olgas), a cluster of monumental rounded rocks, approximately 30km west of Uluru. The international status of this site is highlighted by its listing in the UNESCO World Heritage List in 1987 for its natural values and in 1994 for its cultural significance. Approximately half of all its visitors are from overseas (Brown 1999:680).

Climbing Uluru

It's important to realize that it goes against Anangu spiritual beliefs to climb Uluru, and they would prefer that you didn't. This is because the climb to the top follows in the footsteps of Mala ancestors of the Tjukurpa .... As well, Anangu feel responsible for the safety of all visitors to their land, and are greatly saddened when someone is injured or dies on the Rock. So far 35 have died there, mostly from falls and heart attacks.

Although the number of visitors to Uluru has risen steadily over the years, the number of people actually climbing it is declining. Meanwhile, sales of ideologically sound "I Didn't Climb Ayers Rock" T-shirts are on the rise.

The Anangu call the people climbing up the "Minga Mob." You just have to look at the rock from a distance to get the joke — *minga* means "ant." (Singh et al. 2001:249)

Maintaining Harmony by Appropriate Behaviour

The traditional owners state that this is a very important site, where many ancestors have visited, some still reside at Uluru. All the clues to living in this environment are provided through an understanding of the Tjukurpa (the pattern of life set by the ancestor). The important sites must be approached with respect if we expect all things to stay in harmony. The traditional owners wish that visitors took the time to learn about Tjukurpa and understand the real meaning of the place.

Source: L. Berryman of Anangu Tours, letter to P. Kauffman, 1999, Kaufman

The above paragraph is an excerpt of a new *Lonely Planet Guide to Indigenous Australia*, and illustrates an attempt to instil in visitors a new sense of what constitutes appropriate behaviour on Aboriginal land.

Uluru represents a textbook example of culture conflict at a popular heritage site. An activity popular among visitors is discouraged by the indigenous hosts for reasons of cultural respect. Uluru features an interesting management environment. The Pitjantjatjara and Yankunytjatjara people of Central Australia, collectively known as Anangu, were granted Native Title to the park in 1985, and subsequently entered into a lease-back arrangement with the Australian Government. This arrangement provided for a joint management framework between the Aboriginal owners and the Australian National Parks and Wildlife Service. The park is administered by the Uluru-Kata Tjuta Board of Management, which has a majority representation of traditional owners and is responsible for the development of management plans.

Nevertheless, by the late 1990s, there was no comprehensive visitor management strategy in place at Uluru-Kata Tjuta National Park, nor was there an ongoing process of visitor monitoring (Brown 1999:680). This was surprising in view of the fact that the park had become a major destination for mass tourism. Visitors entered land holding considerable cultural and spiritual significance to its Aboriginal owners. Annual visitor volume had increased from

5,000 in the 1970s to over 300,000 in 1994. A projected increase to 500,000 was expected by the year 2000, with a peak daily visitation probably in excess of 7,000. Visitor counts in the early and mid-nineties showed that typically 1,500 people per day climbed Uluru during busy periods (Ibid.). It was not before early 2000 that Parks Australia published a Visitor Infrastructure Master Plan, which highlighted many of the planning issues associated with the existing infrastructure (Shackley 2004:69). The report confirmed that crowding was viewed as the most significant problem within the Park, and that visitor safety was also a concern. Twenty-seven people have died on Uluru since 1965, and there have been numerous accidents, despite closure of the climb during extreme heat, wind, rain and other inclement conditions (www.deh.gov.au/parks/uluru/vis-info/safety.html). Restrictions on the climb may also be implemented for cultural reasons, for example, following a death in the Aboriginal community.

The controversy surrounding the Uluru climb and evidence of stress of the park's physical and social carrying capacity prompted Brown (1999) to conduct an investigation of the tourists' behaviour. He utilized the Theory of Reasoned Action (TRA), which explores the reasons and influential factors behind a person's behaviour in this case, the decision to climb or not to climb Uluru. According to TRA there are several factors determining a person's behaviour: the perceived implications of an action, an individual's positive or negative feelings about carrying out an action, and the person's perception of social pressures exerted on her or him by outside "referents" or "significant others" (Brown 1999:683). Understanding the rationale behind the visitors' culturally insensitive behaviour could inform potential behavioural control mechanisms aimed at discouraging those large numbers of visitors from attempting the climb.

Brown's study exposed significant differences between the beliefs held by males and females in his sample and between tourists who climbed Uluru and those who did not. Women believed more strongly that climbing the rock might engender negative outcomes or impacts, and they also evaluated these outcomes as more important to them (Ibid.:691). In general, male visitors held a more positive attitude towards climbing Uluru, reflecting their focus on conquering the elements. Earlier research had found men to be more "conquest" focused in the outdoors than women, who tend to be more "connection" focused towards nature and the environment (Knapp 1985, cited by Brown 1999:692). These findings provided a rationale for specifically targeting behavioural change initiatives towards males, for example, by paying special attention to fathers and sons in family groups or all-male bus tours from schools (Brown 1999:692).

The managers of Uluru-Kata Tjuta National Park wish to accively discourage visitors from climbing Uluru. Considering the high value accorded by so many visitors to the experience and accomplishment of the climb, it seems advisable for the park administration to explore closer cooperation with tour operators to promote alternative and culturally appropriate experiences with a similarly strong appeal (Ibid.:693). There is ample evidence in support of the notion that the use of threat or fear arousal is ineffective in behaviour change campaigns, and neither climbers nor non-climbers perceived the climb as difficult or a threat to their health. The most distinct attitudinal differences between climbers and non-climbers turned out to be in their assessment of impact. Thus the most effective avenue to dissuading climbers may be to challenge their attitudes towards the lack of cultural respect associated with climbing Uluru, and the ecological damage resulting from the activity. Such persuasion is most likely to make climbers question their actions sufficiently to cause attitude and behaviour change. Forced compliance with a given behaviour has proven to be ineffective (Ibid.). These findings support the park's current policy to rely on interpretive interventions encouraging visitors to voluntarily abstain from climbing in preference to a strategy of forced closure. This is also reinforced by the importance ascribed by climbers to "external referents" influencing their behaviour, which highlights the potential role of the tourism industry.

The state of affairs at the time of Brown's research suggested that much remained to be accomplished in fostering a sense of responsibility on the part of the tourism industry to promote culturally appropriate activities in the park that are endorsed, rather than just tolerated by the Aboriginal owners (Ibid.:694). But the onus for more ethical conduct is not on the tourism industry alone. Travellers should place greater emphasis on a genuine cultural contact experience. The indigenous community may have to become more proactively involved at the planning and commercial delivery levels of tourism products and programs. Brown detected major shortfalls in visitor access to guided park activities, particularly those involving contact with Aboriginal rangers. He also suggested a more explicit and timely (i.e., prior to or early during a visitor's stay in the park) delivery of messages concerning Anangu and the park's position on the climb, as well as other forms of message delivery such as in-flight videos and a park website.

In 2005 the Park's webpage unequivocally implores the visitor: "Please Don't Climb Uluru" (www.deh.gov.au/parks/uluru/no-climb.html). It also states that the Anangu have not closed the climb, but prefer that the visitor opt against it out of understanding and respect. Visitors are encouraged to visit the Cultural Centre *before* deciding on the climb. Unfortunately, the popular coach tours to Uluru typically involve sunrise viewing, followed by the chance to climb before the heat of the day, and then a visit to the Cultural Centre. Thus visitors are exposed to the displays at the Cultural Centre, which explain why climbing is discouraged, only *after* they have had the chance to climb (Shackley 2004:69). The Park administration and the Anangu hope to phase out the climb, which has decreased in popularity from 90 percent to less than 50 percent of visitors (although few make it to the top). T-shirts are available for both sides of the debate, "I climbed Ayers Rock," as well as the opposite, "I didn't climb Ayers Rock" (Ibid.:70). New activities are devised at Uluru each year, not only to generate revenue, but also to divert people from the climb, and to disperse the crowds. Despite their growing popularity, patronage of less intrusive (and more acceptable to the Anangu) activities is still poor, with only 10 percent of visitors taking advantage of Anangu guided tours, 6 percent embarking on the Uluru Circuit walk, and less than 5 percent going on camel trips or partaking of gourmet dinners with the "Sounds of Silence" (Ibid.:69f).

There is, however, yet another aspect to the "discourse of sacredness" (Whittaker 1994) of Uluru: that of its sacredness for white Australians. This perspective clearly separates the "white Australian" from "the tourist" (Ibid.:317). The latter is stereotyped by these white Australian "pilgrims" to Uluru as profane, thoughtless and insensitive to mysterious and spiritual qualities and, often, American:

> Rather, what *is* evoked is the moral and existential rights of white Australians to make a pilgrimage, to the Mecca of *all* Australia, Ayers Rock. As befits the notion of pilgrimage, the route is depicted as difficult, the climb dangerous and a true test of spiritual endurance. The whole undertaking is described as "our biggest initiation ceremony."
>
> ....
>
> The prospective initiate is frequently reminded that many have *not* met the tests of initiation and have actually died in the act of climbing, and some after the attempt. In appraising the danger and the mystery, it is seen as surprising that not more initiates have encountered their maker on the slopes of the Rock. The mys-

tery of the quest and the possibility of perishing in the throes of initiation are reinforced at the base of the Rock, where memorials are erected to all those who have died in scaling the edifice [sic]. The experience resembles, in spiritual awe, the reverence demanded by the cemetery at the Swiss village of Zermatt, which honors those who perished on the Matterhorn. Barely a couple of decades ago, a visit to the Rock resembled some of the hardships of the Crusades, and initiates prepared for the spiritual test in tents pitched in the very shadow of the challenge. Those who made the "true pilgrimage" at that earlier time refer with disdain to the touristic version, to the appearance of a multimillion dollar Sheraton and the luxurious Yulara tourist complex. These establishments and the tour buses that transport the initiate to the base of the Rock presumably violate the true sanctity of the experience.

....

Given this mystical and sacred communion, many white Australians claim that it is a lifetime dream to climb the Rock and that it should be accomplished before one dies. The spiritual quest, even dying for it, is tantamount to being a true Australian. To be deprived of this experience, the implication continues, would be against all Australian principles of spirituality and the sanctity of religious practice.

....

By all rights, such sacredness must be protected and, above all, shared and not restricted merely to Aborigines. The implication is that, in the face of such powerful sanctity and reverence, notions of property and ownership are self-serving and profane. (Ibid.:318f, italics in original)

Climbing Uluru has not been the only action at issue in the national park. Since 1985, when Uluru-Kata Tjuta was transferred into Aboriginal ownership, the administration has placed large areas of the park off-limits to all professional photographers and closed some walking trails to the general public (Barnett 1994:32). Most restrictions do not yet apply to the average tourist, but any film maker, professional photographer or commercial artist who wants to visit Uluru must apply for a permit to work within the park. Strict guidelines, spelt out in a nine-page document, stipulate what can or cannot be depicted. These actions were taken in accordance with the wishes of the Anangu traditional owners, who believe that uninitiated members of their society face serious consequences if they view images of certain places (Ibid.). Such rules have caused consternation and a moral dilemma among artists and photographers. They acknowledge the traditional owners' right to make decisions about their ancestral land, but also feel that Uluru and Kata Tjuta have great significance for non-Aboriginal Australians, and that, as a result, they should be allowed to produce and use such archetypical images of Australia without undue restriction.

This situation has also created a conflict regarding the Australian government's role as the custodian of a UNESCO World Heritage site, which is understood by some as a responsibility to ensure access to such site. As one photographer, Darwin-based landscape specialist Peter Jarver, puts it, the Olgas (Kata Tjuta) are a "geological gift from the planet," which should be freely enjoyed by all, Anangu or otherwise (Ibid.:33). The current guidelines have not stopped the publication of the many hundreds of photographs that were taken before 1985. Uluru-Kata Tjuta National Park features by far the severest photographic restrictions, but the practice has spread to other Aboriginal-owned parks in the Northern Territory, such as Kakadu, Keep River, Nitmuluk (Katherine Gorge) and Watarrka (King's Canyon). Surprisingly enough, views of Uluru, as well as Kata Tjuta, are featured in the new 2001 *Lonely Planet Guide to Indigenous Australia,* which otherwise appears to go to great length to practice and encourage culturally appropriate behaviour.

And then there are the New Agers, flocking to sacred places and indigenous practitioners, genuine in their search, yet utterly alien and, often, offensive to aboriginal people. Uluru became a truly "contested site" (Digance 2003) when it joined the international mystical tour circuit of "Aquarian pilgrims" (Marcus 1988, quoted in Digance 2003:153). Attempts to incorporate Uluru into their own cosmology have often brought these visitors into conflict with the Anangu, as well as with Australian Parks authorities. The contentious issue with New Age visitors is their insistence on accessing sacred Anangu sites. These special places are clearly marked by Park authorities, and off limits to visitors. Penalties exist for non-compliance with access restrictions. Nevertheless, individual travellers, as well as New Age tour operators, openly defy traditional owners' wishes by "using their own universalistic rituals as a way of connecting with the Other" (Digance 2003:154):

> There are, it is suggested, three reasons why the Anangu
> are unhappy with the increased interest by modern secu-

lar pilgrims wanting to conduct their own rituals and
religious ceremonies at Uluru and Kata Tjuta. The sensitivity of their sacred sites has already been noted. The
second reason is linked with the first: by allowing non-
Anangu to tap into the *Tjukurpa* [the Dreaming], they
are giving away their power and control over their cosmology. One of the intrinsic appeals of Uluru is the
Anangu's connection with the *Tjukurpa*, and the often
explicit message is that non-Anangu cannot access this
merely because the outsider is not Anangu. Finally, the
adverse publicity associated with use of the park by New
Age groups and individuals could dissuade mass tourists
from visiting the park. (Ibid.)

Uluru-Kata Tjuta may be a textbook example for tourism-related
conflicts at indigenous sacred sites, but similar scenarios present
themselves all over the world. Indigenous people everywhere are
becoming increasingly vocal about who has the responsibility for
managing their sacred cultural heritage. Such locations often consist
of what the Western world is accustomed to calling natural features, and for most aboriginal people the notion of a sacred site
carries with it a set of rules and proscriptions regarding visitor
behaviour, and implies a set of beliefs grounded in the non-empiri-
cal world (Shackley 2001:7). Tourism-related conflicts at Native
American sacred sites abound in the United States: for example, at
Rainbow Bridge in Utah, Devil's Tower National Monument in
Wyoming, Paha Sapa (Black Hills) in South Dakota, and at cultural
sites such as the Bighorn Medicine Wheel in northern Wyoming,
the "great kiva" at Chaco Culture National Historical Park in New
Mexico, and the Lions' Shrine at New Mexico's Bandelier National
Monument. Many of the issues encountered are reminiscent of
those occurring at Uluru: the practice by land managers of relying
on voluntary behaviour modification on the part of visitors; the ac-
cusation of reverse discrimination by those white Americans who
claim to revere certain sites in their own way; and the valid
question of who can claim a genuine cultural link with a certain
site.

A trend of great concern to indigenous peoples in the developing world is evidenced by the commercialization of the Great Pyramids at Giza, Egypt: The Egyptian Antiquities Organization's rental
of interior chambers for private use by New Age tour groups highlights the direction that revenue-strapped governments may be taking. Particularly worrisome are the larger New Age tour companies,
such as *Power Places Tours & Conferences*, which may run dozens

of these kinds of itineraries annually, focusing on certain UNESCO World Heritage Sites (Attix 2002:53). This is compounded by the widespread misconception of well-known sacred sites like Machu Picchu as simply examples of archaeology:

> Reinforcing this is the advertisement by a major credit card company in 1999, which featured a photo of Machu Picchu and the text: "Susan went to Peru for the People. Specifically the ones that have been dead for 500 years." In reality, the Quechua people are barred by racism and the U.S.$10 entrance fee from visiting their own sacred site, while enduring deplorable working conditions servicing the multi-million dollar Machu Picchu industry (Johnston 2000:95).

Environmental Perception: Where Worlds Collide

Sacred places in nature may be viewed as the culmination of different environmental perceptions among cultures; as one Aborigine put it quite succinctly (referring to white perceptions of Uluru), "All they see is a big rock, poor buggers" (Horwitz 1986, cited by Whittaker 1994:317). But just as "special places" cannot be isolated from their surroundings, their veneration cannot be separated from more generally held differing views of the environment, which have important implications for tourism. Images of landscape are a crucial component of tourism marketing and destination interpretation. As Taylor (1999) points out, there is a constant tension between what is portrayed and interpreted as nature and what constitutes, in fact, cultural landscape shaped by human intervention.

Furthermore, this distinction between nature and culture is only made in the Western tradition. For most indigenous peoples there are no boundaries between nature and culture. The environment and its creatures are part of their social universe. Much of what is presented to Western travellers as "pristine" landscape owes its special character and habitat characteristics (and often its perceived "attractiveness") to the activities of its indigenous inhabitants. Scientific findings indicate that virtually every part of the globe, from the humid tropics to the boreal forests, has been inhabited, modified, or managed throughout our human past (Gomez-Pompa & Kaus 1992:273; Krech III 1999; Blainey 1976). The American and

Illustration 5.2

Natural or cultural landscape? East Africa's celebrated savannah ecosystem with its wealth in wildlife owes much of its character to pastoralists' activities. Lake Manyara National Park, Tanzania.

Australian continents, for example, have been and to some extent still are extensively impacted by aboriginal burning practices; the same is true for the East African savannah, which owes much of its character to the pastoral activities of the Maasai and other livestock herding peoples. At a less tangible level, for many indigenous people their "land" or "country" is both a physical and a spiritual entity, something that has been made or created by spirit ancestors or superior beings; and the process of interaction with its human and non-human inhabitants is ongoing, with ties to the past and consequences for the future.

While the imagery of such perception has been usurped by the tourism industry, particularly in North America and Australia — as reflected by brochures, postcards, T-shirts and other "Symbolic Souvenirs" (Taylor 1999:70) — an understanding of its substance and implications is slow in coming and has remained mostly shallow. In this context it is hardly surprising that there is a growing indigenous objection to the appropriation of designs and motifs that

Illustration 5.3

Like Canada, Australia uses Aboriginal images for "branding" purposes to highlight the country's uniqueness as a destination for distant markets. This postcards's caption reads: "Awakening. Aboriginal people, the first Australians, have been part of this ancient continent for many thousands of years. They have shaped the environment just as the land has shaped them. At the start of a new millennium Australia is awakening to their cultural and spiritual message."

Source: (Pc-20) made in Australia by Astrovisuals. Copyright by James Widdowson; www.imagec.com.au. Reprinted with permission of James Widdowson Production Pty Ltd.

relate to Aboriginal people's spiritual connection with their environment.[1]

It is not coincidental that the inscription of New Zealand's Tongariro National Park in the World Heritage List came first on the basis of its natural heritage characteristics. The same happened in the case of Uluru-Kata Tjuta. In 1994 and 1995, respectively,

---

1 It is noteworthy that the "pirating of Aboriginal designs" has had consequences for some players in the tourism industry. In Australia, in 1989 the matter of copyright of Aboriginal art on T-shirts was brought before the courts under the Copyrights Act of 1968 and the Trade Practices Act of 1974 (Whittaker 1999:39). The issue of indigenous intellectual property rights is subject to an ongoing and heated debate, and not only in the tourism industry.

they were reinscribed as associative cultural landscapes, paying tribute to their Maori and Aboriginal significance, which had been previously marginalized by the Western environmentalist tradition of separating culture and nature (Taylor 1999:81). There is a tendency in tourism to continue this separation, even though there are major differences depending on what kind of tourism we are looking at. In this context, one of the most enduring myths is that of "wilderness." This has major implications for indigenous people (and their environment), who are involved in or affected by tourism development.

According to the 1964 U.S. Wilderness Act, wilderness is a place "where man himself is a visitor who does not remain." (Gomez-Pompa & Kaus 1992:271). This concept of wilderness as an area without people has influenced thought and policy throughout the development of the Western world, in particular with regard to the conservation movement. It is a thoroughly urban construct, which has viewed "wild lands" as a challenge, as a frontier to be tamed and conquered and, more recently, as outdoor laboratories and natural resource banks of biodiversity (Ibid.:272). None of these interpretations has any notion of humans being a part of the natural environment. For most people in Western society today wilderness is a concept the reality of which they have not personally experienced, and this also applies to the growing urban populace of the newly industrialized countries. In terms of recreation and tourism, wilderness has always been associated with solitude, a notion that has become severely challenged over the past three decades as more and more people are seeking it. Another important recreational and tourism ingredient of the wilderness experience is the idea of challenging oneself and conquering the elements.

Only very recently have more people come to appreciate the idea that their concept of wilderness — which is evolving, but remains a Western one — often includes homelands of indigenous peoples (Klein 1994:4). This development has come about with an evolution and refinement of the "green movement" and in the tourism field, with an evolution of the concept of ecotourism (see next chapter). As the tourism industry becomes increasingly sophisticated and diversified, it also becomes more and more evident that even subtly different varieties of tourism can have profoundly different implications for indigenous hosts' involvement in and benefit from tourism activities. Quite commonly, no clear distinction is made between ecotourism on the one hand and adventure tourism on the other hand. Both are perceived as being nature-based, active and experiential, and focused on an "exotic" and interesting environment. Moss (1994) offers an excellent discussion of the implications of both in his article on Katannilik Territorial Park, near Lake Harbour, Nunavut:

> It might be valuable for planners, administrators, visitors, and resident Inuit to recognize the sometimes conflicting desires of these two approaches. Ecotourism is one thing; adventure tourism, another. They intersect, but their adherents come to Katannilik for quite different reasons, and their impact on the park and on the people who are its guardians is quite different (Moss 1994:23).

> There is excitement in such a venture [NorthWinds Arctic Adventures' rafting trip], the development of skills, plenty of camaraderie. There is exhilaration, exhaustion, a sense of achievement at "conquering the wilderness." But there is virtually no time for contemplative or passive appreciation of the natural environment, no time to discover or appreciate the ways of the native people in the past or present. *What one learns in adventure tourism is about the self — and little about the world* (Ibid.:24; emphasis added).

Ecotourists *were* interested in learning about the world of their hosts (Ibid.). While not necessarily needing guides to find their way around, they would welcome local people as interpreters to travel with them, explaining the traditional way of life on the land and the flora and fauna from an Inuit perspective. In addition to hiking and rafting in the park, they enjoyed community involvement in the form of catering, country food, and opportunities to buy carvings and encounter people on a personal basis. As pointed out by Moss (Ibid.:25), the results were most telling when considering the financial breakdown of the visitors' impact on the community. Ecotourism companies, such as the *Sunrise, Country Walkers*, and *Wanapitei* groups, dispersed more than $600 per person into the local economy; the *NorthWinds* clients spent less than $40 each. Such figures are somewhat misleading, however, since *NorthWinds* is a Baffin enterprise (based in Iqaluit), while the other tour companies are from southern Canada and the United States:

> The environment as a challenge, conquest of the wilderness, these are catchword phrases among adventure travellers — and anathema to the genuine ecotourist. Yet both groups care passionately about the environment; both are committed to engagement with the natural world; both make substantial sacrifices of money and comfort to participate in what they think of, and I have

> been describing as, "wilderness." Often, both lose track
> of the fact that, what to them is wilderness, to the indig-
> enous people, the Inuit, is *home* — not territory occupied
> in a residential sense, but landscape they have lived
> within, beyond memory, even beyond story, beyond time
> (Moss 1994:25; italics in original).

On the surface, indigenous tourism resources and interests appear
to be well matched by the demands and sensitivity of ecotourists.
The rhetoric associated with both types of tourism places a high
priority on the welfare of the natural environment, along with
the interests of the local hosts. Hinch, however, suggests that
a closer examination of indigenous hosts' and ecotravellers' fundamental views of humanity's place in nature reveals that the match
between these groups is not as perfect as it appears (Hinch
1998:12). While both groups are likely to share an ecocentric
world view, where humans are seen as just one part of the ecosystem, Hinch feels that in all probability the sensibilities of many
ecotourists would be offended by longstanding cultural practices of
indigenous people. In particular, he refers to the hunting of whales,
but also to other hunting and trapping activities. The apparent endorsement of such activities by visitors enjoying a feast of country
food is a far cry from actually witnessing a hunt and its aftermath
in all its bloody detail by people unaccustomed to tracing their own
food beyond their local supermarket.

From the local community perspective, the worst case scenario
of such an incident would be the release and widespread distribution of video footage shown out of context, which could then be
used to apply pressure to shut down future hunts. From the tourism point of view, the prospect of disturbed or distraught guests is
equally undesirable (Ibid.:122). In order to avoid such outcomes at
all costs, it is common practice in northern Canadian communities
to separate tourists from hunting activities in a temporal or spatial
manner. This can be accomplished in various ways. The Inuvialuit
of the western Arctic have addressed this problem in a proactive
manner by means of their *Tourism Guidelines for Beluga-Related
Tourism Activities* and their unequivocal statement of priorities (see
Chapter Two). In contrast, Grekin and Milne (1996) report on the
delicate relationship between tourism and Inuit hunting activities in
Pond Inlet, Nunavut, and the adoption of an unwritten policy to
conceal hunting from tourists. To further complicate matters, there
is also potential conflict between different types of nature/wildlife-
based tourism: namely ecotourism and sport hunting (Notzke
1999b).

Big game sport hunting is the variety of tourism with the deepest roots and longest history in northern communities. Hunters are the largest per capita spenders in the tourism industry; they demand less of a tourism infrastructure than many other tourists, and they do not on ideological grounds object to a northern land-based harvesting way of life. Promotion and marketing of sport hunts is by word of mouth through satisfied clients, and via established linkages with local or regional clubs and associations. All this makes them very attractive clients for aboriginal communities. On the other hand it must be acknowledged, that trophy hunting is, at best, a stable industry, whereas growth potential lies with ecotourism and adventure tourism: i.e., non-consumptive outdoor activities. What is the relationship between these two important subsectors of the tourism industry? Not surprisingly, there are different opinions on this subject.

Peter Lamb of Parks Canada (Interview in Inuvik, July 13, 1995) feels that the long history of big game outfitting and the extensive participation in it by many communities is one of the reasons ecotourism will only be able to evolve in the North over a long period of time. While big game outfitting and ecotourism are both resource-based, they require profoundly different people skills from the aboriginal operator. Aboriginal operators themselves express less ambivalence about combining the two, as long as common sense rules are followed, such as cleaning up the hunting camp and keeping the operations separate (Interviews with Maureen Pokiak, Tuktoyaktuk, July 18, 1995, and Randel Pokiak, Tuktoyaktuk, July 19, 1995). Aboriginal people do not necessarily perceive disharmony among the various ways the land and its resources sustain them, be it by harvesting, guiding sport hunters, or catering to ecotourists. James Pokiak of Tuktoyaktuk, who pursues all three activities, expresses it best when he says: "There is a time to harvest the animals, and there is a time to just sit back and enjoy them ...." (Inuvialuit Communication Society & Parks Canada 1995).

The number of hunters welcoming tourists into their camps will likely remain small, but at least among the Inuvialuit there are numerous strong believers in the educational function of tourism. These individuals feel that wherever there is a willing host, tourism can go a long way in changing outsiders' views of harvesting activities. An element of risk remains, though: "How do you control information, once you have given it?" (Interview with Richard Binder, Inuvik, July 24, 1995). But with an increasing measure of control on the part of the harvesters and improving education of tourists, more aboriginal hosts may be willing to take this leap of faith.

Returning to the issue of an ecocentric world view, Hinch cautions both ecotourists and indigenous hosts against claiming moral high ground. He feels that even the more "pure" ecotourists would be hard pressed to acknowledge that the Inuit are a natural part of the predator-prey relationship in the Arctic ecosystem (Hinch 1998:122). In his estimation, there is a greater likelihood that those ecotourists who can accept the hunt will do so by rationalizing the practice as the behaviour of a less civilized culture. Only a select few are likely to avoid such a paternalistic attitude and accept hunting as integral part of the ecosystem.

What about the indigenous host? It is beyond the scope of this chapter to engage with the many contentious issues pertaining to the real and perceived sustainability of traditional subsistence practices, the fit of modern technology with traditional ethics, the presence of waste and litter in northern communities. Indigenous people would not be human if their world view were not characterized by its own ethnocentric perspectives on the relationship between humans and the environment:

> There do not appear to be any pure ecocentric positions on the part of the ecotourists or indigenous peoples although if placed on a continuum running from anthropocentric to ecocentric, indigenous people seem to be closer to the ecocentric end. Regardless of this positioning, the lack of ecocentric purity is not really the critical issue. Ecotourists and indigenous hosts hold different views of their relationship with nature because of their distinct cultural backgrounds. What is problematic is that a false assumption exists in some quarters that there is no difference. It is this assumption which is dangerous. A failure to recognise these differences, to develop a deeper understanding of them, and to consciously take these differences into account when planning and managing indigenous tourism development is likely to lead to debilitating frustration on the part of both ecotourists and indigenous hosts (Hinch 1998:123).

Indigenous Peoples and Protected Areas[2]

The topic of protected areas, such as national and territorial parks, has already been touched on in the previous two sections of this chap-

---

2 For a detailed treatment of this topic and further references see Chapter 8 in Notzke, 1994b.

ter. This is hardly surprising since, as Ryan and Huyton (2000b:27) point out, parks represent a nexus of different cultures, "Western concepts of the hedonistic and scientific, and Aboriginal concepts of identification of self with place as living entities." The record of the relationship between indigenous peoples and protected areas worldwide is a checkered one (Lewis 1990; Notzke 1994b; Shelton 1983; Wells & Brandon 1992; West & Brechin 1991).

The maintenance of national parks (and other protected areas in the same mould) is beset by numerous problems. One set of problems is inherent in the concept itself. Machlis and Tichnell (1985) put it in a nutshell:

> We must always remember that national parks, for all their seeming wildness and the apparent dominance of Nature are partly social creations. They are conceived, established, maintained, and in turn threatened by society. Lost in the philosophical debates between "environmental protection" and "resource development" is the fact that the perpetuation of national parks does not depend upon one or the other; it depends on both (1985:95).

> The conflict originates from the paradoxical mandate that parks provide opportunities for public enjoyment in environments that are to be preserved (Ibid.:22).

National park problems arising from this dual mandate are universal and well known. Another set of problems, however, is caused by circumstances that have until recently received far less attention. The national parks idea is a product of Western industrialized society. Without any adjustment, this concept has been transplanted into different cultural and social environments. In the process, aboriginal populations have either been physically displaced or their socio-economic base has been severely disrupted. Such cultural insensitivity and failure to integrate protected areas into regional socio-economic systems may not only have disastrous consequences for local indigenous populations, but, in the long run, will also jeopardize the very resources protection areas are designed to preserve (see also Chapter Two).

Not only do aboriginal people lack a concept in their languages for what is commonly referred to as a "park," but the two main ingredients of the park idea, preservation and recreation or leisure, are utterly alien concepts in most aboriginal cultures:

This distinction between work and leisure is largely an artifact of industrial society. Leisure, however, requires not only time but also space and resources. The need for wilderness parks, and for the recreational use of wildlife, well known to wildlife managers, is that of an industrial as opposed to an agrarian or a foraging society .... What is more-or-less unified in Aboriginal cosmology is fragmented in our own. The division of knowledge into branches such as law, political theory, economics, and biology, the distinctions between work and leisure, between man and nature, among the attributes of land and the incidents of property, are essentially foreign to Aboriginal tradition (Usher 1984:400).

This is no less true for the concept of preservation that is based on a notion of "apartness" between man and nature. Preservation and conservation are often taken to mean exactly the same thing; namely, to keep things undisturbed or in an unchanged condition. In practice, however, and in particular with regard to the natural environment, the two terms have assumed quite different meanings. Preservation is most commonly used in reference to non-use of a resource and non-interference with the processes of nature. In contrast, the concept of conservation is entirely compatible with sustainable utilization of resources:

Conservation and development-policy-making and -planning often seem to assume that we, the Aboriginal peoples, have only two options for the future: to return to our ancient way of life or to abandon subsistence altogether and become assimilated into the dominant society. Neither option is reasonable. We should have a third option: to modify our subsistence way of life, combining the old and the new in ways that maintain and enhance our identity while allowing our society and economy to evolve. As original conservationists, we now aim to combine development and conservation, and to put into practice the concept of equitable, culturally appropriate, sustainable development. As such, the goal of the World Conservation Strategy is our goal too (Erasmus 1989:93f).

These words by George Erasmus, former National Chief of the Assembly of First Nations and also a director of World Wildlife Fund Canada, indicate that a meeting of the minds between indigenous people and society at large may be possible after all. This is also suggested by a neologism Inuit use to describe a park, namely "mirnguiqsirvik," "a place to rest and relax" (Bruce Rigby, correspondence of July 26, 1993). The fact that numerous places that have been designated as parks also have sacred value and special significance for native people has a potential for complicating as well as facilitating such understanding. This has already been highlighted in the first section of this chapter. Mount Rainier in Washington State, the Banff Hot Springs in Alberta, and Gwaii Haanas (South Moresby) in British Columbia are further examples from North America.

Whereas the ingredients of the Euro-American parks concept are alien to aboriginal ways of thinking, veneration for and protection of special places are not. Thus the management scenario for protected areas is cluttered with a multiplicity of concepts, deeply ingrained in respective cultures and societies and, more often than not, incomprehensible to the other party. Furthermore the situation is complicated by legal and political factors, and by the question of legal and moral rights. The tourism industry is only one of many players on this crowded and complicated stage, but has nevertheless much potential to affect the lives of the indigenous players, as well as the fate of their homelands. This will be illustrated by examples from Australia, northern Canada and Botswana. We will encounter the indigenous inhabitants of the land as landlords, co-managers and displaced persons, aided and hindered in various ways by tourism development.

Aboriginal Landlords of Australian Parks

Australia's Northern Territory (NT) exhibits numerous similarities to Canada's northern territories: both regions have historically been treated as hinterlands; they have become the focus of mineral development activity; and they contain large indigenous populations actively engaged in attempts to retain control over their land and resources in order to safeguard traditional lifestyles. In Australia's Northern Territory, Aboriginal people comprise 22 percent of the population, and Aboriginal land, held under unalienable title, totals nearly half a million square kilometres or about 34 percent of the NT (Altman 1989:457). The territorial economy is characterized by a narrow base (focused almost entirely on the public sector, mining and primary industries) and its high dependency on federal funding. Tourism constitutes the territory's second largest and fastest growing industry, contributing 4.6 percent of Territory product (Ibid.:457f).

The NT capitalizes on two major drawing cards in terms of tourist attractions: the environment and Aboriginal culture. This is of double significance, as the two most important tourist destinations, Kakadu and Uluru-Kata Tjuta National Parks, are owned by Aboriginal people, and leased back to, and run by, the federal Australian National Parks and Wildlife Service (ANPWS). This creates a peculiar tension: the NT Government is vehemently opposed to Aboriginal land rights and the management of some of its national parks by the federal government (Australian national parks are usually managed under state legislation) but, on the other hand, depends on Aboriginal interests for the implementation of its "developmentalist" policies in the tourism field (Altman 1989:460).

Consultation with Aboriginal people is required in Australian Northern Territory legislation for park agency management of:

(a) Land vested in an Aboriginal or Aboriginals, or in a body corporate that is wholly owned by Aboriginals; (b) Land held upon trust for the benefit of Aboriginals, or (c) Any other land occupied by Aboriginals (Territory Parks and Wildlife Conservation Ordinance of 1976 and National Parks and Wildlife Conservation Act of 1975, quoted in: Gardner & Nelson 1981:341).

Furthermore, the terms of the leases clearly define a native role in Kakadu and Uluru.

Uluru-Kata Tjuta National Park was originally founded as the Ayers Rock-Mount Olga National Park in 1958. It was transferred to Aboriginal ownership in 1985, after a prolonged political struggle, with the passage of the Aboriginal Land Rights (Northern Territory) Amendment Act. A condition of the 1985 land grant was that the National Park be leased back to the Australian National Parks and Wildlife Service. The park comprises 1,325km^2 and is surrounded by Aboriginal land except for an enclave of some 104km^2 north of the park, excised for the Yulara township site in 1976. In the mid-1980s the Aboriginal population of the park fluctuated between 120 and 150. As mentioned earlier, tourism to Uluru has increased rapidly during the last decades. This was greatly facilitated by the development of accommodation facilities outside the park in the tourist village at Yulara:

While Uluru National Park is now managed on a day-to-day basis by the ANPWS, policy is formulated by a board of management (the Uluru-Kata Tjuta Board) with an Aboriginal majority. This means that while the Park has been leased back to ANPWS for 99 years, decisions about visitor use of the Park are determined by the Board. However, the NT Government and private sector interests own and control Yulara where almost all tourist facilities are located. This gives them economic control over regional tourism (Altman 1989:462).

The establishment of Kakadu National Park was linked to the Ranger Uranium Environmental Inquiry, which promoted National Park designation for the original sanctuary. But, as reported by Hill (1983:166), the traditional Aboriginal owners were the first to suggest that if they were successful in their claim to the land covered by the proposed park, they would be willing to lease the land to the Director of the Australian National Parks and Wildlife Service. Their motivation was not so much based on a clear understanding of what the national park concept was all about as on the fear that alone they might be powerless to protect the land from competing interests (i.e., uranium mining), and on the feeling that the establishment of a national park in the area was likely to create a management regime that would be sympathetic to their aspirations and interests. As one traditional owner put it: "Whatever this national park thing is, whatever else it does, the land will be safer" (Fox 1983:163):

> Under the terms of the Lease Agreement the Director accepted certain obligations. These include commitments to train local Aboriginals in skills necessary to enable them to assist in Park management; to employ as many traditional Aboriginal owners as is practicable under conditions that recognize their special needs and their culture; to promote among non-Aboriginals a knowledge and understanding of Aboriginal traditions, culture and languages; to engage Aboriginals in park interpretation programs; to consult regularly with the NLC [Northern Land Council] about policy so that the opinions of the traditional owners are taken into account; and (as part of the Plan of Management), to have due regard for the needs of the Aboriginal owners in their use of and movement throughout the Park. In accordance with the Agreement, Aboriginals are involved in planning for and managing the Park at both the consultative and employment levels.
>
> Aboriginal agreement is required before any development or management action affecting them may proceed.

Illustration 5.4

Illustration 5.5

(Illustrations 5.4 and 5.5) Kakadu National Park in Australia's Northern Territory attracts many visitors with its spectacular landscape and unique rock art galleries.

Illustration 5.6

A sign at the Ubirr site within the Park introduces the visitor to the area's traditional owners. It explains that the landowners have the responsibility to ensure that no harm comes to the paintings, and that the stories associated with them and the land are passed on to the next generation. It also points out that the visitor can help by keeping to the marked track, showing respect for the art and by not drinking alcohol at the site.

> Depending on the project or action that is proposed, consultation may take place with individual traditional owners, a group of owners, the Gagadju Association to which all traditional owners of the Park belong or the Northern Land Council. The traditional owners determine the level at which the consultation takes place. They also use the consultative process to put forward their own proposals for the Park. (Hill 1983:166)

Unlike Uluru, in Kakadu there is no formal institutional structure (such as a management board with an Aboriginal majority) to safeguard Aboriginal interests. Instead, this function is assumed by the Northern Land Council (land councils in general have become para-governmental institutions), which represents the interests of traditional owners, and by informal consultative processes.

When Kakadu National Park was proclaimed in 1979, no more than 20 percent of its traditional owners lived there, but by 1982 the proportion had risen to 75 percent. This is not only an indication of people's confidence in the management of the area, but it also relates to the more effective servicing of the outstations (communities) by the Gagadju Association now responsible for utilizing the royalty payments from uranium mining (Fox 1983:165).

In the late 1980s the park's Aboriginal population numbered between 260 and 280 and was distributed over about 15 communities in the Park. Kakadu National Park cannot be viewed in isolation from the large Ranger uranium mine and its mining town which occupy an enclave within the park. Of great significance for the Aborigines is the payment of mining royalty equivalents of about $3 million per annum to the regional Gagadju Association under the Land Rights Act. In the period 1982 to 1987 visitor numbers at Kakadu quadrupled from 45,800 to 195,000. Growth can be linked to improved ANPWS facilities and transport links associated with the Ranger mine, as well as to the World Heritage listing of the park (Altman 1989:462f).

What benefits do Aboriginal people derive from the presence of the parks in general, and their ownership of the land in particular? Obviously there are a variety of economic benefits derived from different kinds of involvement in the tourism industry: employment, ownership of or shares in enterprises, sale of artifacts, commoditization of culture and the lease or sale of resources (Altman 1989:465–468). At Uluru, for example, in 1986 tourism-related employment provided 18 percent of household income, and the manufacture of artifacts a further 6 percent. At Kakadu the impact of the uranium mine and its royalty payments must be borne in mind. In general, local Aborigines do not work at the mine, but prefer employment with ANPWS and the Gagadju Association. Overall, it was estimated that 26 percent of regular household income in 1986 was derived from ANPWS employment alone.

Employment in positions such as that of a ranger holds other, less tangible benefits for Aboriginal people, as it enables them to continue in their function of land stewards. On the other hand, the combined expectations of tribal Elders and the park service put a heavy burden on the shoulders of these individuals. As one Kakadu ranger, Jonathan Yarramarna, puts it:

> There are two sets of laws for us here — Aboriginal law and government law. That means we have to look after the country in two ways, which is pretty hard for us ...
> But we can do it (Breeden 1988:287).

Illustration 5.7

Joint management of national parks has become a widespread practice in Australia. This sign informs visitors that Nitmiluk (Katherine Gorge) National Park is owned by the Jawoyn people and jointly managed by the traditional owners and the Parks and Wildlife Commission of the Northern Territory.

The sale of hunting and ritual culture features prominently in tourism marketing by the NT, but there is little evidence that Aboriginal people are interested in supplying it (Altman 1989:467).

One of the more surprising facts is that Aboriginal parties receive only a small proportion of the tourism rent (or profits) generated by the resources they own. This is most apparent in the case of Kakadu. The leaseback agreement concluded with ANPWS in 1978 stipulated an annual lease payment of $7,502. Jon Altman hypothesizes that this "peppercorn rental" was probably acceptable to traditional owners, because they receive over $3 million per annum in mining royalty and rental payments from the Ranger uranium mine (Ibid.:467). At Uluru National Park, under the memorandum of lease signed between members of the Uluru-Kata Tjuta Land Trust and the Director of ANPWS in 1985, Aboriginal owners are paid $75,000 annually plus 20 percent of any gate fees. In 1986, this amounted to over $100,000. Within just over a decade, in 1997–1998, it increased dramatically to US$2.75 million (*25 percent* of Park income according to Digance 2003:152), of which 20 percent goes towards running the local community, and the remainder is distributed among the traditional owners on a family unit basis:

> It is of interest that while Aboriginal people are provided with a statutory guarantee of a share of mineral rent raised on Aboriginal land, there is no such guarantee with tourism rent. This distinction might be based on an assumption that mineral resources are finite, whereas tourism resources are inexhaustible. However, such an assumption may prove false in situations when excessive tourism pressure results in environmental (and associated cultural) degradation (Altman 1989:474).

Aboriginal people at Kakadu and Uluru are feeling the tourism pressure and associated economic and non-economic costs. Land use by tourists potentially reduces Aboriginal access to land for hunting, gathering and fishing, and thus reduces Aboriginal income-in-kind. Some Aborigines in Kakadu felt that their hunting and fishing rights were not adequately protected (Kesteven 1984:17, quoted in Altman 1989:472). Their position as landowners enables Aboriginal people at least to close communities and sacred sites to visitors; and where they are able to gain a majority of policy formulating bodies like the Uluru-Kata Tjuta Board, they can regulate tourism within the park to a certain extent.

The Aboriginal experience in Uluru and Kakadu National Parks has shown that even where parks are revenue generating tourist destinations, property rights do not necessarily translate into financial returns. Altman also advises that it is absolutely crucial for Aboriginal people to ensure that their interests are given statutory recognition and protection before, and not after, tourism growth (Altman 1989:474). In their struggle for recognition of their land rights, the Gagadju at Kakadu and the Anangu at Uluru Kata Tjuta were compelled by circumstances to place their ancestral lands within the confines of a concept they only vaguely understood. While Aboriginal people as "park landlords" have a degree of leverage in these locations, they still find themselves in a situation where the concept of a national park and the phenomenon of mass tourism have been imposed on them:

> [A] factor working against success is an apparent narrowness of the management authority's understanding of the term management. For instance, Aboriginals have always voiced their fear of tourism throwing large numbers of Eu-

ropeans against the Arnhem Land boundary at the East Al-
ligator River [in Kakadu]. Yet they see ANPWS improving
access roads, setting up attractive facilities, producing color
ul brochures and displays, all primarily aimed at controlling
visitor use but in fact increasing demand. Aboriginals are
involved in discussing the proposed developments, in guiding visitors, and in providing information for signs and
leaflets. They are involved in the implementation of management but not in the management decision-making process itself. This is not to say that ANPWS didn't want to
allow full involvement but that the political climate did not
allow time for traditional consultative processes to work.
Often short-term political solutions caused destabilization
for the traditional people and it is in the field of middle
management decisions that the Aboriginals perceive the
Service excluding them most of all. (Fox 1983:165)

The formation of joint management structures in Australia's national parks originated with the compulsory leaseback agreements
described above, whereby the government recognized Aboriginal
ownership of the land, yet required the immediate lease-back of the
land and negotiation of joint management arrangements within the
framework of a national park (Wearing & Huyskens 2001:191).
Some would call this blackmail. Joint management of national parks
has since spread beyond the Northern Territory, independently of
land ownership, to South Australia, New South Wales, Western
Australia and Queensland, with somewhat mixed success. The overall picture appears to remain one of "Competing Interests" (the title of a review by Woenne-Green et al. 1992, quoted by Wearing &
Huyskens 2001:195) between traditional owners, conservationists and
tourists, more reflective of the tacit acceptance of *involvement* on
the part of Aborigines than of the acknowledgement of their *rights*.
Despite the good will of many of those involved, Wearing and
Huyskens (2001) claim that joint management regimes must be considered essentially Western cultural models of management with an
inherent Anglo-Australian bias. They contend that improvement will
only occur after the adoption of a truly cross-cultural paradigm that
accommodates indigenous cultural values and the formulation of
policies within the framework of ecotourism principles.

Co-Management of Northern Canadian Parks

In contrast to Australian (and United States) federal agencies, Parks
Canada requires outright public ownership of national park land

(Gardner & Nelson 1981:209). But the fact that aboriginal people do not own park land does not necessarily mean that they derive less control or fewer benefits from the establishment of protected areas on their ancestral land.

Traditionally, in the older established parks in most of the provinces, native people have been effectively excluded from protected areas, to which they had originally retained user rights if not ownership. This applies to lands under federal and provincial jurisdiction. Wood Buffalo National Park (located in Alberta and the Northwest Territories) is an exception to this rule, since it constitutes the only example where aboriginal people have a history of participation in the use and management of the park.

Large parts of Canada have recently been involved in or still anticipate both the settlement of comprehensive aboriginal claims and the establishment of new protected areas. As exemplified by Gwaii Haanas, and on a smaller scale, Meares Island, aboriginal groups in British Columbia have proceeded with the establishment of their own protection areas (and the management of visitors). This was done partly because protection from resource exploitation could not wait for government action, and also because it constituted the assertion of jurisdiction. These actions in no way precluded access by non-natives to the protected areas, but they established aboriginal systems of visitor guidance and control. In the case of Gwaii Haanas these efforts eventually resulted in the establishment of a national park reserve under a unique joint management regime (see Notzke 1994b, chapter 8, for more details). British Columbia, with its unsettled aboriginal claims, recently also established the first provincial park under a joint management system, Nisga'a Memorial Lava Bed Park (Copeland 1999:95–98; Pfister 2000:130ff). Great care is taken here to interpret not only the natural, but also the cultural landscape, and to do this in accordance with proper Nisga'a cultural protocol.

The greatest opportunity for and evidence of innovative approaches to the establishment and management of protected areas can be found in Canada's territorial North. This huge region is covered by comprehensive claims of Dene, Metis and Inuit peoples, whose settlement has reached different stages of implementation and negotiation. Inuit make up 80 percent of the population in the recently (1999) established territory of Nunavut. Aboriginal people constitute about 10 percent of the population of the Yukon, and approximately 50 percent of the Northwest Territories (Atkinson 2001:142). Claims settlement usually involves exclusive or preferential harvesting rights for aboriginal people on Crown lands within their claimed territory and aboriginal people's involvement in the management of resources. The latter is accomplished by schemes that allocate control of resources among competing interests and facilitate the merging of knowledge (Notzke 1993:395). For example, the 1984 *Inuvialuit (Western Arctic) Final Agreement* engendered a complex co-management scheme, encompassing all aspects of renewable resource management, environmental impact assessment and review, and the establishment and management of new national parks (see also Chapter Two).

The necessity for designing co-management schemes in the northern park context stems from three facts:

- a profound lack of fit between the conventional Euro-Canadian park idea and northern aboriginal people's stake in the northern environment and its resources;
- the ongoing process of the creation of new national parks in areas subject to comprehensive aboriginal claims;
- the enduring importance of renewable resources to northern Aboriginal mixed economies.

To make allowance for potentially conflicting interests, the involvement of aboriginal parties has become an integral part of the establishment of new northern parks. Where new national parks are established in conjunction with the settlement of land claims, the negotiation of a joint management regime for the planning and management of the new park is an integral part of the settlement agreement. Where claims remain unsettled, national park reserves are established. Park reserves are practically parks-in-waiting: Their boundaries are provisional; they do not compromise native land claims, but they are subject to national park legislation in all other respects.

There are now three national parks within the Inuvialuit Settlement Region. Tuktuk Nogait National Park and Aulavik National Park on Banks Island were established in the 1990s, and the design of their co-management regimes was part of the establishment agreement. In contrast, Ivvavik (formerly Northern Yukon) National Park was a direct result of the Inuvialuit Final Agreement (IFA) of 1984. An Inuvialuit role in the management and administration of this park is firmly entrenched in the IFA. In addition to the role Inuvialuit co-management bodies play in the management of land and resources in the Inuvialuit Settlement Region in general, several sections of the IFA pertain specifically to rights and privileges for Inuvialuit beneficiaries inside the park. These provisions cover a variety of items, including harvesting rights, employment preference in the operation and management of the park, preferred rights to economic opportunities arising from the park etc. The Inuvialuit also played a key role in the preparation and final approval of the Park Management Plan. The stipulations contained in the Aulavik Park Establishment Agreement are even more detailed. The most recent establishment agreement for Tuktuk Nogait calls for a formal advisory board for park operations and management planning (Budke 1999:8f).

When it comes to tourism development under the IFA co-management regime, it was already illustrated that the regime is empowering in some respects, but acts as a constraint in others (see Chapter Two). This is also true for tourism in the national parks. In their recent study of tourism planning for Aulavik National Park on Banks Island, Wight and McVetty (2000) found tourism to be extremely limited in the park: about 20 tourists per year. This is not really surprising, since the park is some 250km from Sachs Harbour, the only settlement on the island, and the only access is by charter plane. Visitor activity is concentrated on the Thompson River. People mainly canoe or kayak, but also hike, sightsee, visit archaeological sites, watch wildlife and birds and take photographs. They may also visit culturally significant sites. Park visitors do not use outfitting or guiding services, since no one in the community of Sachs Harbour is licensed to provide such services in the park. They spend little or no money, and spend no time in the community. As a result park visitors provide little net economic benefit for either the community or Parks Canada (Ibid.:19f).

Geography only partially accounts for this situation. Evidence suggests that even experienced tour operators find trying to operate in Western Arctic Parks increasingly complex, time consuming, expensive and uncertain, and some have actually pulled out from commercial river trips. Much of this has to do with the claims regime. Good intentions notwithstanding, the layering of various bureaucracies has created an operational gridlock, which makes the licence application and consultation process and timelines extremely cumbersome for prospective local tourism outfitters as well as those from "outside" (Ibid.:21). The Park Establishment Agreement for Aulavik stipulates that 50 percent of the park's business quotas shall be awarded to Inuvialuit enterprises. Outside outfitters (with a positive track record in other Arctic destinations) are being turned down or getting no response to their applications from local agencies, who are required to approve applications in fulfilment of the park co-management regime. Locals see this as a way to prevent outsiders from "muscling in."

Since no Inuvialuit businesses have applied, however, the prospects of *any* outfitted tourism in the park appear dubious. Outside operators have clearly expressed a willingness to hire local people or to work with the community. Yet residents seem unaware of the potential benefits of such partnerships. As a result, visitors will either embark on independent unguided trips into the park with little opportunity to interact with Inuvialuit, or they will stay away altogether. There is also more potential for visitors harming the park environment unwittingly. Thus part of the draft park management plan's mandate seems to have been undermined: namely to protect the environment while facilitating tourism, increasing community benefits, and increasing park visitation (Ibid.):

> One main obstacle preventing Banks Island from realising its optimal tourism outcomes has been the failure of Aulavik National Park's co-management parties (Parks Canada and the Inuvialuit Regional Corporation) to address the total tourism context, and to realize that two solitudes of wishful thinking have developed:
>
> • that the park will be a premier tourist destination; yet that
> • Sachs Harbour will provide services to park visitors with the attendant economic benefits and infrastructure.
>
> The result has been minimal visitor use and extremely negligible benefits.
>
> ....
>
> The next step is for co-management partners to examine their mechanism for partnerships, and establish appropriate partnership conditions, to help park stakeholders, local peoples (sic) and outside operators to get benefits. These co-management policy goals must be tempered by a shared understanding of what constitutes realistic outcomes in the Banks Island environment. Whether or not these mutual benefits are realized from park-related tourism will depend on further pragmatic efforts from all parties (Wight & McVetty 2000:25).

This example clearly shows how important the legislative and policy environment can be for tourism planning, and that the empowerment of local communities does not automatically guarantee the desired outcome and tangible benefits from tourism. There are, however, positive developments in Nunavut's three national parks, particularly Auyuittuq (Baffin Island) (see Notzke 1994b:254 and Chapter Seven). Similarly, Katannilik Territorial Park has enjoyed the full support of the people of Lake Harbour (Baffin Island) as a result of their direct involvement in its development and management. The economic impact is already considerable: Airfare and hotel accommodation are major factors in the regional economy, whereas guiding services, other hosting activities and carving sales stimulate the local economy.

Canada exhibits an increasing variety of cooperative management, joint stewardship and co-management scenarios in its protected areas. Some are a result of policy decisions, as exemplified by management practice in older, established national parks like Riding Mountain in Manitoba, where a stakeholder roundtable (including three First Nations) acts as an advisory committee (Budke 1999:13). Others are based on aboriginal peoples' statutory and constitutional rights and are an integral part of modern treaties: namely, in British Columbia and the North. Particularly in the latter case, aboriginal people have gained ownership in the process, and it is largely up to them to direct the process to their optimum advantage.

Grekin and Milne (1996:85ff) call our attention to the fact that literature in general has downplayed the role that local people can play in influencing tourism's development path. This is particularly true for Canada's northern communities. While the results of the claims process are by no means satisfactory to all parties, the resultant co-management regimes have empowered aboriginal communities to take an active role in local tourism development. Canada's northern communities are in a much better position than local communities in many other parts of the world to ensure that tourism remains sustainable and does not undermine its natural and socio-cultural resource base.

Dispossessed Basarwa in Botswana

The reader has already encountered indigenous tourism issues in Africa in Chapters One and Two, as exemplified by recent initiatives and experiments with community-based wildlife management and tourism development. The cases of the Maasai in Kenya and of the San in Namibia represent enlightened initiatives, though they are anything but devoid of problems. An April 2002 court decision in Gabarone, Botswana, sealed the fate of a group of Basarwa (San, Bushmen[3]), who against all odds, had continued to reside in the Central Kalahari Game Reserve. Within the framework of the Botswana Government's

---

3   Refer to Isaacson 2001, Sanders 1989, Van der Post & Taylor 1984 and Wilmsen 1989 for more information regarding Bushman/San/Basarwa terminology, history and current issues in Botswana.

Remote Area Development Program, the last 800 San were forcibly removed from their homes, loaded on trucks and moved to the village of New !Xade. Twenty-four mostly old bushmen remained behind in the Kalahari, steadfastly refusing to abandon their land (*Die Welt,* April 23, 2002). Critics cite diamond mining prospects, tourism development and cattle grazing as the true reasons for this expulsion; the Botswana government claims it can no longer afford to provide the desert dwellers with water and social services.

Ironically the Central Kalahari Game Reserve (CKGR) was not originally conceived as an exclusive park, but was established upon the recommendation of an anthropologist, George Silberbauer, in 1961, in order to preserve the people, wildlife and habitats of the central Kalahari region. In the early 1990s the reserve was inhabited by approximately 1,200 San (down from 5,000 in 1960) in several villages, although the number of people utilizing it varied with rainfall and resource availability, and as many as 3,500 people claimed to have land rights in the reserve (Hitchcock 1985:32; 1991:10). The majority of these people no longer followed a "pure" hunting and gathering way of life but rather subsisted in a mixed economy that involved hunting and gathering as well as some livestock raising and crop cultivation and Botswana government drought relief assistance. By 1982, !Xade (site of a permanent water source, drilled in 1962) had become a small permanent village whose residents were pressing for further development assistance (Hitchcock 1985:34).

In 1985 the government of Botswana called for a commission of inquiry to assess future options for the Game Reserve. This commission recommended that portions of the reserve be turned into a Wildlife Management Area, where people would be allowed to continue to reside and utilize local resources. These recommendations were rejected by the Ministry of Commerce and Industry, which oversees parks and reserves in Botswana. Instead, the minister argued that the San population "is undermining the integrity of the Game Reserve" (*Botswana Daily News,* December 2, 1986, p.1, quoted in Harden 1989:9). Subsequently several reasons were advanced as to why resettlement was necessary. First of all, the move would ensure conservation of the resources in the reserve. Second, the move to other areas would improve people's access to social services and development assistance. And finally, it was argued that such a move would enhance the tourism potential of the region and would serve to increase economic opportunities for local people in the tourism industry (Hitchcock & Brandenburgh 1990:23).

The reasons behind the pressure for relocation of the San were complex and had very little to do with their actual impact on the wildlife of the Kalahari. The resettlement plans were part of a strategy to pacify environmentalists who had been pressuring the European Economic Community to withdraw its subsidies to Botswana's cattle industry (Harden 1989:10f; Hitchcock 1991:12). The environmental community's outcry, however, had not been caused by the Game Reserve's human population, but rather by the death of hundreds of thousands of antelope on account of disease control fences blocking their migration routes out of the CKGR to water and dry season grazing (Owens 1985:292–308, 319–321). In the late 1980s pressure to turn the CKGR into a "true" game reserve or national park, where people would not be allowed to live or hunt and gather, somewhat subsided, but did not disappear completely, while a modest degree of political mobilization occurred in the San communities. In November, 1990, Botswana government planners suggested that the CKGR be nominated as a biosphere reserve under UNESCO's Man and Biosphere Program. Within its framework continued residence and sustainable utilization of resources in the Reserve would be permitted (Hitchcock 1991:12). In the late 1990s the Basarwa residents of the reserve asked the government to allow them to co-manage the CKGR with the Wildlife Department (Currington 1999:14). Nothing came of these proposals, and throughout the 1990s pressure for removal of the San grew again.

It is ironic that conservation and tourism were employed as arguments to dispossess indigenous people in the Kalahari (Hitchcock & Brandenburgh 1990:23). The Basarwa constituted part of the attraction of the CKGR for many visitors. While the controversy was unfolding, the San in the Central Kalahari Game Reserve and other parks and reserves in Botswana were involved in the tourism industry in an opportunistic manner, but were never in a position to dictate the terms of the engagement or to use tourism in a constructive way to strengthen their position with regard to a land base. According to Hitchcock and Brandenburgh (1990:22), the impacts of tourism on the Basarwa were mixed, due to the lack of control by the visited over the encounter. While any influx of cash, however small, was welcomed, the local communities suffered from sudden social stratification and resultant disharmony, disruption of subsistence activities, and the frequently degrading nature of the tourism encounter, when people were expected to remove their clothes to be photographed. Such negative experiences were counterbalanced by excellent working relationships between some Basarwa groups and certain safari companies, who lobbied on behalf of the Basarwa and actively assisted in community development. The mixed blessings of tourism were further evidenced by a cultural revival of practices and crafts on the one hand, and problems associated with the demonstration effect, particularly on young people, on the other hand.

The controversy regarding government policy toward the bushmen (not only in the CKGR) is intensified by Botswana's extreme sensitivity regarding issues of race and ethnicity (Kelso 1993:54). The Botswana government refuses to acknowledge a collective identity, special rights or indigenous status of minority groups within the population. The country's approximately 50,000 Basarwa constitute three quarters of Botswana's so-called Remote Area Dwellers, or RADs, the rural poor, who live outside urban centres and gazetted villages (Hitchcock 1995:2).

Botswana's Remote Area Development Program (RADP) is in line with the government's reluctance to run separate development schemes for the benefit of ethnic groups. It may also be viewed as an attempt to divert international attention away from the much publicized "plight of the Bushmen" and towards the government's national social welfare program (Sanders 1989:181). One of the key objectives of the Remote Area Development Program is the concentration of Remote Area Dwellers in established settlements, yet without giving them the security of land tenure necessary to protect their resources from the incursion of outsiders and their cattle. Many Basarwa, on the other hand, would prefer less centralized settlement, and they desire their own land base. The issue of the Basarwa, tourism and protected areas must be considered within this broader framework. The Basarwa will only be able to harness tourism for their benefit if they advance from being "culture providers" to "culture managers", or if they are enabled to benefit from a resource base in a manner similar to Namibia's area conservancies. Both could be assisted by their continued residence even on the outskirts of game reserves or national parks, but would be much more likely to happen if their collective status and land rights would be reconsidered by the government. One of Botswana's four main planning objectives is, after all, to promote social justice (Hitchcock & Brandenburgh 1990:23).

Finally, it should be added, that like other southern African countries, Botswana pursues a program of community-based natural resource management, but at least in some cases the policy implementation process seems to have been characterized by a planner-centred rather than people-centred (Michener 1998), form of participation, and by manipulation and dominance in dealing with local people rather than community empowerment, regardless of ethnicity (Twyman 2000). On the other hand, there are also reports of a qualified success of some initiatives, as exemplified by the village of /Xai-/Xai (Gujadhur & Modshubi 2001).

Summary

Not only does "the land" provide the stage for the encounter between "the stranger" and "the native", but it also constitutes an important medium whereby the tourist experiences indigenous culture. The intricate relationship between aboriginal people and their land accounts for a large part of the unique character of indigenous tourism, but it also engenders contentious issues that need to be addressed in a tourism setting. This chapter explores three closely related topics: the management of sacred sites; differences in environmental perception and resultant behaviour between hosts and guests; and the challenge to accommodate indigenous interests in protected areas.

Indigenous people's sacred sites are often sacred places in nature that frequently elicit tourist behaviour that is unacceptable to their traditional stewards. Central Australia's Uluru is chosen to document various aspects of the problematic relationship between the stranger, the native and sacred land. One kind of conflict arises when visitors to the site fail to appreciate its sacred nature and engage in what aboriginal people view as disrespectful behaviour, such as climbing Uluru as a physical challenge or for the view. The problem becomes even more complicated whenever outsiders do not necessarily disrespect the sacred place in question — quite the opposite — but do fail to recognize local ownership and stewardship of the site. In Uluru's case, many white Australians, who do not view themselves as tourists conduct regular pilgrimages to the rock with the purpose of climbing it. For them, Uluru (or rather Ayers Rock) has become part of their own national mythology, and thus disconnected from the Aboriginal Dreaming. The same is true for New Age travellers, who also want to incorporate Uluru (and many other sacred places) into their own cosmology, but who do not acknowledge and respect local ownership and spiritual authority.

In many ways, the issues arising from these competing mythologies/cosmologies pose even more serious challenges than imbuing visitors with respect for sacred places. Successful responses to both types of challenges remain to be devised, but it appears that unilateral solutions are not going to work. Effective communication among all players, including indigenous stewards of sacred sites, park authorities (or other government agencies where applicable), tour operators and travellers, is of paramount importance to allow for respectful and enriching visitation of sacred places. While every effort should be made to enable visitors and the travel trade to become part of the solution, aboriginal and non-aboriginal authorities may have to rethink approaches that rely on voluntary behaviour modification on the part of outsiders.

Special places cannot be isolated from their surroundings, and their veneration (or lack thereof) grows out of specific views of the environment. Such environmental world views have important implications for tourism. Nowhere else does this become as clear as when considering the concept of wilderness. "Wilderness" implies the notion of man's apartness from nature, a notion utterly alien to indigenous cultures. But wilderness appreciation is central to the tourism experience sought by many travellers. Only recently have more people come to realize that the wilderness they seek often includes the homeland of indigenous people. Tourism market segments respond differently to this circumstance. An example from Canada's high Arctic demonstrates the relative implications for indigenous people of ecotourism and adventure tourism. It becomes clear that ecotourism offers more potential benefits to aboriginal communities than adventure tourism. While adventure tourism tends to focus on the natural environment as a challenge, ecotourists are interested in connecting with, and learning about, the environment, including a view of this environment through the eyes of its aboriginal stewards. Natural and cultural tourism experiences are thus combined. But a word of caution is in order: There are risks associated with overestimating the commonalities between aboriginal and ecotourism world views. Exposing visitors to the harsh realities of hunting and trapping activities should be approached with extreme caution by aboriginal hosts. Misrepresentation of the harvesting way of life or distraught visitors can both result in serious repercussions for indigenous communities and their tourism industry.

The discussion of differing world views of indigenous peoples and tourists inevitably leads to the topic of protected areas. Like tourism, this notion is firmly rooted in Western industrialized society, yet its constructs have been applied to the homelands of indigenous people, who value the lands in question for their own reasons. The tourism industry plays an important role in the dialogue between aboriginal and non-aboriginal parties with interests in protected lands. Aboriginal people have reached different degrees of accommodation with these foreign concepts, and in some cases they have failed to do so. This is demonstrated by three examples that introduce the indigenous inhabitants of the land as landlords, co-managers and displaced persons.

One would expect aboriginal owners of protected areas to be able to derive the greatest benefits from, and exert the strongest control over, tourism activities on their lands. That this is not necessarily the case is shown by Australian national parks, particularly by the Northern Territory's most important tourism destinations, Kakadu and Uluru-Kata Tjuta National Parks. In both cases joint management structures originated with compulsory leaseback agreements, whereby the government recognized Aboriginal ownership of the land but required the immediate leaseback of it and negotiation of joint management arrangements within the framework of a national park. The Aboriginal owners of the parks have a degree of leverage in managing visitors and derive economic benefits from tourism returns. Yet they have been unable to control the onslaught of mass tourism, to have a decisive voice in management decision-making, and to derive financial returns commensurate with their position as owners of high revenue producing tourism destinations.

The situation is somewhat different in Canada's territorial North. Here aboriginal people do not own the land of protected areas within their comprehensive claims regime, but they do, nevertheless, have substantial control over management decision-making as to whatever happens in these northern parks. This includes tourism development. The co-management regime established by the Inuvialuit Final Agreement, for example, enables its beneficiaries to have decisive input in admitting outside tourism enterprises and reserving business opportunities for themselves. This does not necessarily result in an optimum realization of opportunities. Nevertheless, by and large, Canada's northern claims regimes have empowered aboriginal communities to take an active role in tourism development, and it is largely up to them to direct the process to their greatest advantage.

Finally, with Botswana we encounter a country whose government does not acknowledge a collective identity, special rights or indigenous status of minority groups within its population. Issues pertaining to race and ethnicity are an extremely sensitive topic. This, combined with the government's unwillingness to grant disadvantaged groups security of tenure in land and resources, has serious implications for Botswana's Basarwa. It is exemplified by the forcible removal of 800 San from the Central Kalahari Game Reserve. Ironically, conservation and tourism were employed as arguments to dispossess the indigenous people of the Kalahari. This is a sad example of a Third World government utilizing an outdated version of an alien concept (the protected area) to further its own interests.

6

Indigenous Participation in Ecotourism

Introduction

The previous three chapters have investigated the interplay of "the stranger," "the native" and "the land" as the key elements of indigenous tourism. The kind of tourism where these three elements come into sharpest focus is ecotourism. Various aspects of indigenous people's involvement in ecotourism have been discussed throughout this book, but due to its real and perceived importance for aboriginal people, ecotourism deserves its own chapter.

Over the past two decades there has been a plethora of definitions of ecotourism. Nevertheless, just about every scholarly journal article about ecotourism starts out with a statement that "there is no consensus on the definition of the term *ecotourism*" (Weaver 1999:793) or "there is considerable debate over what ecotourism really means" (Campbell 1999:535), and that "ecotourism still means different things to different people" (Buckley 2000:443). There seems to be some agreement, however, that ecotourism can be defined in terms of a "product" as well as an operating "principle" (Ibid.), that it is driven by ethics, by a certain ideology (that of sustainability). There can also be little argument with the fact that the perception of ecotourism and the way various stakeholders have engaged with the concept have shifted over the years. This shift is very relevant for indigenous people's involvement with ecotourism.

Boyd and Butler (1999:126) illustrate how priorities have shifted over time from the exploration of and education about natural settings to promoting biocentric positive impacts both in terms of environment and cultures present (Table 6.1). Other tourism scholars and researchers like Honey have added the elements of local empowerment and support for human rights and democratic movements (Honey 1999):

> Properly defined, then, ecotourism is travel to fragile, pristine, and usually protected areas that strives to be low impact and (usually) small scale. It helps educate the traveller; provides funds for conservation; directly benefits the economic development and political empowerment of local communities; and fosters respect for different cultures and for human rights (Honey 1999:25).

What all this seems to illustrate is a strengthening of the social and cultural dimension within the concept and approach of ecotourism, which in turn reflects a rethinking of man's place in nature.

Interestingly enough, this evolution coincides with an era of increasing empowerment and politicization of indigenous peoples in Canada and worldwide. Nor is it surprising that aboriginal people

Table 6.1   The Evolution of Ecotourism

Period	Characteristics of Ecotourism
Pre-1950s	Exploration and education
1950–1980	Special interest/education
1981–1988	Nature (culture) observation and study
1988–1991	Nature/culture study with local economic benefits
Post-1991	Biocentric positive impacts (environmental and socio-cultural)

Source: Boyd and Butler 1999:126

in many areas are taking an ever-increasing interest in this particular brand of tourism. People's motivations vary widely. While in Canada economic factors rank most important for involvement in any kind of tourism, indigenous federations in Ecuador, for example, have adopted ecotourism as an important tool for consolidating their land rights movement (Wesche 1994). Establishing a presence on the land by means other than harvesting also ranks important with some northern groups in Canada. Furthermore, participation in an industry gives people an element of control over developments that may occur anyway, with or without them. While disadvantaged in so many other economic ventures, aboriginal people have a competitive edge in ecotourism:

- They are frequently in control of, and knowledgeable about, vast, remote areas.
- They may be able to capitalize on the widespread "image" of indigenous people living in harmony with their environment.
- While many visitors may be interested in nature per se, the opportunity to see the land through native eyes and to experience native cultural activities adds an extra and unique element to the trip.

Whatever motivates hosts and guests, we must bear in mind ecotourism's most important characteristic, namely the fact that it is a resource-based industry. Access to and management power over land and resources is a *sine qua non* for equitable aboriginal participation in the industry. This fact cannot be stressed enough, because what sometimes passes for ecotourism can have disastrous implications for indigenous people without land rights. Thus it is not surprising that there are also many voices of caution and vigilance against ecotourism (Campbell 1999; Johnston 2000, 2001). In this context it is important to realize that the ecotourism phenomenon has featured two trends (which continue in the present). On the one hand there has been a global growth of ecotourism, driven by industry and national governments, which has resulted in the invasion of indigenous lands and of "authentic" or "exotic" indigenous cultures and lifestyles. It is this type of ecotourism that Johnston (2000:90) refers to as "any form of industry monopolized tourism that commercializes indigenous biocultural heritage, including collective property and/or the homeland of the 'host' people."

On the other hand, there has been a trend for indigenous communities to creatively use ecotourism to protect their lands and lifestyles, in both a proactive and reactive manner. Johnston (2000:91) points out that many indigenous organizations clearly distinguish between ecotourism as conceptualized and practised by the tourism industry and indigenous models for ecotourism, where initiatives are community driven and reflect local values and priorities. Others would argue that ecotourism has been mislabelled and mishandled by governments and industry (Epler Wood 2002:25), and that tourism initiatives that are viewed as a threat by indigenous people, by definition, do not constitute true ecotourism. Semantics aside, the fact remains that globally there are major differences both in the degree to which indigenous peoples can harness ecotourism for their own purposes or are likely to be victimized by what is marketed as ecotourism. The major dividing line appears to be between the global North and South. The situation in countries like Canada, the United States, Australia and New Zealand, where there is at least partial recognition of indigenous title to lands and resources, is vastly different from that of most indigenous peoples in the developing world.

This chapter will explore indigenous ecotourism in Canada, where there are major regional differences in potential and actual ecotourism development. Then the issue will be investigated in the developing world, exemplified by Belize and Ecuador. These two countries were selected for their particularly interesting examples of indigenous communities employing ecotourism to realize their own ideas of a sustainable future. The chapter will conclude with some thoughts about the ambiguous relationship between indigenous peoples and ecotourism.

Indigenous Ecotourism in Canada

Amongst Canada's aboriginal people interested in tourism development there is a strong philosophical predisposition for and endorsement of

Illustration 6.1

Illustration 6.2

Illustration 6.3

(Illustrations 6.1, 6.2 and 6.3) Northern Canada offers considerable potential for ecotourism: a pristine environment, aboriginal management power over land and resources, and a live connection between the land and its stewards. Scenes from Banks Island: Twenty-four hour daylight; peregrine falcon chick and Geddes Wolke caring for his dogteam.

ecotourism development: in particular, ecotourism development that capitalizes on an indigenous identity. This is evident, for example, from the title and message of the Canadian National Aboriginal Tourism Association's (CNATA) video *The Stranger, the Native and the Land* (CNATA 1994b), from the endorsement and promotion by CNATA president Barry Parker of "cultural ecotourism" as *the* form of indigenous tourism development (Parker 1996), and from the motto of the Aboriginal Tourism Association of British Columbia, "*...where the land and the people are one*." (www.atbc.bc.ca)

The potential for the development of aboriginal ecotourism in Canada (defined for the purpose of this chapter as majority indigenous-owned and operated and capitalizing on an indigenous identity), however, is determined by several factors that vary across the country:

- a pristine and attractive natural environment
- access to and management power over renewable resources

- "connectedness" with the land (and/or water) in physical as well as spiritual terms
- sophistication of industry knowledge and/or access to industry partnerships
- capital
- skilled manpower

Not surprisingly, the challenges faced by aboriginal people involved in the industry are vastly different depending on whether they live in northern communities, where a land-based way of life still prevails, or whether they are residents of southern reserves.

Northern Canada

In northern Canada, particularly in the territorial North (Yukon, the Northwest Territories and Nunavut) the first three ingredients tend to be present: a pristine environment, access to and management power over land-based resources and a living connection with the land. These aspects are circumscribed by a unique operational environment, namely the presence of mixed economies and co-management schemes, which were already discussed in detail in other chapters of this book. There is a lack of industry knowledge but frequently there are successful partnerships with experienced tour operators, some of them aboriginal. Capital and skilled manpower tend to be in short supply. In the provincial north aboriginal people often face intense resource pressure and competition from extractive resource industries, such as clear-cut forestry, mining and hydro-carbon development. The destruction of Alberta's boreal forest, for example, constitutes a severe threat for ecotourism development in general (as well as big game hunting and birding) (Western Canada Wilderness Committee 1993).

What is the extent of indigenous ecotourism development in this huge region? In short, the potential is vastly under-utilized. *Bathurst Inlet Lodge* in the central Arctic (western Nunavut) is an example of a high-end eco-lodge and a native/non-native partnership. It was established as a naturalist lodge in 1969 by longtime (non-aboriginal) northerners, long before the term "ecotourism" was even coined. It became an Inuit partnership in the mid-1980s, when Kingaunmiut Ltd. was formed to take care of the financial interests of the people of Bathurst Inlet, and the Inuit became co-owners of the Lodge. They participate in all aspects of the operation, from directors on the board to kitchen staff and wildlife guides (Butler 1990:43). Community members play a particularly vital role in the Lodge's educational programs (Burt et al. 1993). The economic impact on this small community is considerable, since the Lodge sells a high-priced and high value product.

The majority of ecotourism enterprises in northern Canada are wholly or partially owned by local people (Raitman 2002:2). Elu Inlet Lodge, 240km from Bathurst Inlet, is the first majority Inuit-owned facility in the Kitikmeot Region of Nunavut. Similar to Bathurst Inlet, guests are treated to a cultural immersion and experience the land from the Inuit perspective: fishing for arctic char, visiting ancient stone fox traps, observing wildlife and witnessing traditional Inuit games and drum dancing. As already described for the western Arctic (see Chapters Two, Three and Five), ecotourism is playing an increasingly important role in the economy of the new territory of Nunavut:

> In April of 1999, the Inuit officially reclaimed their traditional lands, effectively separating Nunavut from the Northwest Territories (NWT). Today, Nunavut, representing one-fifth of Canada's landmass, truly belongs to the Inuit, and many ecotourism enterprises directly enhance the well-being of this native people by boosting the economy, preserving social ties and protecting the environment.
>
> As making a living solely as a trapper, hunter or gatherer has become increasingly more difficult, Arctic ecotourism has enabled the Inuit to survive in a wage-based economy. By facilitating up to 8,000 tourists per year, Nunavut residents have secured jobs in hotels, restaurants and airlines and benefited from the revenue created by such enterprises. Ecotourism has also enabled the Inuit to serve as interpretive guides and ecolodge owners, provided carvers and other artisans with another market to sell their handicrafts and encouraged hunters and fishermen to sell "country foods" like caribou steaks and fresh scallops.
>
> ....
>
> But Arctic ecotourism provides more than jobs and revenue. By showcasing their traditions, the Inuit can bring worldwide attention to their unique culture, revitalize cultural activities that have been abandoned during the 20th century and strengthen bonds between Inuit elders and youth (Raitman 2002:4f).

The environmental education effect of ecotourism can be very multi-faceted and may result in a two way learning process. Clearly visitors are the main beneficiaries of the process, gaining an appreciation of what is involved in living off the land in modern times as well as learning something about the timeless aspects of northern life. But the learning process is not one-directional. In the western Arctic Maureen Pokiak remarked that her husband really "had his eyes opened" about "no trace camping" by working as a guide for *Ecosummer Yukon Expeditions* (a Whitehorse-based company). As a result, the couple not only adopted the practice in their own newly established tour company, but also observe it privately and are passing it on to their children (personal communication in Tuktoyaktuk, July 18, 1995). Raitman (2002:5) reports a similar local influence on Bathurst Inlet, where over the years local habits improved regarding both littering and wasting meat. Thus, for many aboriginal people, an engagement with ecotourism results not only in a new validation of traditional conservation practices, but also the adoption of modern sustainable habits.

More commonly, however, the "ecotourism focus" in aboriginal tourism ventures is implicit rather than explicit. Visitors undergo various degrees of cultural immersion by participating in community tours, visits to hunting and fishing camps, and guided cultural or naturalist tours. The focus is on a living northern culture rather than "aboriginality." The hosts are very keen on teaching southerners about northern life and everything it entails. Visitors want to learn about people's daily lives from the people themselves. There is a strong emphasis on personal encounters (Notzke 1999). Even though many, or even most, indigenous tourism ventures operate outside protected areas, conservation purposes are being served, because tourism contributes to the viability of northern land-based economies and communities, thus strengthening their stake in healthy northern ecosystems.

Southern Canada

In southern Canada the situation is somewhat different, but quite varied. **British Columbia** exhibits some similarities with the North insofar as contemporary treaties are in the process of being negotiated, and in the interim, a number of co-management regimes for renewable resources are in operation, giving First Nations a stronger voice in management decisions than in most other provinces. Also, aboriginal people in this province, particularly on the west coast, have been able to maintain closer physical and spiritual ties to their traditional resource base, the salmon and its habitat, than, for example, those First Nations living on the Plains. The oceans, rivers and forests of west coast peoples may be threatened and their resources over-harvested and damaged, but they have not undergone such total transformation as some other habitats in southern Canada, such as the prairies.

Therefore we may conclude, with regard to ecotourism "ingredients," that many aboriginal people in British Columbia do live in close proximity to spectacular (though not always unspoilt) scenery, have access to and some management power over renewable resources, have maintained economic and cultural ties to these resources, and also tend to exhibit greater sophistication in industry knowledge pertaining to ecotourism than their northern counterparts. This may in part be due to a relatively sophisticated general tourism environment in British Columbia. Aboriginal people do experience shortages in human and financial capital, but the situation is improving. As a result, the number of aboriginal tourism enterprises with an explicit eco-focus is increasing, offering the visitor an experience of the natural and cultural environment of such groups as the Haida, Kwagiulth, or Nuu-chah-nulth.

Klemtu Tourism is an interesting example. This company is a community-owned and operated venture which — according to its website — appeals to nature enthusiasts, sea kayakers, and those interested in learning about coastal native culture. Klemtu and the Kitasoo/Xaixais Traditional Territory are located on the Central Coast of British Columbia, which is also home to the famous white Spirit or Kermode Bear, a rare genetic variation of the black bear. The First Nation's tourism venture is an integral part of its landmark land use plan for its traditional territory (developed in 2000) which set aside 40% of the land as protected area, to safeguard cultural and biodiversity values. The remaining 60% of the traditional territory are managed according to ecosystem-based principles as integrated use areas (Klemtu home page 2002 at http://members.shaw.ca/inventive/klemtuhomepage/homepage2002.htm). Other examples are *Gwaii Eco Tours* (www.gwaiiecotours.com/) and *Skeena Eco-Expeditions* (www.kispioxadventures.com) located on Haida Gwaii (Queen Charlotte Islands) and in Gitxsan-Wet-suwet'en territory respectively. The former is a family business, "100% Aboriginal owned and operated" and in operation since 1982, which offers Haida canoe paddling, sea kayaking and camping combined with cultural immersion. Their mission statement claims: "To see firsthand is to learn, to learn is to understand, to understand is to help preserve." This may be taken to apply to both Haida nature and culture. The *Skeena Eco-Expedition* website does not explicitly refer to its ownership status but focuses on introducing its Gitxsan guides for its outdoor and cultural activities. Both the Haida and Gitxsan have a tradition of taking a *very* proactive stance in the protection of their terrestrial and marine environment (Notzke 1994b).

Illustration 6.4

Illustration 6.5

(Illustrations 6.4 and 6.5) Despite limited potential for "ecotourism pure," many southern Canadian Indian reserves exhibit great scenic beauty, as exemplified by the Stoney Reserve in southern Alberta. Some places are off limits to tourism development, such as the Stoney

Circumstances are different in other parts of Canada — for example the **Prairie Provinces** — where aboriginal people have signed historical treaties with the Crown, been confined to reserves and have had to witness a complete transformation of their traditional lands and an elimination of their traditional livelihood. Context and contents of aboriginal tourism are quite different here, and the potential for ecotourism is much more limited. Reserve communities often constitute patches of a "third world environment" within a Western industrialized nation. The land no longer provides a lifestyle that nurtures culture and social structure. With regard to access to off-reserve land and resources, aboriginal people must deal with provincial legislations, many of which have a history of being unsympathetic towards aboriginal interests. By and large, aboriginal people south of the 60th parallel have very little influence over their operational environment with regard to tourism (Notzke 2000, 2004).

As a result, major ingredients for ecotourism, such as unspoilt and unique scenery, access to and management power over land and resources, and unbroken ties to the land, are often missing. There tends to be an overall lack of industry knowledge with regard to tourism in general and ecotourism in particular and a shortage of capital and skilled manpower. Nevertheless, there is great scenic beauty on many reserves, and there are success stories of socio-cultural tourism on Indian reserves. Some of them call to mind evolving concepts, such as eco-cultural tourism (Singh 2001), or the emergence of new tertiary ecotourism destinations (Boyd & Butler 1999), which may exhibit characteristics quite different from traditional "classic" ecotourism attractions; and we may also want to consider the arbitrariness of the distinction between natural and cultural landscapes (Taylor 1999). Tourists immersing themselves in historical aboriginal culture while staying in tipi or cultural camps, or going on trail rides or guided hikes through Indian country, are acquiring practical knowledge as well as environmental ethics of timeless relevance, which, albeit indirectly, contributes to conservation and social and cultural empowerment — key characteristics of ecotourism.

Indigenous Ecotourism in the Developing World

Tourism does not happen in a vacuum. This is particularly true for indigenous ecotourism. The degree to which aboriginal people are able to determine their place in the industry so as to maximize its benefits and minimize its negative impacts depends on their overall socio-economic, political and legal status in the country in which they live. The case of ecotourism puts aboriginal people's relationship with their land and its creatures into a particularly sharp focus. At the same time tourism can be harnessed for economic as well as political empowerment of indigenous groups, and ecotourism in particular can serve as a tool for aboriginal people to protect and nurture their natural as well as cultural resources (Epler Wood 1999). It has already been demonstrated how community-based wildlife management regimes in Africa have resulted in empowerment of indigenous communities, and ecotourism has been an important conduit in this process. Indigenous ecotourism is probably experiencing its greatest proliferation in Latin America, in so-called "ecotourism meccas," such as Belize, as well as in countries where indigenous tribal territories are subject to intense resource pressure, as exemplified by Ecuador.

Belize: Sustainable Tourism for Sustainable Development

Much has been written about ecotourism development in Belize, the small Central American country that along with Costa Rica has come to occupy a key position in the worldwide ecotourism wave (Munt & Higinio 1993:12). Tourism is an important industry for Belize, second only to sugar production in foreign exchange earnings. The former colony of British Honduras, which gained its independence in 1981, is blessed with an abundant natural heritage, including a magnificent barrier reef (second only to Australia's Great Barrier Reef), extensive well-preserved tracts of tropical rainforest, and idyllic tropical island cayes. Furthermore, Belize boasts part of the renowned archaeological legacy of the ancient Maya civilization, now a major attraction within the regional *Ruta Maya*. Belize has garnered international praise for the widely publicized commitment of consecutive governments to pursue the path of sustainable tourism development with a strong emphasis on community-based ecotourism (Horwich et al. 1993).

However, questions have been raised as to whether the term "ecotourism" is being indiscriminately applied to any tourism project located in an attractive natural setting, and a large proportion of the country's tourism industry is in the hands of a small but powerful expatriate community (Munt & Higinio 1993). Nevertheless, research shows that there are success stories of ecotourism in Belize, where tourism that is focused on protected areas contributes to the economic well-being of local residents and, consequently, increases their support for conservation. Lindberg, Enriquez and

Sproule (1996) investigated three case studies: the Hol Chan Marine Reserve and the adjacent communities of San Pedro and Caye Caulker; the Manatee Special Development Area and the adjacent community of Gales Point; and the Cockscomb Basin Wildlife Sanctuary with the adjacent indigenous communities Maya Center and Maya Mopan. In their evaluation the authors concentrated on quantitative aspects of the financial benefits of tourism: e.g., financial support for protection and management of natural areas, economic benefits for communities located near natural areas, and support for conservation among residents, in part due to the economic benefits (Ibid.:543f). Using positive net financial impact as a standard, tourism did not achieve the first objective, but could easily do so with implementation of a modest user fee.

The other two ecotourism objectives, however, were being achieved, with all communities expressing a high level of support for adjacent protected areas, and tourism being identified as the primary reason for such favourable attitudes. In a similar vein, Possum Point Biological Station in central Belize meets the economic criteria for ecotourism by feeding back tourist monies for environmental and community support, including donations for a sugar mill site and a scholarship fund (Kangas, Shave & Shave 1995). The Community Baboon Sanctuary, established as a private reserve to protect black howler monkeys, is another tourism initiative in central Belize, which since its inception in 1985 has been upheld by the government of Belize as a prime example of a working model of participatory ecotourism development (Alexander 1999:21; see also Horwich et al. 1993). Local reviews of this initiative have been somewhat mixed, with unresolved issues pertaining to the distribution of tourism benefits and management input. Yet, overall there is strong community endorsement of both habitat protection and tourism development.

None of these small scale and relatively successful ecotourism initiatives truly corresponds with the idea of an "indigenous model of ecotourism," "that of community-defined and controlled projects, where initiatives reflect indigenous values and priorities" (Johnston 2000:91; 2001:44). There is, however, such a case in Belize, one that also lives up to Honey's demanding definition of ecotourism (See p.202 of this chapter). What renders the accomplishments of the **Toledo Ecotourism Association** particularly intriguing is their context of peripheral development, which in this particular case is turned into an asset rather than a liability. Using Canada's Northwest Territories as an example and applying a variation of Butler's Tourist Area Cycle of Evolution (Butler 1980), Keller (1987) demonstrates the pitfalls of peripheral tourism development and discusses strategies to avoid the centre-periphery conflict. In a familiar pattern, this conflict is evidenced by peripheral tourism development being "taken over" by outside interests, with local resource use being dictated by outside agendas. Similar to Canada's far North, the Toledo District is a peripheral region in the national context of Belize, often referred to as "the forgotten district" (Timothy & White 1999:231).

In a further analogy to Canada's North, the southernmost district of Belize is home to the country's most pristine natural habitat, in this case lowland rainforest, and an indigenous population, namely Kekchi and Mopan Maya in villages throughout the Toledo District, and Garifuna — a people of mixed African and indigenous Carib lineage — in Punta Gorda, the district capital, and nearby communities. The Toledo Ecotourism Association (TEA) was established in 1990 in an effort to improve the standard of living of village residents in this remote part of the country, and to broaden the region's economic base, which had, until that time, consisted almost entirely of slash-and-burn agriculture. What made this initiative unique was its grassroots beginning and continuing control and management at the grassroots level (Ibid.:228). The potential for ecotourism development in Toledo is considerable. The very conditions that cause this region to appear underdeveloped and isolated make it attractive as a destination (Ibid.:232). The combination of rainforest, Mayan ruins and living local cultures constitutes a prime resource base for tourism. Nevertheless, the Toledo District was virtually ignored by the government in its efforts at national tourism development, and the region's tourism infrastructure remained underdeveloped.

One of the first locally initiated tourism projects was a trail system — on ground, underground, and high above ground. It started out with a nature trail surrounding Punta Gorda (a town of less than 4,000 people). The Punta Gorda Trail project (which in 1999 was still under construction) had several objectives that transcended tourism development. Besides providing jobs for local people as trail guides, rangers, service providers and artisans, it was also intended to establish a Homesite Farmer's Fund, which was to be used to develop alternative agricultural techniques that were less destructive to the rainforest than the traditional slash-and-burn methods (Ibid.). Demonstration of sustainable agricultural technology was incorporated into the tourism product.[1] Other trails enabled the visitor to explore underground cave systems and forest canopies.

The first endeavour to develop indigenous ecotourism outside the city occurred in 1990 — the Village Guesthouse Programme

---

1 The issue of agroecological change, however, must be viewed in a broader and more complicated context of cultural change under the pressure of Protestant missionary activity, and insecure land tenure policies (Steinberg 1998).

(Ibid.:233). The idea was born after Punta Gorda hosted a series of community-sponsored workshops on ecotourism that brought Mayan participants into contact with representatives from environmental organizations, health agencies and local businesses. Aided by one of the workshop organizers as a volunteer consultant, 19 men from five villages formed the Toledo Ecotourism Association in order to plan, control and benefit from ecotourism in their villages:

> The aim of the programme was to help revitalise and strengthen traditional arts and crafts and protect the natural resource base in a sustainable manner. Opportunities were to be available for all those who chose to participate. Supplemental employment and income for housekeepers, cooks, guides, and entertainers would be provided. Workers would be chosen on a rotating basis and, to minimise stress levels on natural and cultural resources, the number of tourists would be regulated as well. This was to ensure that each village would get its share of tourists. A percentage of the profits from the programme were to go to the village aid fund for community services to finance health care, education, training programmes for tourism and financial management, craft development, and homesite agriculture. Homesite farming, a method of same-site agriculture that concentrates on soil renewal from recycled farm waste and fertiliser, was viewed as a more sustainable alternative to the traditional slash-and-burn forms of agriculture, which were the primary cause of deforestation in the area. After implementation, the programme was supposed to be monitored to see that these goals were met (Timothy & White 1999:233f).

Despite a slow start, the program soon created a positive economic impact on the villages with an increase in some village incomes of 25 percent (Ibid.:236). The guesthouse program was complemented by jungle trails, where guided walks were conducted. By 1997 a dozen villages were participating. At this time, approximately 80 percent of the program's profits went directly to the service providers. The remaining 20 percent was directed to the TEA general fund which was supposed to be channelled into different expenditures: 55 percent to administrative costs, 15 percent to health and education, 10 percent to village conservation, 10 percent to marketing, and 10 percent to taxes. During the late 1990s, however, most of these public funds were used for training workshops for tour guides, hospitality-related skills, handicraft marketing and business accounting. There were also eco-awareness workshops at the village level addressing such topics as reforestation and sustainable agriculture.

Predictably, there were some bumps in the road. The introduction of business and competition into a setting characterized by egalitarianism and cooperation produced some rivalries and local political squabbles between and within villages. A problem of a different nature (which many may not view as such) was represented by the Government of Belize, which, at the program's inception, had been conspicuous by its absence. Because of its innovative approach to tourism development, the Toledo Ecotourism Association was the focus of considerable international attention during the late 1990s. For example, the Secretary General of the World Tourism Organisation awarded the Socially Responsible Tourism prize to the TEA, which suddenly found itself the object of increased government interest. Many residents viewed this outside involvement as undesirable, since their original goal had been to develop small-scale tourism that would be entirely locally owned and managed (Ibid.:237).

Two prevalent ideologies emerged among community members regarding the future of the association. There was a pro-government ideology in support of state assistance, and there were those who suspected that government involvement in the Toledo Ecotourism Association was nothing clsc but an attempt to undermine the efforts of the Mayan people to work together as a collectivity (Ibid.:238). Other challenges pertained to physical and market accessibility. As in many developing countries, travel outside urban centres in Belize can be challenging. Finally, few attempts have been made to promote the guesthouse project internationally. Nevertheless, some tourism websites on the internet, such as *Belize Online* (www.belize.com/index/toledo), do feature the various components of the project, and interested visitors are encouraged to contact the program office for more information.

Returning to the concept of peripherality, it becomes clear that one of its main criteria does not apply here, namely, lack of local control. The communities seem to have succeeded in transferring their comparative independence as subsistence farmers to their tourism ventures. There has been little outside investment, and little, if any, of the land has been alienated from local control. It is still difficult to arrange a stay in the villages from abroad, and consequently there is no leakage to travel trade intermediaries (Ibid.:239). Profits from such small-scale ecotourism projects may be small, but they seem to be sustainable and have minimal negative impact. The Toledo District's peripheral location has aided unrestricted local involvement, in addition to being an attraction in its own right.

Another outstanding characteristic of the Toledo project is the way sustainable tourism is being employed to further sustainable development on a broader scale. Tourism has improved the villagers' standard of living and has broadened their economic base. It is also closely integrated with other efforts to use the rainforest environment in a more sustainable fashion, the most important instance of which is a modification of traditional farming practices. Other endeavours extend to small-scale selective lumber cutting and an experimental farm (combined with a bed-and-breakfast inn) using photo-voltaic technology to achieve energy self-sufficiency (*Belize Online*).

Ecuador: Ecotourism to the Rescue

In the central plaza of Misahualli, an eight-foot tall cut-out of a Huaorani tribesman stands at the entrance to a shop advertising jungle tours and local crafts. The cutout is crudely painted, depicting a tall, strong man with long straight black hair. He is carrying a spear, wearing beads and is naked but for a traditional penis strap around his waist. The image is obscene; not the nudity, but the blatant commercialization that demeans a proud people, using their long-gone nakedness as a sales tool for tourism (Marks 1999:53).

"We don't want to see tour guides or tourists because they bring disease that the Huaorani can't cure; tour guides and tourists enter our houses when we are working in the fields, they hunt and fish for the food we need, they leave garbage. Tourists are paying US$20–30 per day for this and we are being exploited and receive nothing. Therefore we resist tourism and want the tours to leave us alone. If necessary we will oppose tourism with our spears" (Moi Enomenga, community leader and coordinator of the first Huaorani National Assembly, quoted in the *Lonely Planet Guide to Ecuador* by Marks 1999:54).

Sadly, the above paragraphs provide a condensed version of many Indian nations' encounter with the tourism industry in Latin America. Blatant voyeurism and commercialization combined with total disregard for cultural and environmental pollution have reduced many indigenous people to passive tourist attractions or bitter opponents of foreign visitation. And yet, Moi Enomenga, the same man who voiced such spirited opposition to tourism, was guiding invited guests to his community only a few years after his comments. The key to this apparent contradiction lies in the type of tourism involved and his motivation for hosting foreign guests. The kind of tourism involved is simply tourism on **Huaorani** terms: small scale, strictly controlled, and paying a fair price. His motivation for hosting tourists is equally straightforward: a need for money to fight the oil companies, to protect his land and his people from the relentlessly encroaching industrialized world (Marks 1999:54). This theme is a recurrent one in the Amazon basin.

Similar to the Maya villages in Belize, indigenous peoples here are searching for a sustainable livelihood in a world that sometimes seems to have spun out of control. But there is an extra edge and sense of urgency to the situation due to the imminent threat to the rainforest environment posed by advancing national development frontiers — in the case of Ecuador, primarily oil and gas exploration and production. In such a scenario, tourists can serve a twofold purpose: First, they contribute a cash income and thus aid in the economic (and political) emancipation of indigenous communities. Second, by becoming educated about people's relationship with their land and their struggle to protect it, they become witnesses and messengers. Such a role for travellers has been well documented for other geographical locations like Tibet (Schwartz 1991).

It goes without saying that it takes a special kind of traveller and a special kind of tourism to measure up to this challenge, and the answer seems to lie in community-controlled and initiated ecotourism. In the Huaorani case, Moi Enomenga's village, Quehueri'Ono, is earning more per person than other villages are making from a group of 20. By limiting the numbers and charging a fair price, the community is able to attract people with a genuine interest in Huaorani culture who do not disrupt the local way of life (Marks 1999:55). In return, visitors are treated to a genuine immersion experience, but are not spared witnessing the environmental degradations caused by oil exploration. Despite the personal nature of the encounter, great care is taken to avoid undue pressure on the Huaorani's fragile cultural and natural resources. Thus, the visitors' accommodation in a couple of traditional huts is located a 20-minute walk away from the village, and visitors bring their own supplies of food and water, as well as a naturalist tour guide and cook, while the villagers provide a local guide, boatman and cook's help. The income earned through these and other prearranged services is spent on communal purposes, such as a solar panel to charge a battery for a radio transmitter as a link to the outside world, or funding representatives to fight for Huaorani rights in political campaigns (Ibid.:56).

This tourism project was set up in 1996 as a community initiative with the help of a British conservationist and ecologist who is also president and owner of *TROPIC Ecological Adventures*, an Ecuador-based ecotourism operator. The initiative was not embarked upon without careful assessment and discussion of an estimated limit of acceptable change by both the tour operator and the community. In this case, cultural limits are likely to be exceeded before environmental risks occur, which necessitates a careful selection of indicators and constant monitoring (Drumm 1998:206ff). While the risk of unpredictable cultural impacts is ever present, the benefits transcend the usual tourism pay-off:

> Both TROPIC and the Huaorani intend that the initial visit will simply be the beginning of a longer-term relationship between the tourists and their hosts. An important element of TROPIC's programs is the aim to inspire and motivate the visitors so that on returning to their own country, they work to raise funds and consciousness on behalf of the people and places that they have visited. In this way TROPIC has created a constituency of foreign-based supporters for Ecuador's Amazon peoples and rainforests. This has generated letter writing; cash donations to finance training workshops, HF radios, and solar panels; and helped facilitate the establishment of a non-profit foundation — Accion Amazonia — which focuses, full time, on generating political and economic support for those Amazon communities seeking help to defend their environmental and cultural integrity (Ibid.:207).

The Organization of the Huaorani People, ONHAE, regards the Quehueri'Ono experience as a pilot program, one that could possibly be implemented in other Huaorani communities. It is hoped that such an approach may eventually displace the prevalent operation type, which tends to be based in Amazon frontier towns, focus on low-budget and backpacker travellers, rely on untrained (non-native) guides, and put low cost above cultural and environmental considerations. These operations have widespread negative impacts: the hunting of wildlife and dynamiting of rivers to catch fish to supply cheap food, low or no income generation, and blatant disrespect for culture (Ibid.:208).

Initiatives where communities react to outside pressure in the form of resource exploitation and/or inappropriate and exploitative tourism and capitalize on fortuitous partnerships with individuals or non-governmental organizations have become increasingly common. In the early 1990s Macdonald of *Cultural Survival* reported on Indians vying for space and resources with colonists, cattle ranchers, and workers for extractive industries such as logging and mining. He described an Indian movement as falling clearly within what could be called "The ecology of cultural ecotourists" (Macdonald 1993:14). In this context he highlighted examples of conventional nature-based tour itineraries of local and national tour companies being enriched by day trips to Quechua and Cofan Indian communities:

> With the additions of the day trips to the standard itinerary, simple nature tours have been subtly transformed into ecotours. It becomes clear to travellers that "nature" is more than a series of spectacular wild species that exist in isolation. They can see that the environment is an interrelated, ever-changing landscape in which people play a part. They observe the ways in which new settlers and extractive industries have affected the unique flora, fauna, and Indian cultures of the forest. They learn how social and economic changes have become as important a part of the environment as the velvety orchids and scarlet macaws. They also see how these changes threaten the social and biological diversity — the very elements that attract tourists and scientists and, perhaps more importantly, secure part of the earth's future as well (MacDonald 1993:14).

Some indigenous groups in the Upper Amazon have opted out of tourism and post signs that proclaim "No Tourists Allowed." It is often those who have increased their control over land and resources, who invite outsiders to witness and support their management of natural and cultural resources. Wesche and Drumm have documented more than 30 community-based ecotourism projects in the Ecuadorian Amazon alone (Epler Wood 2002:42). Another example from the same region as the Huaorani territory is that of the **Quichua Indian village of Caspira** (also near the river port of Misahualli), where the villagers decided that rather than continuing to serve as either objects of curiosity for tourists or workers for non-Indian guides, they would themselves design and manage tours to their community. They set aside a nature reserve within their territory, carved out a nature trail and constructed a guest house, where visitors are served local food and are engaged in a cultural exchange. They are also made to bear witness to the dangers threatening this natural and cultural environment (Macdonald 1993.:15).

Fear of oil exploitation in the region has generated larger scale developments. The Quichua community of **Capirona** pioneered community-based ecotourism in the Upper Napo valley of eastern Ecuador. Villagers built a traditional style lodge and developed a program offering visitors a window onto Quichua culture (Colvin 1994:1). In 1992 the community invited a small team from the University of California Research Expeditions Program (UREP) to assist in developing long term management strategies for the project. One of the most important outcomes of this initiative was a set of guidelines for visitors.

A decade later there have been some changes. Capirona has expanded its program and added some visitor comforts. More important, it is part of a network of 10 Quichua communities in the Upper Napo valley who have organized to form an ecotourism program called *RICANCIE* (Indigenous Community Network of the Upper Napo for Intercultural Exchange and Ecotourism) under the sponsorship of the provincial indigenous federation, Federation of Indigenous Organizations of the Napo (FOIN) (*http:// ricancie.nativeweb.org/* accessed in June 2003). In 2003 the organization offered five different five-day tour programs, featuring village stays with a variety of cultural programs, rainforest hikes and dugout canoe trips, visits to community projects involving the rescue of endangered animals, ethnobotanical instruction and participation in community work. Obviously, such intimate cross-cultural encounters in remote areas have their share of risks for the indigenous host:

> Over a mid-afternoon snack on the deck at Runa Huasi, a guide and a director of RICANCIE quickly recount a laundry list of the complaints they have heard about the dangers of bringing foreign tourists into communities and selling Quichua culture to them. The elders were worried about the evils of too much money. The women had initially resisted cooking with onions and garlic for the tourists. The men were concerned about being looked at as another kind of animal in the jungle. Visiting bishops had voiced concerns that sex and intermarriage with tourists would destroy Quichua culture. Foreign development workers had pointed out that the guides and directors themselves were the most vulnerable to "acculturation."
>
> The history of RICANCIE has proven all of these concerns to be valid, some more than others. Surprisingly, one of the most significant issues for RICANCIE administrators has consistently been the question of sexual rela-

tions between guides and tourists. While anthropologists and development workers worry that contact with the consumer goods of the global market might contribute to materialist behaviors, the real cultural action has been much more physical than psychological. In response to the problem, RICANCIE instituted rules against sexual interaction and against intermarriage in RICANCIE communities. The rules, according to administrators, have largely taken care of the problem. Development workers continue to worry about the acculturation of the RICANCIE guides, but most of the other concerns faded as the operation overcame its initial growing pains or as problematic communities dropped out of the network. (Edeli 2002:4f)

Overall, the impact of ecotourism on *RICANCIE* communities seems to have been mostly positive. The reinvestment of tourism revenue at the community level permits the development of other sustainable economic activities such as handicraft production, small animal raising, aquaculture and agroforestry. New services are provided in the form of radio communication and motorized canoe transport (Drumm 1998:209). Rather than leading to a demonstration effect, the project has resulted in a cultural renaissance (Edeli 2002:5). When meeting Westerners, the Quichua were surprised by their visitors' interest in and appreciation of traditional architecture, music, food and other cultural manifestations. Young and old Quichua have a newfound admiration for their culture, as traditional knowledge and indigenous stewardship of the land are validated and traditional crafts are revived (Ibid.; Colvin 1994:3). Furthermore, the cross-cultural contact is creating an international network of support from individuals and groups who visit the communities and, at least in the case of Capirona, letter writing campaigns by former visitors were instrumental in staving off oil exploration (Colvin 1994:4). The visitors' interest in healthy rainforest ecosystems also reinforces the importance of rainforest conservation to the villages, as a result of which *RICANCIE* communities seem to have lost less of their primary and secondary forest than neighbouring communities (Edeli 2002:6). This is not to say that there are no challenges for the Quichua. In their effort to satisfy tourist notions of "authenticity", communities face the risk of a "museumization" of certain aspects of their culture (Colvin 1994:3). The challenge of operating within a competitive business environment and the risk of tying the economic well-being of local communities to global market forces are everpresent. Undercapitalization and lack of marketing serve to undermine the project's competitiveness at a time when the tourism industry experiences unprecedented challenges.

The latter problems could be more effectively addressed with a stronger involvement of the private sector. However, as Rodriguez points out, the lack of communication and trust between indigenous groups and the private sector has been the principal hurdle for development in Latin American countries:

> Indigenous organizations have seen private enterprises as abusive institutions eager to exploit indigenous culture and resources. The private sector, on the other hand, tends to consider indigenous people untruthful and indolent. If these misunderstandings are resolved, a new niche for socially responsible development will evolve which can provide important economic and social benefits, and create space for tolerance and learning (Rodriguez 1999:43).

A final example from Ecuador, however, shows how private capital investments can be integrated with local community goals with a minimum of environmental and cultural disruption, in an environment of largely non-monetized economies. The **Achuar**, or people of the achu palm, live in the remotest area of southeastern Ecuador and northeastern Peru, and had practically no contact with Westerners prior to the arrival of missionaries in the late 1960s. Remaining nearly self-sufficient in their territory even today, the Achuar nevertheless find themselves confronted with the modern world and inspired by the desire to present their children with genuine options for the future. Like the Maya, Huaorani and Quichua, they, too, chose ecotourism as a crucial tool to realize their aspirations for a sustainable future, but they adopted a somewhat different approach. Whereas the above-mentioned cases represent exclusively community-owned projects (with occasional input from indigenous organizations), *Kapawi* represents a new model in the implementation of sustainable ecotourism, based on the respectful relationship between a private enterprise and the Achuar. The private sector enterprise is *CANODROS*, an Ecuadorian tour operator, who joined forces with OINAE, the Organization of Ecuadorian Achuar Nationalities, to develop the Kapawi Ecological Reserve with a minimum of environmental and cultural disruption (www.ladatco.com/rfd-kpwi.htm accessed on June 14, 2003). Their objectives are twofold:

1. To implement a $2 million project in an indigenous territory, by leasing their land, sharing benefits, and passing the know-how and installations to the

Achuar. At the end of a 15-year period, the project will be owned and managed by the Achuar. Meanwhile Kapawi seeks to recover the investment and to obtain a profit.

2. To facilitate the Achuar's request for partnership with the outside world by contributing to the creation of a not-for-profit organization that provides access to technical expertise and funding for a variety of Achuar projects. These projects are all intended to enhance the Achuar's ability to manage integration with the modern world on their own terms and to defend their lands against encroachment (Rodriguez 1999:43f).

The project was begun in 1993, the lodge opened in 1996, and the entire establishment will revert back to the Achuars in 2011. This "most expensive ecotourism project in the Ecuadorean Amazon Baain" (Ibid.:44) is very different in character from the previously described community projects of the Huaorani and Quichua. Despite its remote location and resultant restrictions on luggage, *Kapawi* can be classed as luxury accommodation with 20 double cabins, each with private bathroom and private terrace, a combination of international cuisine and local foods, and a well stocked bar. The design combines the best of vernacular architecture with exogenous, sustainable technology. The architecture is completely Achuar in character, with not a single nail being used. The latest environmental technology is employed: The lodge is powered by solar energy; tap water is filtered through charcoal filters and purified with UV rays; solar showers provide hot water, and other low impact technologies provide for trash management and electric outboard motors. The land is rented, not purchased, and a rent has been set at $2,000 a month, increasing at a yearly increment of seven percent. At the end of the period, the accumulated rent will total over $600,000. In addition, a $10 fee is charged to every visitor for the exclusive benefit of the Achuar communities. With an estimated average of 1,000 guests per year, this will contribute a further $150,000 through the year 2011.

In the late 1990s, 16 out of 52 Achuar communities of the Achuar Federation based a significant percentage of their economy on ecotourism, striving to substitute ecotourism for cattle ranching as an external source of income. Their involvement in tourism ranges from the direct employment of 22 Achuar at *Kapawi* to cultural programming, handicraft production, and the provision of various services and products. According to Rodriguez (1999:44), the Achuar are actively involved in decision-making processes, at the level of individuals, communities, associations, and the federation. Published guidelines have been developed to further socially and culturally sensitive behaviour on behalf of visitors. Not surprisingly, there are cautionary voices. As Johnston (2000:90) points out in regard to ownership transfers in joint ventures like ecolodges, most indigenous communities have no means of knowing that the typical ecotourism destination loses its unique and thus marketable features within a 15-year time frame. It remains to be seen how sustainable *Kapawi's* combination of environmental best practices and co-management of cultural and natural resources will be in the long term, once we enter the second decade of this millennium.

Ecotourism as *Coyote*

It seems only fitting to conclude with an analogy drawn by Barry Parker of the Okanagan Nation in British Columbia. Ecotourism can be like *coyote* (Parker 1996:1). *Coyote* is a cultural hero and trickster for many First Nations of the Rocky Mountain interior. *Coyote* takes on the guise of many different animals or people, sometimes to trick people, sometimes to teach lessons and to help. Ecotourism can be like that. In theory, ecotourism utilizes Mother Nature as the base of a tourism product or service in such a way that there is minimal impact on the ecosystem, suggesting a focus on conservation and sustainability. But ecotourism is also business the primary focus of which is the financial bottom line. Ecotourism claims the high moral ground, but if pursued in an unsustainable manner, it can be even more damaging than other varieties of tourism. In situations where indigenous peoples are not in control of their lands, their resources and their destiny, their leaders have identified ecotourism as one of the major threats to their cultures and the biodiversity within their homelands (Johnston 2000:89). Others have made ecotourism an integral part of their strategy to remedy such situation.

It would be easy to misrepresent ecotourism. Unlike *coyote*, the trickster, who is the ultimate free agent, ecotourism is not a force in its own right, even though it may sometimes appear that way. Ecotourism is whatever its players and their circumstances allow it to be. In 1999 the UN General Assembly declared 2002 to be the International Year of Ecotourism (IYE). The IYE was intended to help governments and the private sector use tourism "as a tool for sustainable development and conservation of natural and cultural resources." However, Johnston (2001:44) points out that several indigenous organizations protested against the IYE, since governments participating in multilateral UN functions consistently implied that indigenous peoples were mere "stakeholders" in the IYE process rather than holders of collective rights recognized under international law.

This is a crucial distinction. Unauthorized access to and utilization of indigenous homelands by the ecotourism industry has not only resulted in a threat to fragile ecosystems, but also in widespread privatization of collective cultural property (Johnston 2000:92). In this context, what Honey (1999:51ff) calls "ecotourism lite" constitutes a major threat to indigenous interests. She observes that in recent years, there has been a gradual trend for many ecotourists "to be less intellectually curious, socially responsible, environmentally concerned, and politically aware than in the past" (Ibid.:52). Ecotourism is becoming "softer" and more mainstream, with extensive "greenwashing" through advertising images and cosmetic adjustments. Epler Wood (2003:7) expresses similar concerns about green market trends in general and ecotourism market trends in particular. Ecotourism lite is promoted by travel agents, tour operators, airlines and cruise lines, as well as large hotel and resort chains and some international tourism organizations:

> In identifying what is ecotourism lite and determining where genuine ecotourism is being practiced today, we need also to discover ways in which authentic ecotourism can move from being simply a niche market in the category of nature tourism to become a broad set of principles and practices that transform the way we travel and the way the tourism industry functions (Honey 1999:54).

Such a broad set of principles and practices must include rules of engagement for the travel industry and indigenous peoples. Johnston (2000:96) suggests the following principles for future dialogue and partnership building between indigenous peoples, governments and industry:

- Prior informed consent as an industry standard, achieved through supportive national legislation and impact assessment frameworks.

- "Readiness to negotiate" as the guiding principle for consultation and negotiations; i.e., equivalent capacity and access to information at the community level.

- Methods and timelines that enable indigenous peoples to document and share information about their customary uses of an area for planning purposes, without compromising their intellectual property, religious freedom or traditional resource rights.

• A central role for indigenous conservation expertise in joint management decisions concerning protected areas and other places within indigenous homelands receiving tourists, including traditional ways of documenting ecosystem knowledge, such as prophecies and stories.

• Respect for the intent and function of sustainability protocols based on customary law (Ibid.).

In a similar vein, an indigenous working group at a Side-Event at the 2000 Conference of Parties to the Convention on Biological Diversity in Nairobi highlighted some of the indigenous community's key concerns:

1. The need for tools to ensure prior informed consent;
2. The need to undertake a collective review of prior informed consent;
3. The need to determine criteria for cultural diversity within the context of biological diversity;
4. The creation of a process for grievances and conflict resolutions for indigenous peoples;
5. Development of a deeper appreciation for indigenous rights separate from rural communities and others (Epler Wood 2002:45).

Both sets of principles and concerns reiterate once again that aboriginal people's involvement in ecotourism cannot be isolated from their general legal and socio-economic status in their country of residence. Indigenous people want to engage with ecotourism from a position of strength, secure in their rights to land, resources and intellectual property, and cognizant of potential conflicts and means to resolve them.

Once these conditions are fulfilled, indigenous people are in a position to establish their own bottom line. This bottom line may vary from case to case and place to place, but one message has been resonant locally and globally at many indigenous gatherings: If nature and culture are not exploited, but shared with dignity and respect, everyone can benefit. You can even do business. If you can't protect them, don't do it.

Summary

This chapter zeroes in on the type of tourism where the interplay of *the Stranger, the Native and the Land* comes into sharpest focus: indigenous ecotourism. Ecotourism offers very special opportunities to aboriginal people. It is defined by a product that features natural and cultural experiences, and thus can truly capitalize on indigenous people's intimate relationship with their land. What truly sets ecotourism apart from other types of tourism, however, is the fact that it is defined not only by a product, but by operating principles and ethics. This strengthens its potential role as a tool for aboriginal people to be used for their advancement and empowerment.

An investigation of indigenous ecotourism in Canada reveals major regional differences throughout this huge country. Natural endowment, aboriginal access to resources and cultural connection with the land vary substantially in territories and provinces, as do tourism industry-related factors. It becomes clear that the greatest potential for ecotourism development is to be found in Canada's northern territories and, to a lesser degree, in British Columbia. These areas are characterized by the presence of innovative co-management regimes, which facilitate aboriginal people's access to land and resources.

Furthermore, northern Canada features a pristine environment and a "living connection" between the land and its aboriginal stewards. There is a growing number of aboriginal owned and operated ecotourism ventures, but the true potential remains underutilized, particularly in the North. Conditions for indigenous ecotourism development are much more challenging in parts of the country where aboriginal people have been confined to reserves and have witnessed a total transformation of their traditional livelihood. This situation is exemplified by the southern prairie provinces. But even here there are interesting examples of socio-cultural tourism ventures separated from ecotourism by blurred boundaries.

The chapter progresses to explore indigenous ecotourism in the developing world. Belize and Ecuador are selected as examples, since they yield particularly interesting cases of aboriginal people using ecotourism in creative ways to further their own goals. The Toledo Ecotourism Association in Belize effectively demonstrates how peripherality — a phenomenon frequently associated with aboriginal people and their lands, and commonly interpreted as a disadvantage — can actually be turned into an asset aiding people in pursuing truly grassroots driven and sustainable development initiatives. This particular case also illustrates how sustainable tourism may be employed to further sustainable development on a broader scale.

Ecuador presents a somewhat different scenario. In common with Belize's Maya, Ecuador's Indian nations are striving to use ecotourism in their search for a sustainable livelihood. But their situation is characterized by an extra sense of urgency due to the imminent threat to their rainforest environment posed by advancing national development frontiers: in Ecuador's case, primarily oil and gas exploration and production. A different type of disruption of indigenous cultures is represented by exploitative tourism practices. Aboriginal communities have increasingly reacted to such outside pressures by capitalizing on fortuitous partnerships with individuals, non-governmental organizations and, less commonly, private sector enterprises, to develop their own brand of ecotourism. In this context, visitors often become witnesses and messengers. Not only do they contribute the necessary financial means to empower indigenous people economically and politically, but they evolve into an international support and advocacy network. This pattern is illustrated by the examples of the Huaorani, Quichua and Achuar.

The chapter concludes with some thoughts about the ambiguous relationship between indigenous people and ecotourism, using the analogy of *coyote*, the trickster. We must bear in mind that like a trickster, ecotourism may present itself in different guises. Small-scale, community-initiated and controlled ecotourism is only one of them. Ecotourism may also be government and industry-driven and assume characteristics of "ecotourism lite." This type of ecotourism will leave a larger footprint, and feature greater numbers of visitors who are less intellectually curious, socially responsible, environmentally conscious and politically aware. Aboriginal leaders have indeed identified this variety of ecotourism as a major threat. In order to benefit from the ecotourism phenomenon, indigenous people must be able to operate from a position of strength and knowledge.

7

Community-Based Tourism: Facts and Fiction

Introduction

Throughout this book the concept of community-based tourism development has come up several times: for example, the Namibia Community-Based Tourism Association (NACOBTA) (Chapter Two) and the endorsement by indigenous organizations of ecotourism models, where initiatives are community-driven and reflect local values and priorities (Chapter Six). Community-based theory circumscribes a concept of development that defines economic growth within a social and cultural context, enhancing the potential for increased political power and broadened economic options for the future (Reimer 1993:69). Community-based ecotourism management, for example, as introduced in the previous chapter, refers to ecotourism programs that are carried out under the control and with the active participation of the local people who inhabit or own a natural attraction (Drumm 1998:198). This definition can easily be expanded to embrace other kinds of tourism more strongly focused on cultural resources. Community involvement is considered an integral characteristic of "real" ecotourism, but is also a very prominent theme in the indigenous tourism discussion in general.

Furthermore, a community focus takes centre stage in the sustainability debate. In his seminal work *Tourism: A Community Approach,* Murphy (1985) introduced the community as the focus for decision-making and direction, so that tourism planning could become part of the social consciousness of the destination. Two decades later, these ideas have lost none of their relevance, but it has also become abundantly clear that the community approach is by no means a simple and easily implemented concept. While the ethic of local involvement is rarely questioned, and the advocation of a community approach enjoys widespread political correctness, it is, on the other hand, very easy to succumb to a highly romanticized view of communal responsiveness. Communities are not necessarily "one big happy family," and may indeed exhibit a high degree of pluralism. Developments hardly ever evenly impact different sections of society. Caution must be exercised not to create yet another stereotype.

According to Murphy the wishes and traditions of local people should shape tourism development, and yet they are expected to be part of "the community show" (1985:169), and must act as hosts whether they are directly involved in the industry or not (Ibid.:138). It frequently is this type of participation that is evoked in promotional materials about the warmth and hospitality of a community. The promise of a warm welcome and the chance to share the private world of local people seeks to define the community in ways that often lack legitimacy (Taylor 1995:488).

It goes without saying that within any community attitudes towards tourism development will vary considerably. Madrigal (1994) identified three types of community clusters, namely tourism "realists", "haters" and "lovers." Murphy (1985) found important differences between the responses to tourism by residents, the business sector and administration. The degree to which such differences can be resolved by communication or "internal marketing" will depend on the cohesion of the community; that is, whether a community regards itself as a true community or as an association characterized by individualism and competitiveness (Taylor 1995:488). As Aramberri (2002:85) puts it, "Conflicts are," after all, "the stuff of everyday life." Vosa Flyman's observations from Botswana are illustrative for many community scenarios:

> Experience in other Community Based Natural Resource Management projects in Botswana .... have shown that the management of these projects is often taken up by traditional village leaders who are elected during a one-morning meeting. In some cases it is debatable whether these leaders represent the interests in natural resources utilisation of all the residents within the community. It comes down to the number one question asked when dealing with community projects. "Who is the community?" Most often communities are not homogeneous entities. Between residents there are differences in traditional power, economic power, and ethnicity with according social status. There are definitely differences in gender. And most often different groups with different status make different use of the available natural resources. Because the natural resources are common property, there <u>has</u> to be some form of community management. The challenge is to arrive at a management structure that represents the interests of all resource users while ensuring an equitable distribution of costs and benefits (Vosa Flyman 2001:10; emphasis in original).

It has already been illustrated that non-Western societies have widely differing perceptions of tourism, traditions of hospitality, cultural boundaries and communal identities. All of these characteristics will affect a community's reaction to the introduction of tourism. In most cases tourism only benefits a certain proportion of local residents. In a strongly stratified society its introduction may exacerbate social and political divisions. In previously homogeneous societies tourism tends to give rise to diversification as groups exhibit different responses to touristic development. A further complication arises when tourism entrepreneurs are not actually part of the community, when they are outsiders or "marginal" individuals. On the other hand, tourism costs such as intrusion, congestion and inflation are, in most cases, more evenly shared than financial benefits:

> Those in the community with most to gain from the expansion of tourism know how to sell themselves and others. That this represents an insider approach to the community rather than some outside initiative may be politically expedient, appear more empowering and perhaps more acceptable to the "realists." The question of whether, in the end, it is different from any other kind of tourism development is another matter (Taylor 1995:489).

This cautionary note notwithstanding, there is evidence that community-based tourism development approaches can be successful, but no two stories are the same. Success can be measured in many different ways. This will be illustrated by two cases, literally from opposite ends of the earth.

The Different Faces of Community-Based Tourism

The previous chapter concluded with an analogy of ecotourism as *Coyote*. It is tempting to invoke the animal kingdom once more to describe the chameleon-like quality of community-based tourism. In response to different geographical, socio-cultural, political and economic circumstances, community-based tourism development (or, in some cases, what passes for it) can take on many different forms with varying levels and quality of community involvement. Therein lie strengths as well as weaknesses of the concept. Two examples from the high Arctic and Polynesia, respectively, illustrate different approaches and achievements.

Pangnirtung: "Community-Based" Tourism Development in Canada's Arctic[1]

> In 1980–81 we were using a buzz word that no-one really understood — "community based tourism development" —

---

1 For a detailed discussion of this case see Reimer & Dialla 1992.

a catchy new word that implied that the community would
drive the direction of their tourism development (Economic Development & Tourism Baffin Regional Superintendent, quoted by Reimer & Dialla 1992:10).

This new approach by the Government of the Northwest Territories
marked an economic and political shift in Territorial policy, following the political upheaval of the 1970s. At the same time the animal rights movement had been successful in undermining the
market for sealskins, thus curtailing a vital source of cash income
for Inuit in remote Arctic settlements. The government recognized
tourism as one of the few resources to be exploited in the eastern
Arctic. A policy document published by the Government of the
Northwest Territories in 1983 outlined the principles of community-
based tourism:

> The intention of community based tourism is to allow
> communities to use the tourism industry as a means to
> self determination, especially economically. This Govern-
> ment's role in community based tourism is that of a con-
> sultant in the planning stages, and that of a provider of
> direct financial support in the developmental stage (Gov-
> ernment of the Northwest Territories 1983:14).

The policy had as its goal the creation of a private sector industry
in which the government would provide support services (Reimer &
Dialla 1992:11). The Baffin Island community of Pangnirtung was
chosen by the Department of Economic Development and Tourism
and the Baffin Regional Council as the pilot project site for tourism development in the Eastern Arctic. Pangnirtung is located
40km south of the Arctic Circle and constitutes the gateway to
Auyuittuq National Park Reserve. The hamlet is home to a population of approximately 1,200 people, 95 percent of whom are Inuit.
The majority of households continues to be involved in the land-
based economy in combination with wage labour and transfer
payments. Compared to other Baffin communities, Pangnirtung is
characterized by an enterprising spirit and has a well-developed
infrastructure, including a hotel and a campground:

> One goal of the community-based pilot-project was to
> direct tourism development in a way more appropriate to
> the cultural and geographical distinctiveness of the com-
> munity. Another goal was to distribute the benefits of
> tourism among local people. These objectives were to be

Illustration 7.1

Illustration 7.2

(Illustrations 7.1 and 7.2) The Baffin Island (Nunavut) community of Pangnirtung constitutes the gateway to Auyuittuq National Park Reserve.

accomplished by involving people at the local level in all stages of tourism development. As well, training programs would help build local people's capacity to participate in, and ultimately control, the industry. This marked a significant shift in Territorial development policy and in decision-making at the community level: the people of Pangnirtung were presented with the option of development and with the opportunity to participate in all stages of tourism planning and implementation (Reimer 1993:68).

When Reimer embarked upon her evaluation of the pilot project in 1990, it was in its tenth year of implementation. The fact that tourism development in Pangnirtung was still considered a pilot project after 10 years was a matter of some controversy (Reimer 1993:72). This was all the more significant, as the government's approach to community-based tourism development in practice did not imply community control, but merely community involvement (Robbins 1992:135). The government was able to rationalize this with its mandate to promote economic growth in Arctic communities and the fact that the public purse paid the bill for economic projects, even when levels of local participation were low. Throughout the pilot project phase public and private ownership roles often blurred as Government of the Northwest Territories employees functioned as tour operators. This created the paradoxical situation where the government became a competitor to existing local and regional private tour companies, thus competing against its own "community-based" goals (Reimer & Dialla 1992:45). On the other hand, Inuit organizations and academics argued in favour of a devolution of powers, where the development engine would be community driven (Dickerson 1992 quoted in Reimer 1993:71). By implication, it is the mandate that must be devolved, as well as the political and budgetary means to put it into action.

Nevertheless, government initiative has not resulted in socio-culturally inappropriate and imposed tourism development in Pangnirtung. Visitors are attracted by the beauty of the local surroundings to be explored on hiking trails, by craft purchases, sport fishing and Kekerten Historic Park, which showcases local involvement in the 19th and early 20th century whaling industry. First and foremost, however, "Pang" serves as the gateway to Auyuittuq National Park Reserve, where hikers rely on local outfitters to transport them by boat to the trailhead. The Canadian Parks Service is the most active federal player in Pangnirtung's tourism development.

Auyuittuq National Park Reserve was established in the face of considerable Inuit opposition in 1974. Park Reserve boundaries were still being adjusted throughout the 1990s pending the ratification of the Tungavik Federation of Nunavut Final Agreement. In Pangnirtung a Park Advisory Committee (with representatives of various community groups such as the Hunters and Trappers Association, Elders, the Hamlet, etc.) was established in 1981, and became increasingly active and visible during the late 1980s and early 1990s. After almost two decades characterized by communication problems and numerous misunderstandings, this author found that in the early 1990s the Park Reserve's presence was viewed as very positive by the community of Pangnirtung: Auyuittuq's aboriginal employment record was very good (80 percent, aiming for 100 percent); local resource harvesting was not interfered with; people appreciated the cash income derived from tourists and had retained full control over tourism activities outside the Park Reserve; and the local Parks Office (designed in consultation with the community) had become a focus for community activity with regard to broader environmental issues and was being transformed into an environmental resource centre for the local population (Interviews with Japodee Akpalialuk, Mayor of Pangnirtung; Sakiasie Sowdlooapik, Visitor Service Officer — Canadian Park Service; Rebecca Mike, Pangnirtung MLA; and Bruce Rigby, Superintendent Eastern Arctic District National Parks, August 10 and 11, 1992). As Japodee Akpalialuk, Pangnirtung Mayor, summed up the situation, "It is worth it for both sides." The Parks Office adjoins the Angmarlik Visitors' Centre, the latter with an Elders' room, a library and a museum. The two are integrated and open to community functions (Notzke 1994:254).

An important reason for the overall positive reception of tourism is the fact that the industry has been moulded to fit into the local mixed economy in a similar way as was previously described for the western Arctic (see Chapter Two of this book and Notzke 1999). Reimer observed a high level of part-time, domestic and "underground" economic activity associated with the tourist trade (Reimer 1993:70). Thus tourism was enabled to complement and supplement land-based activities rather than competing with them:

> However, this co-existence has created cultural conflicts, evident in Pangnirtung by people's struggle over whether or not to act competitively. For example, younger outfitters who were prepared to compete as individual entrepreneurs were well aware of senior outfitters' endeavours to strengthen the cooperative efforts of the Association [local Outfitters Association]. To date, local outfitters have fol-

lowed a roster system, in which individuals take turns transporting tourists, according to a list kept at the Visitor Centre. The forcefulness of the general attitude of cooperation was evident in some outfitters' attempts to outwardly abide by the Association's decision to "share" clients on the roster system, while secretly they "stole" tourists when it was not their turn. This practice was severely denounced by the Association, as behaviour unfitting to "the Inuit way" and to the good of the community and the local tourism industry. However, it appears that the Association prefers not to enforce any type of regulation in this regard, but rather to label the wrong-doer as someone who is violating Inuit cultural values. (Reimer 1993:70)

Not surprising, the community was by no means homogeneous in its response to tourism opportunities, as exemplified by an overall apathetic attitude among local youth. Reimer (1993:71) attributed this in part to an education system that tended to alienate northern young people from their home environment without preparing them for a modern industrial lifestyle or a balance between the two. This was further aggravated by the failure of the territorial government to match capital development with human resource development (Reimer & Dialla 1992:77). It remains to be seen whether the new territory of Nunavut will be able to provide all sections of its population with a stronger sense of belonging and purpose that will ultimately impact all socio-economic endeavours including tourism. In the meantime, despite its shortcomings, the community-based approach to tourism development has facilitated some important achievements.

In Pangnirtung, the major accomplishment of the community-based approach has been the empowerment of the local community to create its own unique mix of formal and non-formal cash-related activities in the tourism industry, which best meets the needs of local families and the community as a whole. Tourism has supplemented and complemented other elements of the mixed economy and has thus broadened economic options for local residents (Ibid.).

Western Samoa: Tourism for Manono's Future[2]

Oh, and let's get one thing straight. We only want a small number of travellers in Samoa. We are just not

---

2   This section is summarized entirely from Leiataua Vaiao 1994. Refer also to Wylie 1992.

into "mass tourism." We've already explained that we want to keep these islands beautiful. Our ambition now, and hopefully your ambition, is to surruptiously (sic) push our nation towards sustainable development, in this case via sustainable tourism. All that means is that our quality of life keeps rising while at the same time the quality of your visit keeps rising. It means that our natural resources, our culture and our economy are safeguarded for future generations. And if that's the type of holiday contribution that you would like to knowingly make, then that's great (http://home.pi.se/hotel/orbit/public_html/samoa/19sust.html. Homepage of the Samoa Visitors Bureau, accessed on July 1, 2003).

The geographical setting of this example for community-based tourism development, Western Samoa, could not be more dissimilar from the Canadian Arctic, and yet there are important parallels. Like the Inuit after the demise of the sealskin market, the Samoans, too, were faced with a traumatic change in their economic base. Two major hurricanes devastated the islands in 1990 and 1992, destroying people's agricultural base as well as their homes. While the villagers had struggled before to come to terms with modern needs, these natural disasters put their very survival in question. The only immediate solution for many families was to send their young people to work in New Zealand. Few returned. Here, too, people were looking to tourism to fill a gap.

This is where the similarity ends. On the island of Manono tourism started as a community initiative, in opposition to actions imposed from the outside. People were asking themselves the question: "How can we earn enough to rebuild without losing our youth and control of our villages and land?" (Vaiao 1994:2) A committee was formed to address this question with two representatives from each village. It was called KAMA, short for *Komiti Atina'e Manono* or Committee for Manono's future. Hotels were out of the question, due to lack of capital, expertise and a ban on liquor. Like Ecuador's Indian nations, Manono villagers looked back on a tradition of being used as passive tourist attractions for day tours departing from hotels in Apia, the capital. An attempt to charge for this service resulted in cancellation of the tours. The next challenge originated with the government:

In its 1990 tourist development plan, the government proposed to "assist village tourism." When KAMA asked how, they explained that one family in 35 villages was to be selected, trained and financed to establish a "bed and breakfast" for tourists who wanted to see village life. Every chief on Manono had a problem with that idea. *The most important task of a village council is to see that resources are fairly divided between families. If one of them should suddenly get rich by exhibiting its neighbors (sic), there would be no peace until the others brought it down to size again. To keep stability in a village it must be developed as a whole* (Vaiao 1994:2; emphasis added).

A community leader, Leiataua Vaiao, recalled his acquaintance with *Elderhostel* and the fact that this organization's travellers were "not into bars or Club Med entertainment" (Ibid.). They thought of themselves as students rather than tourists. After being approached by them for weekend visits, he also remembered the Samoan belief that villages, not just individuals, form friendship pairs called *so'o* to exchange visits with each other periodically. No village had ever thought of establishing a *so'o* with a group from abroad. The village of Lepuia'i agreed to be the first to try and proceeded to award the *Elderhostel* director a title so everyone would know how to address the group in traditional fashion. *Elderhostel* made some stipulations, such as a pier and flush toilets, and these were met with the help of the Australian High Commission. *Elderhostel* weekend visits offering a genuine cultural immersion and cultural exchange experience were highly successful. Payment assessed as part of the original tour fee was presented in the form of a gift to the village, known as *lafo*, and subsequently banked and distributed according to a formula determined by the village:

> It is their tour. They see that everyone is involved either
> as a host or part of a group entertainment. Everyone
> gives; everyone gets; and the guests benefit from meeting
> the whole community. That's the Samoan way (Ibid.:4).

Similar to the Ecuadorian experiences, the end of the tour does not necessarily signal the end of the relationship established by *so'o*. Many *Elderhostelers* continue corresponding with their host families and have donated books for the school library. Other villages on Manono have found their own *so'o* partners in the form of American university students who spend several weeks in the villages. Unlike elders, these young people are not treated as chiefs but experience the life of young, untitled members of the community, participating in daily chores and receiving cultural instruction, but also helping to teach English in the primary school.

Before long, Manono's experiment was expanded to the national level and customized to accommodate the interests of a large variety of different groups. With the assistance of overseas educated community members, a support agency called *Samoa Customized Tours* was established, acting as a facilitator and tour operator.

In summary, right from the outset, one of the principal goals of this tourism initiative was an even distribution of the benefits of tourism. The host's idea was patterned after a traditional practice, *so'o*, friendship pairs of communities. This Samoan practice was extended to groups from abroad. People were thus operating within a familiar frame of reference. Its implementation involved the entire village in a hosting capacity, in various functions. Guests were ascribed suitable community roles depending on their age. They were not treated as outsiders, where the community was at a loss how to react to them, a frequent occurrence in tourism. They were ascribed a familiar role before they even arrived; people knew "what to do with them." An expansion to the national level undoubtedly presents new challenges to the community-based character of the endeavour, but the track record makes the future look promising.

The Samoa example appears to come very close to the ideal of community-based tourism development: Initiative, process, product and cultural contents, as well as distribution of input and benefits are all truly communal and culturally and socially integrated. A familiar frame of reference is extended to embrace outsiders.

Involving and Empowering Communities

The above examples of community-based tourism from Canada and Samoa may be viewed as representing opposite ends of a spectrum of community involvement in tourism development. Manono's case represents a rare example of a genuine community initiative that is conceived, executed and benefited from within a cultural framework that guarantees collective involvement and remuneration. The "development engine" is clearly located within the community. This contrasts with the scenario of Inuit communities in Canada's Northwest Territories, where the Territorial Government's policy of community-based tourism strives for a maximum of community involvement in decision-making, but for various reasons is hesitant to devolve control and mandate of development. It remains to be seen whether the new government of Nunavut will show more willingness to devolve control to communities, but fiscal constraints render such possibility doubtful.

Both cases show measures of success, but the magnitude and distribution of economic benefits differ, with those in Pangnirtung being more modest and unevenly distributed. The same is true for the opportunity to do things "the Inuit way" or "the Samoan way." There are many stages between these two extremes. There is an abundance of examples where there is an outside impetus for community-based tourism development. Such impetus may come from government, the private sector, non-governmental organizations or individuals. Frequently there is a dual impetus from within and outside a community, as exemplified by indigenous groups in Latin America. In Canada, government promotion of community initiatives in the tourism field is not confined to the North. Throughout the 1980s, the provincial governments of British Columbia and Alberta both underwrote community tourism planning exercises (Murphy 1993:4f). In Alberta a $30 million Community Tourism Action Plan (1987) was intended to encourage small communities to develop their own tourism projects. The program was designed as a matching fund project, with the province providing 75 percent and the municipalities 25 percent of the funds required for a community-defined and approved project. Many aboriginal communities involved themselves in these planning exercises (Hinch 1992).

Namibia's Wildlife Management, Utilization and Tourism in Communal Areas Policy and the establishment of the Namibia Community-Based Tourism Association (NACOBTA) in 1995, as well as the experience of a San group, were already discussed in Chapter Two. NACOBTA is a grassroots membership organization that operates under a constitution, is managed by a committee comprising community representatives and has a small number of permanent employees (Karwacki 1999:2). It operates in rural Namibia and small urban settlements on the periphery of national parks, the location of most of the country's natural and cultural resources. The association provides business advice to member enterprises, initiates cooperation with private industry, assists communities in the development of their human resources, markets members' tourism products and strives to increase community involvement and responsibility in the tourism industry. Its most valuable initiatives include a comprehensive training program for community members. In 1999 the organization provided support to 29 established and 11 new tourism projects, including campsites, rest camps, craft centres, traditional villages, indigenous tour guides, and tourism information centres and museums. NACOBTA-supported projects ranged from wholly community-owned to private enterprises. All projects were geared towards involving as many community members as possible while optimizing their stewardship for natural and cultural resources (Ibid.:4). While the ownership of resources remains in government hands, community members may benefit from resource-based tourism projects through employment, lease of land, levies, or concessions.

In developing countries tour operators and local and foreign non-governmental organizations (NGOs) have played an important role in facilitating community-based tourism development, which has frequently been driven by a dual impetus from inside and outside the community. With regard to ecotourism (but not confined to it) Epler Wood (2002:41) identifies three main types of community-based tourism enterprises. The purest model is represented by a project that is totally owned and managed by the community. All community members are employed by the enterprise on a rotational basis, and profits are allocated to community projects. Manono and the Toledo Ecotourism Association in Belize (see Chapter Six) would qualify as examples.

The second type involves family or group initiatives within communities. This type may be represented by a broad spectrum of scenarios, where a family or group (or even an individual) relies on communal natural and/or cultural resources for a tourism product or service in exchange for more widely distributed benefits. An example is *EagleStar Tours* on the Tsuu T'ina Reserve near Calgary, Alberta, Canada, which is an individual proprietorship that showcases the reserve community, involves a large number of community members and renders services to the community (Chapter Three of this book; and Notzke 2004:37). It may be viewed as a "catch-all" category in recognition of the fact that in most indigenous (and many non-Western) societies even "non-communal" endeavours require community approval or tolerance. In many cases, however, the categorization of such initiatives as "community-based" is open to question. Finally, Epler Wood's third type of community-based ecotourism is a joint venture between a community or family and an outside business partner, exemplified by the Huaorani and *TROPIC Ecological Adventures* (see Chapter Six), certain Iban groups working with tour operators in East Malaysia, Borneo (see Chapter One) and selected San groups in southern Africa, who join forces with tour operators and private guest or hunting farms (see Chapter Two).[3]

Epler Wood (2002:41) concedes that, in practice, it may not be realistic to expect that an entire community can manage and con-

---

3 For another excellent case study from Namibia see Ashley & Jones 2001.

trol ecotourism. Based on their experiences in Ecuador, Wesche and Drumm comment that

> the notion of long-term communal enterprise requires the permanent, consistent commitment of all community members. It has to be learned and reinforced through positive experience. Problems have resulted from the communal enterprise approach such as the slowness of democratic decision making and inconsistent quality of services. The community enterprise model is being adapted to allow for allocation of responsibilities to specialized, trained members of the community (Wesche & Drumm 1999, quoted in Epler Wood 2002:41f).

The challenges encountered by community-based tourism management are indeed daunting. Training is a major issue. As community operations often run at low occupancy levels, new skills such as guiding, languages, food preparation, accounting and administration should not supplant traditional ones, nor should they result in deculturization. Tour companies and NGOs have made important contributions in this area. On the other hand it must be recognized that local people have much to teach outside guides, who continue to play an important role, particularly in ecotourism, due to local guides' lack of fluency in English, German and other languages. Acknowledging indigenous people as trainers and instructors would greatly enhance the skills of outside guides, the quality of the visitors' experience, and the empowerment of men and women of the host society (Drumm 1998:202f).

Connecting the product with the market has been called the Achilles' heel of community-based enterprise (Ibid.:203). Particularly in the developing world, but sometimes even in industrialized countries, the very nature of community-based tourism is rural and remote, without access to the tools of tourism communication — telephone, fax and e-mail. This explains why well-connected private operators often play such a crucial role in mutually beneficial relationships with community-based operations: They provide the link with the market in exchange for low net prices to which the operators add a mark-up. However, in most cases, these agreements lack explicit guidelines on anything other than itineraries and price arrangements (Ibid.:204). Sometimes NGO's take on the role of the market intermediary or, in rare cases, a member of the community takes up residence in an urban centre.

Using ecotourism as an example, there are 10 specific issues critical to eliciting community-based participation when approaching a project. It must be emphasized here that this represents a planned approach contingent upon some kind of catalyst originating with government, an NGO, an institution or an individual. The following citation, summarized from Brandon (1993) and quoted from Epler Wood (2002), highlights "basic steps towards encouraging local participation in nature tourism projects."

- **Understand the Community's Role.** Communities should exercise control over their growth and development. They will in many cases need technical assistance to make appropriate decisions and should be given adequate information and training in advance. Allocate time, funds and experienced personnel to work with communities well in advance. Avoid allowing communities to feel they are powerless to influence patterns of development.

- **Empower Communities.** Participation is a process that is more than just making communities the beneficiaries of an ecotourism project. Jobs are an important benefit, but they do not replace empowerment. Communities must genuinely participate in the decision-making process. This involves more than consultation. Processes must be initiated to ensure that communities can manage their own growth and resources wisely.

- **Urge Local Project Participation.** Project managers must identify local leaders, local organizations, key priorities of the community, and ideas, expectations and concerns local people already have. Information can be gathered for and by the community. The opinions gathered should be disseminated and discussed with the community along with other relevant information, such as government market statistics or regional development plans. Training opportunities must be formulated at this phase to help community members gain planning skills, and also the entrepreneurial skills required to run small businesses.

- **Create Stakeholders.** Participation can be encouraged at two levels — for individuals and for local organizations. Investment in project development areas should be encouraged, either in cash, labor or in-kind resources. Developing lodging by local entrepreneurs and setting standards for local services by local organizations are good examples.

- **Link Benefits to Conservation.** The links between ecotourism benefits and conservation objectives need to be direct and significant. Income, employment and other benefits must promote conservation.

- **Distribute Benefits.** Ensure that both the community and individuals benefit from projects.

- **Identify Community Leaders.** Identify opinion leaders and involve them in the planning and execution of projects. Identify leaders that represent different constituents to ensure that a cross-section of society is involved (including both men and women). Be sure the project has good information on local social structure. Strategize on the effects of the projects on different social groups, and never assume that all parts of society will cooperate or agree. Be strategic and gain appropriate allies early.

- **Bring about Change.** Use existing organizations already working in the community to improve its social well-being through economic development. Development associations or local cooperatives are good prospects. Groups involved in organizing recreation can also be good allies. Community participation through institutions is more likely to bring about effective and sustained change.

- **Understand Site-Specific Conditions.** Be aware that authority structures vary greatly in each region. Consensus is not always possible, nor is the full participation of all sectors of society. (Women are often excluded.)

- **Monitor and Evaluate Progress.** Establish indicators in advance to track tourism's impacts — both positive and negative. Goals such as employment and income levels are only one type of indicator. The project should track negative impacts, such as evidence of rapidly escalating prices for local goods, inflation in land prices, antagonism towards visitors, frequency of arrests, change in youth activities, and evidence of drugs, prostitution and other illicit activities. Ideally, the more the local community is fully involved in ecotourism development, the less these problems should develop. Another important indicator of local involvement is evidence of initiatives within the community to respond to the negative influ-

ences of tourism. (Brandon 1993, summarized in Epler
Wood 2002:39)

The distinction between a *participatory* and a *beneficiary* approach is
crucial when considering the notion of empowerment. "Participatory
approaches involve people in the process of their own development" (Brandon 1993:139). People are empowered to gain control
over their own lives. This goes well beyond the effect of a beneficiary approach, where community members may share in social and
economic benefits without gaining control of their own destiny.
Thus people may benefit from jobs as guides or the sale of products but, at the same time, have no voice in the decision-making
process. As a result they will feel like bystanders rather than stakeholders, let alone owners of the process and outcome.

Scheyvens (1999) designed an "empowerment framework" to
determine the impacts of ecotourism initiatives on local communities. Indicators for *economic* empowerment include opportunities
that have arisen in terms of both formal and informal sector employment and business opportunities, with due consideration of
equitable distribution of such benefits. Economic empowerment or
disempowerment also calls to our attention a community's access to
productive resources in an area newly targeted for ecotourism
(Ibid.:248). Ecotourism can be *psychologically* empowering if it
respects local traditions and reinforces the integral relationship
between a group of people and their land. Disruption of customs
and alienation of land can be psychologically crippling. *Social* empowerment can be effected when ecotourism profits contribute to a
community's sense of cohesion and integrity: for example, by financing social development projects such as schools, health clinics
or water supply systems. Inequitable distribution of economic benefits can result in social disempowerment, evidenced by feelings of
jealousy and social divisiveness. *Political* empowerment refers to the
decentralization of decision-making from the national level to the
community level, resulting in the local community's ability to exert
control over the course of tourism development (Ibid.:249).

Nobody can deny the positive outcomes of community-based
approaches to tourism development, nor can there be any doubt that
the concept is fraught with numerous difficulties. Preceding the benefits of the above-mentioned types of empowerment, first and foremost indigenous people must be empowered to do things their
own way, which brings us to a major *external* obstacle to community-
based approaches to development: the failure of some governments
to recognize the legitimacy of community-based enterprises. Drumm
(1998:209ff) identifies Ecuador's tourism law as one of the greatest

limitations to *RICANCIE*'s plans (see Chapter Six), as it demands that communities convert themselves into companies. The imposition of a corporate structure and culture would leave *RICANCIE* without a system of checks and balances to prevent disintegration into "mini-companies" with internal competition and social and cultural conflicts. After a futile struggle for the right to approach tourism in an alternative manner, unable to access needed credits and hampered by its "illegality" in promotional efforts, *RICANCIE* decided in 1997 to constitute itself as a corporation. Thus, the community approach in many ways seems to be at the heart of indigenous people's struggle to pursue a truly alternative path of development.

Summary

This chapter focuses on the community-based approach to tourism development. This is a popular topic in the indigenous tourism discourse. A widespread implicit assumption that community-based tourism development is the most desirable approach to tourism development in indigenous communities is not always matched by a critical understanding of the challenges presented by this concept. An appreciation of the complexity of most communities is indispensable for grasping the differential impact that tourism development is likely to have on a community. It is easy to succumb to the stereotype of communities as "big happy families," jointly embarking upon and benefiting from innovative tourism enterprises.

In reality, most communities are characterized by a considerable degree of pluralism. Different sections of society will experience a differential degree of impact from tourism development and react accordingly. Community-based tourism development approaches may take different forms with varying levels and quality of community involvement. Correspondingly, success can be measured in different ways. This is demonstrated by examples from Canada's Arctic and from Polynesia. The case of Pangnirtung illustrates the community-based tourism development approach by the Government of the Northwest Territories. In practice, this approach is characterized by community involvement rather than community control. Nevertheless, it has empowered the people of Pangnirtung to mould the tourism industry and their involvement in it in a way that best meets the needs of local families and the community as a whole. Tourism complements and supplements other elements of the mixed economy with a minimum of social and cultural disruption. In contrast, the Samoa example comes very close to the ideal of community-based tourism development. The development engine is clearly located within the community. A familiar frame of reference, rooted in the local culture, is extended to embrace foreign visitors. The initiative to embark on the project, its execution, the tourism product and its cultural contents, as well as participation and distribution of benefits are all truly communal and culturally and socially integrated.

While occupying opposite ends of a spectrum of community involvement in tourism development, both cases show measures of success. At the same time, neither can be simply replicated in a different environment. There is no blueprint for community-based tourism, but there are certain principles for the involvement and empowerment of communities. The impetus for community-based tourism development does not necessarily originate solely from within the community, but may come from outside agents, such as government, the private sector, non-governmental organizations or individuals. Frequently there is a dual impetus from within and outside a community. Cases where an entire community has total ownership of and management power over a tourism enterprise are extremely rare. But regardless of where the initial push for community-based tourism development comes from, and regardless of how large a proportion of the community is directly involved in a tourism venture, it is of crucial importance that the overall approach to development aims for participatory rather than beneficiary involvement of community members. Only when people become stakeholders rather than just passive beneficiaries with regard to tourism development will they have the opportunity to gain ownership of the process and outcome, and as a result be empowered to gain control over their lives.

8

Outlook

Introduction

The past seven chapters have explored the complex interplay of the stranger, the native and the land in many different environments. As observed by Timothy and White (1999:240), sustainable tourism initiatives tend to be highly scale- and place-specific, and nowhere is such individuality more pronounced than with regard to indigenous tourism initiatives. Nevertheless, some broader observations and speculative ideas will be ventured at this point.

Even though numerous governments in developing countries show little inclination to encourage representational democracy, rapid political changes are occurring throughout the world that have resulted in an increased opportunity for indigenous peoples for greater levels of involvement in participatory development and planning (Ibid.). The example of the Toledo District in Belize has shown that peripherality can indeed be a positive agent of change and empowerment by providing a buffer against unwanted government interference in community initiatives.

Indigenous people become involved in the tourism industry for various reasons. For some it may be "just a business venture," with few concerns besides the financial bottom line. For the majority, however, economic goals are closely intertwined with socio-cultural aspirations and concerns, and the development process is embedded in a specific cultural, social, political and economic framework. In non-Western societies and economies tourism can fulfil a variety of functions. For people interested in maintaining traditional aspects of their socio-economic systems within the framework of a mixed economy, tourism can underwrite the expense of pursuing traditional land-based activities or even help transform these into neo-traditional and more sustainable practices. Tourism has also effected cultural validation and revitalization and has contributed to an international network of support for indigenous causes.

On the other hand, the industry may provide those who desire it with an escape from what they perceive as the hardship and confinement of a traditional existence. Tourism can thus act as an agent of conservation or an agent of change or both, ideally providing people with options for the future that would otherwise be lacking. Involvement in tourism will invariably complicate people's lives and introduce some kind of change. Whether such complication and change will ultimately result in empowerment of individuals and communities rather than negative environmental, socio-cultural and economic impacts depends largely on the participatory involvement of the host in the decision-making process and on the quality of planning, including continued monitoring, once tourism development has started.

Planning: A Blueprint for the Future

The importance of an appropriate and effective planning process for indigenous tourism cannot be overemphasized, regardless of whether an individual considers a tourism enterprise or a whole community embarks on a venture. Whenever communal cultural or natural resources are involved, the implications are similar:

> Planning saves time and maximizes resources. A plan is a "blueprint" for action. Community participation in planning is critical for self-determination or for a proactive stance to occur during development. Planning depicts a desirable future. It is aimed at building consensus and gaining participation.
>
> ....
>
> Finding the connection between cultural subsystems is the key to sustainable development, that is long-range development that supports culture as well as the economy. A special feature of planning for sustainable development... is the design of activities that achieve more than one result, such as cultural preservation, substance abuse prevention, or the integration of families, as well as training for employment. The crux of effective planning for proactive development is discovering how one action can accomplish more than one objective.
>
> The planning process is useful for many purposes. Gaining community participation for any anticipated development is an important outcome of the planning process. This can be accomplished through community hearings, surveys, meetings, or interviews. Also, long-range strategies are developed in the planning process that tribal councils, boards, or community committees can adopt for long-term continuity. Plans are also useful for staff to follow once projects are underway. In addition, planning is invaluable for generating funding. Once a long-term strategy is mapped out and the resources are identified to accomplish a project, plans can be shown to prospective funding agencies. Plans not only demonstrate competence to funding agencies but also are a basis for funding applications

.... Finally, planning is closely linked to evaluation. Once goals and objectives are formed in the planning process, these are used to measure progress later in the evaluation process. Evaluation, in turn, is essential to improving the effectiveness of programs and businesses. In short, planning involves the community and creates alignment.

Planning keeps a project on target; one of the key benefits of planning is creating focus. Of particular importance, planning is a tool for linking people together to accomplish a larger result (Guyette 1996:9f).

As is true for sustainable tourism initiatives in general, successful planning needs to be scale and place specific. There are different planning approaches and tools that need to be customized for the case at hand, but the effective ones have in common that they are inclusive, participatory and holistic. In her excellent guide to *Planning for Balanced Development,* Guyette (1996:10–35) describes the "Poeh Center model," a detailed planning process over a six-month period that created a strategic plan for approximately 20 cultural preservation projects. It was focused on the establishment of Poeh Center, a Tewa (Pueblo in New Mexico) cultural centre and museum. The process incorporated 13 steps:

Step 1: Create a Vision (including a cultural vision and an employment vision)

Step 2: Identify Key Issues

Step 3: Define a Strategy (assess future actions)

Step 4: Collect and Analyze Important Data (including Needs Assessment)

Step 5: Do a SWOT Analysis (identifying Strengths, Weaknesses, Opportunities, and Threats that change could bring)

Step 6: Create a Mission Statement (a focused expression of long-term purpose)

Step 7: Form Your Goals

Step 8: Define the Projects

Step 9: Conduct a Resource Audit

Step 10: Calculate Timetables for Development

Step 11: Prepare Financial Projections

Step 12: Write an Executive Summary

Step 13: Plan for Sequential Development

There is no fixed formula for indigenous tourism planning. There are likely numerous unpublicized examples of successful tourism planning in indigenous communities, often involving individuals with some fluency in their own indigenous culture as well as non-native culture and business culture. A good example is an outline of Kwanlin Dun First Nation Tourism Planning in Canada's Yukon Territory, which was shared by Joe Jack of *Aetsi Taen Tours* at a tourism workshop in Yellowknife, Northwest Territories, in 1995. His objective was clear:

> The main purpose of putting an effective tourism plan into place is to: help the healing of Kwanlin people through the revival of cultural practices; reacquaint the local people with their culture and stories; attain respect for the Kwanlin Dun culture through sharing with non-Indian people, share the stories in a positive way, to share who we are; generate revenue for the Kwanlin Dun community; create meaningful employment for Kwanlin Dun members — rather than just creating jobs giving them something to do that they will enjoy; and educate Kwanlin Dun members about tourism and the importance of working with established businesses, organizations and governments (Jack 1995:36).

Kwanlin Dun community response to this exercise was positive, as the approach was inclusive, participatory and holistic. In addition to community input advice was also solicited from outside industry stakeholders. Nevertheless, such a planning exercise can be a major challenge to novice individuals or communities taking their first tentative steps into the business of tourism. In many countries there is an increasing amount of information available through government and industry organizations, as well as indigenous tourism organizations, that specifically addresses the concerns of newcomers to indigenous tourism. In Canada this includes resources produced by the Canadian National Aboriginal Tourism Association (CNATA 1995) and its successor organization, Aboriginal Tourism Team Canada[1] (ATTC n.d. a & b), such as a planning manual, a business planning guide and a "checklist for success". Australia's Aboriginal and Torres Strait Islander Commission produces similar materials (ATSIC 1995). Regional aboriginal tourism associations provide a variety of support services.

In developing countries the situation is somewhat more problematic. Tour operators and non-governmental organizations have made important and positive contributions in assisting indigenous people's

---

1 Currently known as Aboriginal Tourism Canada (ATC).

entry into the tourism industry. Yet, tour operators rarely have the means or motivation to assist communities in a comprehensive planning effort, and non-governmental organizations often lack experience in the field of tourism development, which sometimes induces them to create unrealistic expectations on the part of communities as to the timing and scale of future benefits. This easily results in the building of tourism infrastructure "white elephants" (Drumm 1998:201).

Such situations underscore the importance of an international exchange of experiences among indigenous peoples, and the urgency for researchers to disseminate their ideas among indigenous peoples who aided them in their development. For example, Valene Smith's Four Hs of indigenous tourism — habitat, heritage, history and handicrafts (Smith 1996; Notzke 2004) — are an easily applied analytical tool to evaluate the indigenous tourism potential in any given geographical and cultural environment. Sofield and Birtles (1996) developed an "Indigenous Peoples' Cultural Opportunity Spectrum for Tourism" (IPCOST) that constitutes a means for a community's self-assessment:

> It is designed to ensure that indigenous communities have ownership of a database from which to reach an informed decision about cultural tourism in the context of decision making for change, implementation of those planned changes, and subsequent management of the resources — or alternatively rejection of change, with control over the resources retained wherever possible by the indigenous communities. *The crucial element in the process is that a community will have assessed itself.* Thus, IPCOST provides a community with a mechanism to:
>
> 1. Catalogue its culture in terms of potential opportunities for tourism ventures;
> 2. Carry out its own assessment of its capacity to undertake development generally and cultural tourism specifically;
> 3. Decide whether it should therefore venture into cultural tourism at all;
> 4. And decide which particular option(s) represent the best opportunities to pursue according to a range of cultural and social values as well as economic considerations.
>
> IPCOST has as its underpinning the principles of ecologically sustainable development. This is absolutely

critical because of the "caring for country" relationship which most traditionally oriented societies have with their tribal lands. Any compromise of this would be unacceptable because it would strike at the core of their culture. The mix of traditional values and the principles of ecologically sustainable development constitute a powerful force for conservation, thus providing impetus for the maintenance of both cultural diversity and bio-diversity and the potential to "save" both indigenous peoples' way of life and fragile ecosystems from modernization and inappropriate development (Sofield & Birtles 1996:402f, emphasis added).

This exercise was developed on the Solomon Islands in the South Pacific (Melanesia), but can be executed in any geographical environment and on varying geographical scales. This author encouraged Canadian aboriginal students from all over Canada to apply this approach in an evaluative exercise (as an individual rather than a community exercise) to their own communities, ranging from Arctic and sub-Arctic villages to southern Indian reserves or Metis communities. The exercise was much appreciated by the indigenous students and their results were extremely revealing and interesting.

A "Culture" of Professionalism

The importance for all tourism stakeholders to recognize and consider indigenous interests and sensitivities has repeatedly been emphasized. Understanding, however, must be two-directional. Indigenous tourism is considered a niche product, which increases the importance of *professionalism* in its delivery. Even more than other sectors of the tourism industry, niche products are faced with an extremely competitive marketplace and an increasingly sophisticated clientele. Taking the aboriginal tourism scenario in southern Alberta, Canada, as an example, however, too many aboriginal operators (with excellent ideas and a genuine desire to host visitors) remain ignorant of the nature of the tourism industry and the requirements of tourism businesses: and, what is worse, oblivious of the need to acquire this knowledge. There is no lack of learning opportunities, which are provided in the form of workshops, marketing assistance and other resources by government departments and industry associations (The *Canadian Tourism Commission, Aboriginal Tourism Canada, Travel Alberta* and, until 2003, the *Niitsitapi Tourism Society of*

Alberta[2]), often free of charge and hardly ever prohibitively expensive. Post-secondary education offers additional opportunities. Researchers can do their part by disseminating the results of their investigations to those who may benefit from them, which this researcher is doing. Excellent communication is a must in the tourism industry, and nowadays a presence on the WorldWideWeb is almost a *sine qua non* for a product supplier. And yet, very few aboriginal operators in southern Alberta have a website or an e-mail address. Some of them were assisted by *Niitsitapi* (before its demise) featuring contact information for aboriginal tourism attractions on its website, but many businesses and individuals are notoriously difficult to contact, which signals lack of market readiness to potential visitors and the travel trade alike.

Just as *Visitor Guidelines* and a *Code of Ethics* or *Guidelines for Tour Operators* often assist in protecting fragile cultural and natural resources from the impact of tourism, there may be a need for a *Code of Professionalism* for tourism product suppliers and tour operators, that somehow transcends cultural relativity and socio-cultural embeddedness. While the very nature of certain cross-cultural tourism experiences defies adherence to a strict schedule, such a code should commit enterprises to certain standards of communication, reliability and punctuality, contingency plans in case of alternative personal and social commitments, and consistency of product delivery. A demonstrated commitment to such a code would put travel trade intermediaries and potential clients at ease, and would separate those who choose to dabble in tourism on their own terms from tourism entrepreneurs who expect to make a living from the industry while establishing a long-term presence in the market. Both approaches to tourism are legitimate, but they must be matched with realistic expectations in terms of benefits.

---

2   The *Niitsitapi Tourism Society of Alberta* promoted Alberta's aboriginal tourism. It served as a contact and clearinghouse for information for various industry stakeholders. It had a website that publicized contact information for tourism attractions and responded to inquiries from the media, travel trade and travellers domestically as well as internationally. Even though it was a membership organization, it had only 37 members but served a much larger constituency of aboriginal tourism-related businesses in the province. *Niitsitapi* owed its success to a single dedicated and talented individual, Lori Beaver. Its future, however, was uncertain even before its demise due to health issues. The organization used to receive core funding from *Industry Canada*, which enabled it to operate on a shoestring budget, but this funding source was about to dry up.

Illustration 8.1

Illustration 8.2

(Illustrations 8.1 and 8.2) During the summer of 2004 the author worked as an ecovolunteer on a Przewalski horse release project in Mongolia. Our work involved the tracking of wild horses in their natural habitat, as well as teaching Mongolian biologists English one on one, with plenty of opportunities for cultural immersion with nomadic families. This type of tourism offers many opportunities for aboriginal people.

An Ethic of Caring

The frontier of sustainable tourism development in general and indigenous tourism in particular is being advanced by people who care about other people and the environment rather than just about the financial bottom line. These people are hosts, guests and travel trade intermediaries. Clearly, aboriginal hosts are taking the greatest risk. While they enter the industry with expectations of tangible and intangible benefits, be they economic, social, political or environmental, they are engaging with a highly unpredictable phenomenon that at times appears to take on a life of its own. Even with careful planning and management, tourism is very difficult to control and is affected by many external factors outside of the host society's sphere of influence, such as the global economy and societal trends. Even the internal environment of a community is not as easily controlled as some would hope (Murphy 1993:10). The risk is magnified if indigenous people lack political clout and control over their land and resources. Yet there are cases where aboriginal people have successfully embarked on the risky undertaking of using tourism to rectify this very situation.

The elusive character and extreme changeability of the tourism market remain a challenge. Even among responsible travellers there is a constant waxing and waning in their degree of social responsibility, environmental consciousness, intellectual curiosity and sense of adventure. But there is a special kind of tourist with the potential to make a different kind of contribution to indigenous peoples' interests. Described as "Tomorrow's Travellers" (Cherrington 1997) and as "Extreme, Extravagant and Elite" (Weiler & Richins 1995) these volunteers contribute not just money, but themselves to cultural and environmental conservation and research:

> The generic term "volunteer tourism" applies to those tourists who, for various reasons, volunteer in an organized way to undertake holidays that might involve aiding or alleviating the material poverty of some groups in society, the restoration of certain environments or research into aspects of society or environment (Wearing 2001:1).

> Volunteer tourism can take place in varied locations such as rainforests and cloudforests, biological reserves and conservation areas. Popular locations include countries in Africa, Central and South America. Activities can vary across many areas, such as scientific research (wildlife, land and water), conservation projects, medical assistance, economic and social development (including

agriculture, construction and education) and cultural restoration. Indeed, volunteers can find themselves anywhere between assisting with mass eye surgery operations to constructing a rainforest reserve.... Of interest, however, is that volunteer tourists will almost always pay in some way to participate in these activities (Ibid.:2).

It is difficult to assess the size of this market segment. According to www.VolunteerTourism.com, over 500,000 Americans volunteered internationally in 1999. Growth trends are reflected in the number of organizations offering volunteer vacations. One of the longest published guides to these organizations, *Volunteer Vacations* by Bill McMillon, listed 75 such organizations in its first edition in 1987, whereas there were 275 organizations in the 2003 edition (Brown & Morrison 2003:75). *Earthwatch* is the best known of a number of nonprofit organizations that allow people from all walks of life to join research projects in a variety of fields, including archaeology, anthropology, zoology, ecology, and wildlife management. They are teamed with scientists to work in the field as full-fledged expedition members under often physically challenging conditions. There are opportunities for travelling volunteers to contribute to indigenous cultural survival within the framework of participatory research being conducted under the control and with the participation of indigenous people:

> In this kind of participatory research people do, indeed, visit remote cultures and learn ancient secrets (among other things), but they do so in the service of the culture, not in the interest of voyeurism. In fact, several Earthwatch projects in Australia have helped Aboriginal people to locate and document their prehistoric rock art and to preserve ancient rituals directly. They've protected fragile sites and made videotapes that can be shown to the younger members of tribes to help them appreciate and participate in their own traditions (Cherrington 1997).

Wearing (2001) provides us with an in-depth study of the volunteer tourism experience at the Santa Elena Rainforest Reserve in Costa Rica, administered by the volunteer tourist organization *Youth Challenge International*. He effectively demonstrates the impact of such an experience on the volunteers' value system and sense of identity, and the importance of a shift away from the more traditional emphasis on travel, where tourist pleasure is derived from an exploitation of resources, to one in which tourist satisfaction and fulfilment are achieved through the individual contributing to and learning about natural and cultural environments. Furthermore, the author ventures the idea that in volunteer tourism "the power balance between tourist and hosts can be destabilised" (Wearing 2001:172). With the growth of participatory action research among indigenous peoples throughout the world, there may be enhanced possibilities for mutual enrichment for hosts and guests, but these initiatives must be driven by an agenda that accords highest priority to the welfare of the host's cultural and natural environment.[3]

Finally, aboriginal tourism is also being advanced by private sector entrepreneurs, working with indigenous communities. Theirs has been a particularly important role in the area of ecotourism, but also one wrought with many difficulties, as illustrated by an example from Tanzania:

> The example of Oliver's Camp [on lands used by Maasai] serves to show two points: that successful ecotourism is taking place at the small-scale level, and, that effective cooperation (e.g., leasing arrangements) between local communities and the private sector can be achieved with a commitment on the part of the entrepreneur to bear the financial costs and risks of capacity building (education and training) in the community. Costs associated with this commitment involve organizing meetings to keep the process moving forward, as well as making initial investments in the project, often before a long-term lease or concession agreement is reached. Another type of cost incurred involves time, as local communities do not always respond according to the deadlines set by business investors for a given project. Patience to see the process through is essential if an agreement that is beneficial to all is to be achieved.
>
> Perhaps the largest risk of investing in a tourism venture with a lease agreement signed by a village council involves the fact that the community may or may not have actual rights to the land in question (Christ 1998:186).

Another Tanzanian venture, *Dorobo Tours and Safaris*, operates mobile camps and walking safaris in the heart of Maasailand. After a decade of hands-on experience, *Dorobo* has identified certain issues that have dominated its private sector experience and its challenges with local community involvement:

---

3 The growing complexity of this burgeoning field of research is illustrated by a special 2003 issue of *Tourism Recreation Research* 28(3) with contributions by Broad, Brown & Morrison; Ellis, Halpenny & Caissie; Higgins-Desbiolles; Lyons; and Uriely, Reichel & Ron.

- Extensive time and commitment are needed on the part of the entrepreneur in meeting with the communities involved and working out an effective concession or lease agreement that meets each party's concerns and needs.

- There is still no real official policy, framework, or support from government agencies involved, particularly in developing nations, for how a private-sector entrepreneur can carry out effective community involvement with tourism. There is nothing that says, "Here is what you can do, here is how to proceed, and this is what you must avoid." In this regard, especially at the official level, ecotourism still has a long way to go.

- Capacity building within villages and communities still falls largely on the private sector, and they are often the least able to meet this need (Ibid.:187).

The need for capacity building within communities and the absence of a stable government policy framework are thus the major challenges faced by the tourism trade in many developing countries and likely to scare off many potential private investors. Capacity building includes many different skills, such as basic education in understanding legal documents, financial management training, strengthening of decision-making structures, including village councils and project oversight committees, and tourism enterprise development training, including community-managed cultural centres, craft centres and guiding opportunities (Christ 1998:191).

It is hardly surprising that most of the success stories of private sector involvement with local communities have been on a small scale with one operator or one lodge working with one or two communities. A notable exception is *Conservation Corporation Africa,* one of the world's largest ecotourism companies, which may be considered "a pioneer private-sector ecotourism company willing to tackle the challenge of community planning and involvement in the arena of "large-scale" commercial tourism development" (Ibid.:192). In 1998 the company operated four private sanctuaries (two owned, two leased), and more than 20 lodges and camps, spread across the African continent (Ibid.:189). Between 1991 and 1997, *Conservation Corporation* spent over $1 million through its Rural Investment Fund to underwrite development projects within communities located in the proximity of its lodges, camps and private reserves, primarily in South Africa:

These projects have included everything from building classrooms in village areas to constructing a residential health clinic serving 30,000 people in an area where only limited medical facilities previously existed. *The purpose and focus of these efforts has been to involve communities directly in the economic benefits of tourism by actively seeking a way for local peoples to coexist in a beneficial relationship with nature-based tourism* (Ibid.:190, emphasis added).

Joint ventures between communities and tourism investors are somewhat facilitated in southern Africa by the presence of a broader policy framework of community-based natural resource management — more effective in some countries than in others — which provides communities and investors with a support network to provide advice and information. But even in the relatively supportive environment of Namibia Ashley and Jones (2001:419f) found that there were other critical factors accounting for the success of certain ventures: the role of committed individuals on both sides of the negotiating table and throughout the operation of the project, and a company philosophy that furthers the *spirit* of partnership, regardless of the legislative framework.

Another example of private sector initiatives to not only take but also give back to the indigenous community is represented by operators such as *Turtle Tours* (see Chapter Three). *Turtlewill* is the humanitarian arm of *Turtle Tours*, the American tour company owned by Irma Turtle, which specializes in small group travel to visit tribal peoples worldwide, but particularly in Africa. *Turtlewill* makes varied contributions to the welfare of the tribal peoples on the tours' itineraries, including well digging, livestock purchases, sending sick people to hospitals, providing medical assistance, supporting local schools and funding women's cooperatives. *Turtlewill* started out as a personal initiative by the company's owner, but has since snowballed through the efforts of travellers on many of her trips with remarkable initiatives in the areas of healthcare, education and training to help individuals and communities (www.turtletours.com/twill.htm).

The fact that this is a growing trend is evidenced by the recent Traveller Philanthropy Conference, held at Stanford University, April 12-15, 2004 (*Eco Currents*, First Quarter 2004, pp.4ff). This conference brought together leaders of socially responsible travel businesses involved in corporate giving programs to support community projects in tourism destinations. Projects sponsored by tourism companies spanned the globe and encompassed a great variety of literacy, income generation, environmental conservation, healthcare, and various other grassroots initiatives, supported by large and small tourism businesses. The conference also featured critical perspectives, such as the consideration of unintended "bad consequences" of "doing good," and the recommendation of partnering with well-established local NGOs (Ibid.:5).

One of the most vital positive contributions of ecotourism has been the development of standards and ethics, and a travel philosophy that can contribute to the prospects of sustainability of *all* kinds of tourism, even mass tourism. There are important ongoing initiatives aimed at making the tourism industry a more humane undertaking. One is *Tourism Concern*, a United Kingdom-based membership organization, campaigning for ethical and "fairly traded" tourism (www.tourismconcern.org.uk,). It was founded in 1989 with the mission of "putting people back in the picture." Considered militants by the industry at the time, their message is now accepted as common sense (*Tourism in Focus* 49/50:5, Spring 2004). One of the organization's current campaigns focuses on the improvement of working conditions of porters employed by the trekking industry in Asia and South America. *Tourism Concern* has produced an extensive collection of educational material in printed and audio-visual format. Another initiative is *Indigenous Tourism Rights International* (formerly the *Rethinking Tourism Project*), which explicitly focuses on helping indigenous peoples protect their territories, rights and cultures:

> Our name, Tourism Rights, refers to the rights of indigenous communities to control the ways that tourism affects our lives including:
>
> • the right to choose not to allow invasive tourism imposed from outside the community; and
> • the right to control community-based tourism in a socially appropriate and environmentally sustainable way (www.tourismrights.org).

Based in the United States, it is a non-profit education and networking project, which supports indigenous-directed development initiatives (see also McLaren 1998, particularly the "Resources" section, pp.133–173). Adopting a broader focus, we can hope that the "triple bottom line of 21st century business" (Elkington 1998) will also take hold of the tourism industry, ensuring a consideration not only of economic prosperity, but also of environmental quality and social justice.

Indigenous Tourism in the Age of Globalization

Globalization has been the buzzword of the 1990s, and the trend appears to continue into the new millennium. Since tourism constitutes *the* global industry, the relationship between globalization and the travel industry is bound to be an interesting one. Furthermore, indigenous concerns have enjoyed broad exposure in the raging globalization debate. Definitions of globalization vary considerably. Combining the insights of various writers, Waters (1995:3, quoted in Wood 2000:346) has proposed defining globalization as "a social process in which the constraints of geography on social and cultural arrangements recede and in which people become increasingly aware that they are receding." He argues that this process plays itself out in interrelated but irreducible ways in the realms of the economic, the political, and the cultural. Central to the phenomenon is how global processes disembed local practices from their geographies, re-embedding them in patterns and networks that increasingly have a global dimension. Social relations become partially deterritorialized, less constrained by the various aspects of locality. This in turn sets in motion new types of change and response:

> "The single, clearest, most direct result of economic globalization to date is a massive global transfer of economic and political power away from national governments and into the hands of global corporations and the trade bureaucracies they helped create. This transfer of power is producing dire consequences for the environment, human rights, social welfare, agriculture, food safety, workers' rights, national sovereignty and democracy itself." (International Forum on Globalization, 2000, quoted in Robb 2000:20)

On the other hand, environmentalists, human rights organizations, church groups, trade unionists, and indigenous people's organizations, collectively known as "civil society," have been pursuing their own kind of globalization by building cross-sectoral and cross-cultural networks (Herman 2000:6). An indigenous tourism entrepreneur from the Andes remarked to Edeli (2002:166), "Globalization is coming whether indigenous people like it or not. The only question is whether we will let it erase us, or whether we will take advantage of it." Paradoxically, and at significant risk, aboriginal people all over the world are trying to take advantage of global markets to preserve a local world and culture where the market cannot be king (Ibid.:167). Especially after the September 11th attack, indigenous communities like those of *RICANCIE* (Indigenous Community Network of the Upper Napo for Intercultural Exchange and Ecotourism) are paying the price for tying the welfare of their local economies to the economic health and societal trends of countries halfway around the world. In 2002 *RICANCIE* had a staggeringly low 3 percent occupancy rate and lacked both capital and profit. As Edeli (2002:169) points out, as long as there are Ecuadorian laws to protect communal property and local capital, *RICANCIE* and other enterprises like it may be able to coexist with heavily capitalized foreigners. However, as attempts to liberalize the trade in services throughout the Americas and the world proliferate, tourism services are increasingly being brought under international trade jurisdiction, with mounting pressure for higher capitalization and productivity.

The most important international agreement with direct bearing on tourism is the General Agreement on Trade in Services (GATS). Signed in Morocco in April 1994, GATS is the first multilateral and legally enforceable liberalization agreement covering trade in services, and states its objectives to be "the progressive elimination of obstacles and discriminatory barriers to service trade." (Hoad 2003:213) Intended as a panacea for many of tourism's ills, GATS may indeed pose considerable threats to sustainable forms of tourism, in particular to local communities and local governance frameworks:

> In short, GATS makes it easier for big tourist and travel TNCs [transnational corporations] to invest in the local tourism industries of Third World countries. Among others, it removes restrictions on foreign corporations' abilities to transfer staff from one country to another, and enables them to use trademarks, create and operate branch offices abroad, and more importantly, to repatriate their earnings to their mother companies abroad.
>
> Under GATS, protection of the local tourism industry would be construed as unfair practice and would thus have to be eliminated. TNCs now enjoy the same benefits as local travel and tourism agencies. This opens the local industry to competition from giant TNCs, *which virtually means effectively transferring its control to them* (Chavez 1999:3; emphasis added).

The legal principles on which the GATS rests run counter to many of the principles of sustainable tourism development. The market access provision explicitly prohibits members from discriminating against foreign service suppliers and from imposing restrictive quotas or other limitations. Most-favoured nation treatment prevents member countries from distinguishing between trading partners on the basis of such issues as human rights, labour practices or their environmental track record (Hoad 2003:216). Similar to the general exceptions principle in its predecessor, the General Agreement on Tariffs and Trade (GATT), the general exception article in the GATS provides for the possibility of exemption from trade rules. Such exemption may be granted, for example, to protect public morals or human, animal or plant life and health (Ibid.:217).

It should be noted, however, that in past trade disputes, particularly those under the GATT, the Dispute Settlement panels have invariably ruled against member countries trying to employ general exceptions articles for environmental protection. Precautionary measures to safeguard the natural environment are interpreted as trade restrictive (Ibid.:223). It is easy to see how such a jurisdictional environment would deal with initiatives to protect socio-cultural values or community empowerment. Similar concerns are expressed by Bendell and Font (2004:152):

> Market access principles rule out qualitative and quantitative restrictions (limits and quotas) as sources of potential trade discrimination. Under these rules many of the quantitative and qualitative safeguards which local communities and governments have used to create a space for sustainable tourism development could be challenged. For instance, tourism carrying capacity, frequently mentioned as a tool for controlling the direction and consequences of tourism development, may find itself under threat. Though a much contested concept, the notion of establishing maximal population size and usage in a given tourist area is anathema to free trade and market principles. Market access rules make it very difficult for environmental protection agencies, tourism planners and other stakeholders to establish quotas or limits in areas threatened by high tourist numbers and tourism expansion (Hoad 2003:221).

> One of the key issues for critics of the GATS is that it appears not to complement measures being adopted by communities or regions attempting to create an environment for sustainable forms of tourism. Members outline their commitments before they know what the environmental, social or economic implications might be and at no point in the agreement is there reference to sustainability or environmental protection. The GATS lacks complementary measures to ensure that resources are used in a sustainable way and that protective measures are not misconstrued as discriminatory barriers to trade (Ibid.:225).

> The development of the GATS should be based on broader concerns such as equity, participation and environment rather than open markets and increased global access (Ibid.:226).

In the meantime, different sections of the tourism industry have responded in different ways and are assuming different roles in the ongoing discourse of globalization. One end of the spectrum is occupied by the cruise industry, particularly the Caribbean cruise industry, as an important agent as well as a product of the process of globalization:

> Globalization detaches economic life from the constraints of geography — physical, cultural, political — and nowhere is this more evident than in Caribbean cruise tourism. The companies are entirely non-Caribbean. Their destinations are increasingly under their direct ownership and control; Caribbean cruises are taking on elements of "cruises to nowhere." The ships' laborforce is overwhelmingly non-Caribbean. What these ships do in the Caribbean Sea (including dumping) is outside the jurisdiction of Caribbean states (Wood 2000:364).

> It is a good place to watch how an unusually unfettered form of globalization plays itself out (Ibid.:366).

Indigenous tourism is to be found on the opposite end of the spectrum, as it epitomizes the idea of "a sense of place." Herein lies its vulnerability, as well as its strength. In the discourse of *the stranger, the native and the land*, indigenous tourism communicates the essence of an intimate relationship between the native and the land to the stranger, along with an implied sense of stewardship. In contrast to "cruises to nowhere," here is the potential of imparting the idea of a "home place" to a stranger, who may have but a dim memory of what this notion entails. There is hope that indigenous tourism will not only aid in the liberation of indigenous peoples, but will also contribute to our collective sense of place, locally and globally.

References

References

Aboriginal and Torres Strait Islander Commission (ATSIC). (1995). *The Business of Indigenous Tourism. A Book for Indigenous People and Communities who want to get into Tourism.* Canberra: ATSIC

_____. (1997). *Tourism Industry Strategy.* Canberra: Aboriginal and Torres Strait Islander Commission and The Office of National Tourism.

Aboriginal Tourism Team Canada (No Date a). *Aboriginal Tourism. Business Planning Guide.* Ottawa: Canadian Tourism Human Resource Council.

_____. (No Date b). *Aboriginal Cultural Tourism. Checklist for Success.* Ed. Beverley O'Neil. Ottawa: Canadian Tourism Commission.

Adams, Kathleen M. (1984). Come to Tana Toraja, "Land of the Heavenly Kings": Travel Agents as Brokers in Ethnicity. *Annals of Tourism Research* 11:469–485.

_____. (1995). Making-Up the Toraja? The Appropriation of Tourism, Anthropology, and Museums for Politics in Upland Sulawesi, Indonesia. *Ethnology* 34(2):143–153.

Adams, Vincanne. (1992). Tourism and Sherpas, Nepal. Reconstruction of Reciprocity. *Annals of Tourism Research* 19(3):534–554.

Alexander, Sara E. (1999). The Role of Belize Residents in the Struggle to Define Ecotourism Opportunities in Monkey Sanctuaries. *Cultural Survival Quarterly* 23(2):21–23.

Altman, Jon. (1989). Tourism Dilemmas for Aboriginal Australians. *Annals of Tourism Research* 16(4):456–476.

_____. (1993). Where to now? Some strategic Indigenous Tourism Policy Issues. In: *Indigenous Australians and Tourism: A Focus on Northern Australia.* Proceedings of the Indigenous Australians and Tourism Conference, Darwin, June 1993. pp.86–90.

_____, and Julie Finlayson (1993, 2003). Aborigines, Tourism and Sustainable Development. *The Journal of Tourism Studies* 4(1):38–50 and 14(1):78–91.

Aramberri, Julio. (2002). The Empowerment Riddle. *Tourism Recreation Research* 27(3):83–87.

Ashley, Caroline, and Brian Jones. (2001) Joint Ventures between Communities and Tourism Investors: Experience in Southern Africa. *International Journal of Tourism Research* 3:407–423.

Atkinson, Ken. (2001). New National Parks in the Canadian North. *Geography* 86(2)141–149.

Attix, Shelley A. (2002). New Age-Oriented Special Interest Travel: An Exploratory Study. *Tourism Recreation Research* 27(2):51–58.

Barnett, Ross. (1994). Uluru, Photographers get snappy. *The Bulletin,* March 1, 1994:32–34.

Barnett, Shirley. (2001). Manaakitanga: Maori Hospitality — A Case Study of Maori Accommodation Providers. *Tourism Management* 22:83–92.

Baron, Eve. (1998). Casino Gambling and the Polarization of American Indian Reservations. In: *Tourism and Gaming on American Indian Lands.* Edited by Alan A. Lew and George A. Van Otten. New York: Cognizant Communication Corporation. pp.163–171.

Bendell, Jem, and Xavier Font. (2004). Which Tourism Rules? Green Standards and GATS. *Annals of Tourism Research* 31(1):139–156.

Bennett, Judy. (1999). The Dream and the Reality: Tourism in Kuna Yala. *Cultural Survival Quarterly* 23(2):33–35.

Berno, Tracy. (1999). When a Guest is a Guest. Cook Islanders View Tourism. *Annals of Tourism Research* 26(3):656–675.

Blainey, Geoffrey. (1976). *Triumph of the Nomads. A History of Aboriginal Australia.* Woodstock, New York: The Overlook Press.

Blundell, Valda. (1990). The Tourist and the Native. In: *A Different Drummer: Readings in Anthropology with a Canadian Perspective.* Edited by Bruce Alden Cox, Jacques Chevalier and Valda Blundell. Ottawa: Carleton University, The Anthropology Caucus. pp.49–58.

_____. (1993). Aboriginal Empowerment and Souvenir Trade in Canada. *Annals of Tourism Research* 20(1):64–87.

_____. (2002). Aboriginal Cultural Tourism in Canada. In: *Slippery Pastimes. Reading the Popular in Canadian Culture.* Edited by Joan Nicks and Jeannette Sloniowski. Waterloo: Wilfrid Laurier University Press. pp.37–60.

Bolz, Peter. (1989). Life among the "Hunkpapas": A Case Study in German Indian Lore. In: *Indians and Europe. An Interdisciplinary Collection of Essays.* Aachen: Alano Edition Herodot. pp.475–490.

Bopp, Suzanne B. (1999). Home Away From Home. *Escape* January 1999:86–87.

Borman, Randy. (1999). Cofan: Story of the Forest People and the Outsiders. *Cultural Survival Quarterly* 23(2):48–50.

Boyd, S.W., and Butler, R.W. (1999). Definitely not Monkeys or Parrots, Probably Deer and Possibly Moose: Opportunities and Realities of Ecotourism in Northern Ontario. *Current Issues in Tourism* 2(2&3):123–137.

Broad, Sue. (2003). Living the Thai Life — A Case Study of Volunteer Tourism at the Gibbon Rehabilitation Project, Thailand. *Tourism Recreation Research* 28(3):63–72.

Breeden, Stanley. (1988). The First Australians. *National Geographic* 173(2):266–289.

Brink, Jack. (1995). Aboriginal People and the Development of Head-Smashed-In Buffalo Jump. Paper presented at *"Focusing our Resources"*, A National Forum on Resource Development and Management on the traditional First Nations Territories. April 23–26, 1995, Calgary.

Brown, Dee. (1970). *Bury my Heart at Wounded Knee*. New York: Bantam Books.

Brown, Sally, and Alastair M. Morrison. (2003). Expanding Volunteer Vacation Participation. An Exploratory Study on the Mini-Mission Concept. *Tourism Recreation Research* 28(3):73–82.

Brown, Terence J. (1999). Antecedents of Culturally Significant Tourist Behavior. *Annals of Tourism Research* 26(3):676–700.

Browne, Rita-Jean, and Mary Lee Nolan. (1989). Western Indian Reservation Tourism Development. *Annals of Tourism Research* 16(3):360–376.

Buchholtz, Debra. (1998). The Battle of the Little Bighorn: History, Identity, and Tourism in the 1990s. In: *Tourism and Gaming on American Indian Lands*. Edited by Alan A. Lew and George A. Van Otten. New York, Sydney, Tokyo: Cognizant Communications Corporation. pp.113–127

Buckley, Ralf. (2000). Neat Trends: Current Issues in Nature, Eco- and Adventure Tourism. *International Journal of Tourism Research* 2:437–444.

———. (2003). *Case Studies in Ecotourism*. Wallingford, UK, and Cambridge, MA: CABI Publishing

Budke, Isabel. (1999). *A Review of Cooperative Management Arrangements and Economic Opportunities for Aboriginal People in Canada's National Parks*. Prepared for Parks Canada, Western Canada Service Centre, Vancouver, British Columbia.

Bufo Incorporated. (1992a). *1992 Western Arctic Visitor Survey. Preliminary Analysis*. Submitted to: Government of the Northwest Territories, Department of Economic Development and Tourism. Vancouver: Bufo Incorporated.

———. (1992b). *1992 Western Arctic Visitor Survey. Summary Report*. Submitted to: Government of the Northwest Territories, Department of Economic Development and Tourism. Vancouver: Bufo Incorporated.

Burchett, Chris. (1991). Ecologically Sustainable Development and its Relationship to Aboriginal Tourism in the Northern Territory. In: *Ecotourism incorporating the Global Classroom*. 1991

International Conference Papers. Edited by Betty Weiler. Canberra: Bureau of Tourism Research. pp.70–74.

_____. (1993). A Profile of Aboriginal and Torres Strait Islander Tourism — Its History and Future Prospects. In: *Indigenous Australians and Tourism: A Focus on Northern Australia*. Proceedings of the Indigenous Australians and Tourism Conference, Darwin, June 1993. pp.20–25.

Burt, Page M., et al. (1993). A Course for Teachers about the Arctic in the Arctic. *Information North* 19(3):1–8.

Butler, Elaine. (1990). An Ecotourist in Bathurst Inlet. *Borealis* 1(4):42–46.

Butler, Richard W. (1980). The Concept of a Tourist Area Cycle of Evolution: Implications for Management of Resources. *Canadian Geographer* 24(1):5–12.

Butler, Victoria. (1996). Sampling the hunting and gathering life. *The Globe and Mail* November 20, 1996; A14.

Byrne Swain, Margaret. (1989). Gender Roles in Indigenous Tourism: Kuna Mola, Kuna Yala, and cultural Survival. In: *Hosts and Guests. The Anthropology of Tourism*. Second Edition. Edited by Valene L. Smith. Philadelphia: University of Pennsylvania Press. pp.83–104.

Campbell, L. M. (1999). Ecotourism in Rural Developing Communities. *Annals of Tourism Research* 26(3): 534–553.

Canadian National Aboriginal Tourism Association (CNATA). (1994a). Canadian National Aboriginal Tourism Association Business Plan 1993–94.

_____. (1994b). *The Stranger, the Native and the Land*. VHS Format Videocassette. Produced by Red Mango Pictures for CNATA.

_____. (1995). *For the Love of Nature. Nature-Based Tourism for Aboriginal Peoples. Manual.* Ottawa: CNATA.

The Canadian Tourism Commission (CTC). (1995). *Aboriginal Marketing Program — Operational Plan 1995–96.* Ottawa: CTC.

Cardozo, Yvette, and Bill Hirsch. (1994). An Arctic Cultural Adventure. *Up Here* 10(5):18–22.

Carmichael, Barbara A., and Donald M. Peppard, Jr. (1998). The Impacts of Foxwoods Resort Casino on Its Dual Host Community: Southeastern Connecticut and the Mashantucket Pequot Tribe. In: *Tourism and Gaming on American Indian Lands*. Edited by Alan A. Lew and George A. Van Otten. New York: Cognizant Communication Corporation. pp.128–144.

Chapin, Mac. (1990). The Silent Jungle: Ecotourism among the Kuna Indians of Panama. *Cultural Survival Quarterly* 14(1):42–45.

Chavez, Raymond. (1999). Globalisation and Tourism: Deadly Mix for Indigenous Peoples. *Third World Resurgence* 103. TWN (Third World Network) online: *www.twnside.org.sg.*

Cherrington, Mark. (1997). Tomorrow's Travellers. *People and the Planet* 6(4):32.

Chiago Lujan, Carol. (1993). A Sociological View of Tourism in an American Indian Community: Maintaining Cultural Integrity at Taos Pueblo. *American Indian Culture and Research Journal* 17(3):101–120.

Christ, Costas. (1998). Taking Ecotourism to the Next Level. In: *Ecotourism. A Guide for Planners and Managers.* Volume 2. Edited by Kreg Lindberg, Megan Epler Wood and David Engeldrum. North Bennington, Vermont: The Ecotourism Society. pp.183–195.

Cohen, Erik. (1972). Toward a Sociology of International Tourism. *Social Research* 39(1), reprinted in: McIntosh, Robert W., and Charles Goeldner, *Tourism. Principles, Practices, Philosophies.* Sixth Edition, Toronto: John Wiley & Sons, Inc. 1990. pp.197–208.

_____. (1988). Authenticity and Commoditization in Tourism. *Annals of Tourism Research* 15(2):371–386.

_____. (1989). "Primitive and Remote" Hill Tribe Trekking in Thailand. *Annals of Tourism Research* 16(1):30–61.

_____. (1996). Hunter-Gatherer Tourism in Thailand. In: *Tourism and Indigenous Peoples.* Edited by Richard Butler and Tom Hinch. Toronto: International Thomson Business Press. pp.227–254.

Colvin, Jean G. (1994). Capirona: A Model of Indigenous Ecotourism. Paper presented at the IIPT (International Institute for Peace through Tourism) Second Global Conference on *Building a sustainable World through Tourism.* September 12–16, 1994, Montreal.

Commonwealth Department of Tourism. (1994). *A Talent for Tourism. Stories about Indigenous People in Tourism.* Canberra: National Capital Printing.

Copeland, Grant. (1999). *Acts of Balance. Profits, People and Place.* Gabriola Island: New Society Publishers.

Cornell, Stephen, and Marta Cecilia Gil-Swedberg. (1995). Sociohistorical Factors in Institutional Efficacy: Economic Development in Three American Indian Cases. *Economic Development and Cultural Change* 43(2):239-268.

Cornell, Stephen, and Joseph P. Kalt. (1990). Pathways from Poverty: Economic Development and Institution-Building on

American Indian Reservations. *American Indian Culture and Research Journal* 14(1):89–125.

Crawshaw, C., and J. Urry. (1997). Tourism and the Photographic Eye. In: *Touring Cultures — Transformation of Travel and Theory.* Edited by C. Rojek and J. Urry. London: Routledge. pp.176–195.

Creedon, J. (1998). God with a Million Faces. *Utne Reader* 8(4):42–48.

Crystal, Eric. (1989). Tourism in Toraja (Sulawesi, Indonesia) In: *Hosts and Guests. The Anthropology of Tourism.* Second Edition. Edited by Valene L. Smith. Philadelphia: University of Pennsylvania Press. pp.139–168.

Cukier, Judith. (1996). Tourism Employment in Bali: Trends and Implications. In: *Tourism and Indigenous Peoples.* Edited by Richard Butler and Tom Hinch. Toronto: International Thomson Business Press. pp.49–75.

Currington, Matt. (1999). On the Trail of the Bushmen. *Geographical* 71(2):12–19.

Dahl, Jens, and Espen Waehle. (1993). Editorial. *IWGIA (International Work Group for Indigenous Affairs) Newsletter,* No.2, pp.2–3.

Daltabuit, Magali, and Oriol Pi-Sunyer. (1990). Tourism Development in Quintana Roo, Mexico. *Cultural Survival Quarterly* 14(1):9–13.

D'Amore, L.J. (1990). Tourism: The World's Peace Industry. *Recreation Canada* 48(1):24–33.

Davis, James A., and Lloyd E. Hudman. (1998). The History of Indian Gaming Law and Casino Development in the Western United States. In: *Tourism and Gaming on American Indian Lands.* Edited by Alan A. Lew and George A. Van Otten. New York: Cognizant Communication Corporation. pp.82–92.

Dayton, Sandra A., and Renae Prell. (1994). Tourism for the 21st Century — Maya Echo. Paper presented at the IIPT (International Institute for Peace through Tourism) Second Global Conference on *Building a Sustainable World through Tourism.* September 12–16, 1994, Montreal.

Dearden, Philip, and Sylvia Harron. (1994). Alternative Tourism and Adaptive Change. *Annals of Tourism Research* 21(1):81–102.

Digance, Justine. (2003). Pilgrimage at Contested Sites. *Annals of Tourism Research* 30(1):143–159.

Dodson, Mick, and Toni Baumann. (2001). Responsible Tourism In: *Guide to Indigenous Australia.* Edited by S. Singh et al. Melbourne/Oakland/London/Paris: Lonely Planet Publications. pp.118–125.

Doubleday, Nancy C. (1989). Co-Management Provisions of the Inuvialuit Final Agreement. In: *Co-Operative Management of Local Fisheries.* Edited by Evelyn Pinkerton. Vancouver: University of British Columbia Press. pp.209–227.

Doucette, Virginia. (2000). The Aboriginal Tourism Challenge: Managing for Growth. *Canadian Tourism Commission Communique* 4(11):1.

Doxey, G. (1976). When Enough's Enough: The Natives are Restless in Old Niagara. *Heritage Canada* 2(2):26–27.

Dressler, Wolfram H. (1999). *Nature-Based Tourism and Sustainability in the Beaufort-Delta Region, N.W.T.: an Analysis of Stakeholder Perspectives.* Unpublished Master of Natural Resource Management Thesis. Natural Resources Institute, University of Manitoba, Winnipeg.

Drumm, Andy. (1998). New Approaches to Community-Based Ecotourism Management. Learning from Ecuador. In: *Ecotourism. A Guide for Planners and Managers.* Volume 2. Edited by Kreg Lindberg, Megan Epler Wood and David Engeldrum. North Bennington, Vermont: The Ecotourism Society. pp.197–213.

Dubois, Daniel. (1993). Indianism In France. *European Review of Native American Studies* 7(1):27–36.

Dworski, Susan. (1994). The Black Ghost of Borneo. *Escape* Spring:15–16.

Dyer, Pam, Lucinda Aberdeen and Sigrid Schuler. (2003). Tourism Impacts on an Australian Indigenous Community: A Djabugay Case Study. *Tourism Management* 24:83–95.

Edeli, David. (2002). Selling Culture without Selling Out. Community Eco-Tourism in the Global Economy. *Re Vista,* Tourism in the Americas, *Harvard Review of Latin America.* Winter 2002. Accessed via *http://ricancie.nativeweb.org/* on June 13, 2003.

Ehrentraut, Adolf W. (1996). Maya Ruins, Cultural Tourism and the Contested Symbolism of Collective Identities. *Culture* 16(1):15–32.

Elder, Bruce. (2000). Land of the Dreaming. In: *Australian Outback.* Discovery Travel Adventures. Edited by Scott Forbes. Singapore: Discovery Communications, Inc. Insight Guides. pp.30–35.

Elias, Peter Douglas. (1995). Northern Economies. In: *Northern Aboriginal Communities. Economies and Development.* Edited by

Peter Douglas Elias. North York: Captus University Publications. pp.3–31.

_____, and Martin Weinstein. (1992). *Development and the Indian People of Fort Ware: Predicting and Managing Consequences.* A Study for the Kaska Dena Council and the Community of Fort Ware. September 1992. Unpublished Report.

Elkington, John. (1998). *Cannibals with Forks. The Triple Bottom Line of 21st Century Business*. Gabriola Island: New Society Publishers.

Ellis, Claire. (2003). Participatory Environmental Research in Tourism. A Global View. *Tourism Recreation Research* 28(3):45–55.

Epler Wood, Megan. (Ed.). (1999). Ecotourism, Sustainable Development, and Cultural Survival: Protecting Indigenous Culture and Land through Ecotourism. *Cultural Survival Quarterly* 23 (2).

_____. (1999). Ecotourism in the Masai Mara: An Interview with Meitamei Ole Dapash. *Cultural Survival Quarterly* 23(2):51–54.

_____. (2002). *Ecotourism: Principles, Practices & Policies for Sustainability*. Paris: United Nations Environment Programme and Burlington: The International Ecotourism Society.

_____. (2003). Community Conservation and Commerce. *Epler Wood Report* by Epler Wood International. October 2003.

Erasmus, George. (1989). A Native Viewpoint. In: *Endangered Spaces. The Future for Canada's Wilderness*. Edited by Monte Hummel. Toronto: Key Porter Books Ltd. pp.92–98.

Fagence, Michael. (2000). Ethnic Tourism in Developed Countries: Special Interest or Specialized Mass Tourism. *Tourism Recreation Research* 25(2):77–87.

Feest, Christian E. (2002). Germany's Indians in a European Perspective. In: *Germans and Indians. Fantasies, Encounters, Projections*. Edited by Colin G. Calloway, Gerd Gemuenden and Susanne Zantop. Lincoln: University of Nebraska Press. pp.25–46.

Fennell, David A., and David C. Malloy. (1999). Measuring the Ethical Nature of Tourism Operators. *Annals of Tourism Research* 26(4):928–943.

Finlayson, Julie. (1991). Issues in Aboriginal Cultural Tourism: Possibilities for a Sustainable Industry. In: *Ecotourism incorporating the Global Classroom*. 1991 International Conference Papers. Edited by Betty Weiler. Canberra: Bureau of Tourism Research. pp.66–69.

Fisheries Joint Management Committee (FJMC). (1991). *Beaufort Sea Beluga Management Plan*. Inuvik: FJMC.

Fox, Allan. (1983). Kakadu is Aboriginal Land. *Ambio* 12(3–4):161–166.

References

Frantz, Klaus. (1999). *Indian Reservations in the United States*. Chicago and London: The University of Chicago Press. Originally published as *Die Indianerreservationen in den USA,* Stuttgart: Franz Steiner Verlag, 1993.

Frideres, James S. (1988). *Native Peoples in Canada: Contemporary Conflicts.* 3ʳᵈ Edition, Scarborough, Ontario: Prentice Hall Canada Inc.

Gardner, J.E., and J.G. Nelson. (1981). National Parks and Native Peoples in Northern Canada, Alaska, and Northern Australia. *Environmental Conservation* 8(3):207–215.

Gartner, William C. (1996). *Tourism Development. Principles, Processes, and Policies.* New York, Detroit, London etc.: Van Nostrand Reinhold.

Ginsberg, Steve. (1994). Roughing It. *Escape* Fall 1994:91–93

Gomez-Pompa, Arturo, and Andrea Kaus. (1992). Taming the Wilderness Myth. *BioScience* 42(4):271–279.

Goodman, Ric. (2002). Pastoral Livelihoods in Tanzania: Can the Maasai Benefit from Conservation? *Current Issues in Tourism* 5(3&4):280–286.

Gordon, Robert, J. (1992a). Anthro-Tourism: A new Market in Development. *Development* 1992(4):42–44.

_____. (1992b). *The Bushman Myth. The Making of a Namibian Underclass.* Boulder, San Francisco, Oxford: Westview Press.

Government of Canada. (1984). *The Western Arctic Claim: The Inuvialuit Final Agreement*. Ottawa: Department of Indian Affairs and Northern Development.

_____. (1988). *The Native Tourism Product.* A Position Paper. Tourism Canada. March 10, 1988.

Government of the Northwest Territories. (1983). *Community-Based Tourism. A Strategy for the Northwest Territories Tourism Industry*. Yellowknife: Department of Economic Development and Tourism, GNWT.

_____. (1995). *1994 NWT Exit Survey. General Report on Visitors to the Northwest Territories*. Yellowknife: GNWT, The Economic Planning Section, Policy, Planning & Human Resources.

Grekin, Jacqueline, and Simon Milne. (1996). Toward Sustainable Tourism Development: the Case of Pond Inlet, NWT. In: *Tourism and Indigenous Peoples.* Richard Butler and Tom Hinch eds. Toronto: International Thomson Business Press. pp.76–106.

Gujadhur, Tara, and Charles Motshubi. (2001). "Among the Real People in /Xai-/Xai". SNV/Botswana. Retrieved from <www.cbnrm.bw> on June 24, 2004.

Guyette, Susan. (1996). *Planning for Balanced Development. A Guide for Native American and Rural Communities.* Santa Fe: Clear Light Publishers.

Guyette, Susan. (1998). *Strategic Tourism Plan.* Prepared for New Mexico Indian Tourism Association. Santa Fe: Santa Fe Planning & Research.

Hall, C. Michael. (1996). Tourism and the Maori of Aotearoa, New Zealand. In: *Tourism and Indigenous Peoples.* Edited by Richard Butler and Tom Hinch. Toronto: International Thomson Business Press. pp.155–175.

Halpenny, E.A., and L.T. Caissie. (2003). Volunteering on Nature Conservation Projects: Volunteer Experience, Attitudes and Values. *Tourism Recreation Research* 28(3):25–33.

Hanbury-Tenison, Robin. (2000). Touring with the Tuareg. *Geographical* 72(11):36–41.

Harden, Blaine. (1989). Botswana: Goodbye to the Kalahari — San Forced to Abandon their Territory. *IWGIA Newsletter* 58:8–19.

Hart, F., Steadman, A. & Woods, P. (1996). *A Market Analysis for Aboriginal Theme Tourism Products in Saskatchewan.* Prepared for Federation of Saskatchewan Indian Nations. Saskatoon: KPMG. Project Report and Summary Report.

Herman, Tamara. (2000). Let the People Speak. *Alternatives Journal* 26(1):6–7.

Higgins-Desbiolles, Freya. (2003). Reconciliation Tourism: Tourism Healing Divided Societies. *Tourism Recreation Research* 28(3):35–44.

Hill, Michael. (1983). Kakadu National Park and the Aboriginals: Partners in Protection. *Ambio* 12(3–4):158–169.

Hinch, Tom D. (1998). Ecotourists and Indigenous Hosts: Diverging Views on Their Relationship With Nature. *Current Issues in Tourism* 1(1):120–124.

Hinch, Thomas, and Richard Butler. (1996). Indigenous Tourism: a Common Ground for Discussion. In: *Tourism and Indigenous Peoples.* Edited by Richard Butler and Tom Hinch. Toronto: International Thomson Business Press. pp.3–19.

Hinkson, Melinda. (2003). Encounters with Aboriginal Sites in Metropolitan Sydney: A Broadening Horizon for Cultural Tourism? *Journal of Sustainable Tourism* 11(4):295–306.

Hitchcock, Robert K. (1985). Foragers on the Move. San Survival Strategies in Botswana's Parks and Reserves. *Cultural Survival Quarterly* 9(1):31–36.

_____. (1991). Game Park vs. the San. Conservation and Sustainable Development in Kalahari. *IWGIA Newsletter* 1:7–12.

_____. (1993). Indigenous Peoples, the State, and Resource Rights in Southern Africa. *IWGIA-Document* No.74. Copenhagen: International Work Group for Indigenous Affairs (IWGIA) and Centre for Development Research. pp.119–131.

_____. (1995). *Settlement and Survival: What Future for the Remote Area Dwellers of Botswana?* Paper presented at a National Institute of Research (NIR) Seminar at the University of Botswana, Gabarone, Botswana, October 13, 1995.

_____., and Rodney L. Brandenburgh. (1990). Tourism, Conservation and Culture in the Kalahari Desert, Botswana. *Cultural Survival Quarterly* 14(2):20–24.

Hoad, Darren. (2003). The General Agreement on Trade in Services and the Impact of Trade Liberalisation on Tourism and Sustainability. *Tourism and Hospitality Research* 4(3):213–227.

Hollinshead, Keith. (1996). Marketing and Metaphysical Realism: the Disidentification of Aboriginal Life and Traditions through Tourism. In: *Tourism and Indigenous Peoples*. Edited by Richard Butler and Tom Hinch. Toronto: International Thomson Business Press. pp.308–348.

Honey, Martha. (1999). *Ecotourism and Sustainable Development. Who Owns Paradise?* Washington, D.C. and Covelo, Ca: Island Press.

Horwich, Robert H., et al. (1993). Ecotourism and Community Development: A View from Belize. In: *Ecotourism: A Guide for Planners & Managers*. Edited by Kreg Lindberg and Donald E. Hawkins. North Bennington, Vermont: The Ecotourism Society. pp.152–168.

Horwitz, Tony. (1986). Everyone Wants a Bit of The Rock. *Sydney Morning Herald*, April 19, 1986:7.

Howard, Jonathon, Rik Thwaites and Brenda Smith. (2001). Investigating the Roles of the Indigenous Tour Guide. *The Journal of Tourism Studies* 12(2):32–39.

Immink, L. (2000). Learning from Education and Youth Market. *Inside Tourism* (December 7).

Ingles, Palma. (2002). Welcome to my Village: Hosting Tourists in the Peruvian Amazon. *Tourism Recreation Research* 27(1):53–60.

International Institute for Environment and Development (IIED). (1997). *Evaluating Eden. Exploring the Myths and Realities of Community Wildlife Management*. A Global Collaborative Research Programme Coordinated by IIED, 1996–1999. Working Project Document, 14 April 1997. London, England: IIED.

_____. (1999). *Newsletter of the Evaluating Eden Project,* April 1999, London, England.

International Resources Group. (1992). *Ecotourism: A Viable Alternative for Sustainable Management of Natural Resources in Africa.* Washington, D.C.: International Resources Group.

The International Work Group for Indigenous Affairs (IWGIA) and Christian Erni. (Ed.). (2000). *The Indigenous World 1999–2000.* Copenhagen: IWGIA.

Inuvialuit Communication Society and Parks Canada. (1995). *"Nutakaptingnun Qimaksavut"* or *"Our Children's Legacy".* VHS Format Videocassette.

Isaacson, Rupert. (2001). *The Healing Land. The Bushmen and the Kalahari Desert.* New York: Grove Press.

Jack, Joe. (1995). Kwanlin Dun–First Nation Tourism Planning. Paper presented at *Tourism and Interpretation....a Developing Partnership.* Interpretation Canada. North of 60 Section Workshop. Annual General Meeting. Yellowknife, NWT, May 10–13, 1995. Proceedings, pp.36–39.

Jafari, Jafar. (1989). Tourism as a Factor of Change: An English Language Literature Review. In: *Tourism as a Factor of Change: A Sociocultural Study.* Edited by J. Bystrzanowski. Vienna: European Coordination Centre for Research and Documentation in Social Sciences. pp.17–60.

Johnston, Alison. (2000). Indigenous Peoples and Ecotourism: Bringing Indigenous Knowledge and Rights into the Sustainability Equation. *Tourism Recreation Research* 25(2):89–96.

_____. (2001). Ecotourism and the Challenges Confronting Indigenous Peoples. *Native Americas* 18(2):42–47.

Johnston, C.R. (Ed.). (1990). Breaking out of the Tourist Trap. *Cultural Survival Quarterly* 14 (1&2).

Jones, Brian T.B. (1995). *Wildlife Management, Utilization and Tourism in Communal Areas: Benefits to Communities and Improved Resource Management.* Research Discussion Paper Number 5. Windhoek, Namibia: Ministry of Environment and Tourism.

_____. (1996). *Institutional Relationships, Capacity and Sustainability: Lessons learned from a Community-Based Conservation Project, eastern Tsumkwe District, Namibia, 1991–1996.* Research Discussion Paper Number 11. Windhoek, Namibia: Ministry of Environment and Tourism.

Kalt, Joseph P. (2000). Sovereignty and Economic Development on American Indian Reservations: Lessons from the United States. *First Perspective,* May 2000, pp.10–11. Reprinted from *Sharing the Harvest*: *The Road to Self Reliance*, Royal Commission on Aboriginal Peoples.

Kangas, Patrick, Mary Shave and Paul Shave. (1995). Economics of an Ecotourism Operation in Belize. *Environmental Management* 19(5):669–673.

Karwacki, Judy. (1999). Indigenous Ecotourism: Overcoming the Challenges. *The Ecotourism Society Newsletter*. First Quarter:1–2,4.

Kaufman, Paul. (2000). *Travelling Aboriginal Australia. Discovery and Reconciliation*. Flemington, Vic.: Hyland House Publishing Pty Ltd.

Keller, Peter C. (1987). Stages of Peripheral Tourism Development — Canada's Northwest Territories. *Tourism Management* 8(1):20–32.

Kelso, Casey. (1993). The Landless Bushmen. *Africa Report* 38(2):51–54.

Kesteven, S. (1984). *Summary of Report to the Minister of Aboriginal Affairs on a Fieldtrip to Kakadu National Park to Discuss Tourism with Aboriginal Traditional Owners and Residents of the Park Area*, 21–31 March 1984. Unpublished Report, Department of Aboriginal Affairs (File 83/465), Darwin.

King, Joan Marie, and Elliot McIntire. (1998). The Impact of the Indian Gaming Regulatory Act on Tribes in the U.S. In: *Tourism and Gaming on American Indian Lands*. Edited by Alan A. Lew and George A. Van Otten. New York: Cognizant Communication Corporation. pp.48–56.

Klein, David R. (1994). Wilderness: A Western Concept Alien to Arctic Cultures. *Information North* 20(3):1–6.

Klotzbach, Kurt. (1982). Als Buffalo Bill in Deutschland ritt. *Magazin fuer Amerikanistik* 2/1982:34–41.

Knapp, C.E. (1985). Escaping the Gender Trap: The Ultimate Challenge for Experiential Educators. *Journal of Experiential Education* 8(2):16–19.

Krech III, Shepard (1999). *The Ecological Indian. Myth and History*. New York, London: W.W. Norton & Company.

Krippendorf, Jost. (1989). The Motives of the Mobile Leisureman — Travel Between Norm, Promise and Hope. In: *The Holidaymakers*, J. Krippendorf, Oxford: Butterworth and Heinemann, pp.22–29.

Kroshus Medina, Laurie. (2003). Commoditizing Culture. Tourism and Maya Identity. *Annals of Tourism Research* 30(2):353–368.

Kuper, Adam. (2003). The Return of the Native (CA Forum on Anthropology in Public). *Current Anthropology* 44(3):389–402.

Kyle, R. (1995). *The New Age Movement in American Culture*. Lanham, M.D.: University Press of America.

Langley, Greg. (1997). Germans are enchanted with Native North America. *Windspeaker's Guide to Indian Country* June 1997, pp.10&13.

Laxson, Joan D. (1991). How "We" see "Them". Tourism and Native Americans. *Annals of Tourism Research* 18:365–391.

Lee, Gary. (2001). Women and the Didjeridu. In: *Guide to Indigenous Australia*. Edited by S. Singh et al. Melbourne/Oakland/London/ Paris: Lonely Planet Publications. p.138.

Lew, Alan A. (1996). Tourism Management on American Indian Lands in the USA. *Tourism Management* 17(5):355–365.

_____. (1998). American Indians in State Tourism Promotional Literature. In: *Tourism and Gaming on American Indian Lands*. Edited by Alan A. Lew and George A. Van Otten. New York, Sydney, Tokyo: Cognizant Communications Corporation. pp.15–31.

_____, and George A. Van Otten. (1998). Prospects for Native American Reservation Tourism in the 21st Century. In: *Tourism and Gaming on American Indian Lands*. Edited by Alan A. Lew and George A. Van Otten. New York, Sydney, Tokyo: Cognizant Communications Corporation. pp.216–221.

Lindberg, Kreg, Jeremy Enriquez and Keith Sproule. (1996). Ecotourism Questioned. Case Studies from Belize. *Annals of Tourism Research* 23(3):543–562.

Lovatt Smith, David. (1997). Maasai Hopes and Fears. *People and the Planet* 6(4):12–13.

Lyons, Kevin D. (2003). Ambiguities in Volunteer Tourism: A Case Study of Australians Participating in a J-1 Visitor Exchange Programme. *Tourism Recreation Research* 28(3):5–13.

MacCannell, Dean. (1973). Staged Authenticity: Arrangements of Social Space in Tourist Settings. *American Journal of Sociology* 79(3):589–603.

_____. (1976). *The Tourist. A New Theory of the Leisure Class*. New York: Schocken Books.

MacDonald, Theodore. (1993). Ecotourism and Indigenous People: From Endangered Species to Resource Managers. *Tour & Travel News Supplement*, October 25, 1993:12–15.

Machlis, Gary E., and David L. Tichnell. (1985). *The State of the World's Parks*. Boulder and London: Westview Press.

Madrigal, R. (1994). Residents' Perceptions and the Role of Government. *Annals of Tourism Research* 22(1):86–102.

Marcus, J. (1988). The Journey out to the Centre. The Cultural Appropriation of Ayers Rock. *Kunapipi* 10:254–274.

Marks, Guy. (1999). A Delicate Equation. *Geographical* 71(7):52–57.

Marshall, John. (2002). *A Kalahari Family* (A Five Part Series). Watertown MA: Kalfam Productions. Documentary Film.

Martin, Brenda M. (1998). Return of the Native: The Big Picture for Tourism Development in Indian Country. In: *Tourism and Gaming on American Indian Lands.* Edited by Alan A. Lew and George A. Van Otten. New York, Sydney, Tokyo: Cognizant Communication Corporation. pp.32–47.

McClintock, Walter. (1910). (1968) *The Old North Trail. Life, Legends and Religion of the Blackfeet Indians.* Lincoln and London: University of Nebraska Press.

McGregor, Andrew. (2000). Dynamic Texts and Tourist Gaze. Death, Bones and Buffalo. *Annals of Tourism Research* 27(1):27–50.

McIntosh, Alison J. (2004). Tourists' Appreciation of Maori Culture in New Zealand. *Tourism Management* 25:1–15.

McKercher, Bob (1993). Some Fundamental Truths About Tourism: Understanding Tourism's Social and Environmental Impacts. *Journal of Sustainable Tourism* 1(1):6–16.

McLaren, Deborah. (1998). *Rethinking Tourism and Ecotravel. The Paving of Paradise and What You Can Do to Stop It.* West Hartford, Conn.:Kumarian Press.

Michener, V.J. (1998). The Participatory Approach: Contradiction and Co-option in Burkina Faso. *Wld Dev.* 26(12):2105–2118.

Microsoft Corporation. (1998). New Age Movement. *Microsoft Encarta Encyclopedia.*

Ministry of Environment and Tourism (MET). (no date). *Community-Based Natural Resource Management Programme.* Windhoek, Namibia.

Morgan, N., and A. Pritchard. (1998). *Tourism, Promotion and Power: Creating Images, Creating Identities.* Chichester: Wiley.

Moscardo, Gianna M., and Philip L. Pearce. (1989). Ethnic Tourism: Understanding the Tourists' Perspective. Paper presented at *Travel and Tourism Research Association, Twentieth Anniversary Conference*, Honolulu, Hawaii, June 11–15, 1989.

_____. (1999). Understanding Ethnic Tourists. *Annals of Tourism Research* 26(2):416–434.

Moss, John. (1994). Engineering Wilderness. *Arctic Circle.* Spring 1994:10–13, 22–27.

Mosser, Sasha, and Douglas Michele Turco. (2000). Native American Tourism Web Sites Review. *International Journal of Tourism Research* 2:363–365.

Mowaljarlai and Jutta Malnic. (2001). (1993) *Yorro Yorro — everything standing up alive. Rock Art and Stories from the Austra-*

lian Kimberley. Broome, Western Australia: Magabala Books Aboriginal Corporation.

Munt, I. And E. Higinio. (1993). Belize — Eco-tourism Gone Awry. *Focus* Autumn 1993, No.9:12–13.

Murphy, Peter E. (1985). *Tourism. A Community Approach*. New York and London: Routledge.

Murphy, Peter E. (1993). Community Development: Maintaining the Right Perspective through Appropriate Tourism Management. In: *Communities, Resources and Tourism in the North*. Edited by Margaret E. Johnston and Wolfgang Haider. Thunder Bay: Lakehead University, Centre for Northern Studies. pp.1–15.

Northern Territory Tourist Commission. (1994). *Masterplan*. Darwin, NT: Northern Territory Tourist Commission.

_____. (1994). *Aboriginal Tourism in the Northern Territory*. Discussion Paper. Darwin, NT, June 1994.

_____. (1996). *Aboriginal Tourism Strategy*. Darwin, NT, May 1996.

Notzke, Claudia. (1993). Aboriginal Peoples and Natural Resources: Co-Management, the Way of the Future? *National Geographic Research & Exploration* 9(4):395–397.

_____. (1994a). Aboriginal People and Protected Areas. Paper presented at *"Saskatchewan's Protected Areas, A Conference Workshop"*, University of Regina, June 20–21, 1994.

_____. (1994b). *Aboriginal Peoples and Natural Resources in Canada*. North York: Captus University Publications.

_____. (1995a). The Resource Co-Management Regime in the Inuvialuit Settlement Region. In: *Northern Aboriginal Communities. Economies and Development*. Edited by Peter Douglas Elias. North York: Captus University Publications. pp.36–52.

_____. (1995b). Partners in Conservation: Co-Management, Protected Areas and Ecotourism. Paper presented at *"Focusing our Resources"*, A National Forum on Resource Development and Management on the traditional First Nations Territories. April 23-26, 1995, Calgary.

_____. (1995c). A New Perspective in Aboriginal Natural Resource Management: Co-Management. *Geoforum* 26(2):187–209

_____. (1996). Co-Managing Aboriginal Cultural Resources. *MUSE* 14(3):52–56.

_____. (1999a). Indigenous Tourism Development in the Arctic. *Annals of Tourism Research* 26(1):55–76.

_____. (1999b). Aboriginal Community Involvement in Wildlife Tourism: The Canadian Experience. In: *Northern Eden. Community-Based Wildlife Management in Canada*. Leslie Treseder et al. Edmonton: Canadian Circumpolar Institute (CCI) Press. pp.45–62.

_____. (2000). Aboriginal Tourism Development in Canada: A Northern and Southern Perspective. Paper presented at the *51ˢᵗ Arctic Science Conference*, September 21–24, 2000, Whitehorse, Yukon, American Association for the Advancement of Science and Yukon Science Institute.

_____. (2004). Indigenous Tourism Development in Southern Alberta, Canada: Tentative Engagement. *Journal of Sustainable Tourism* 12(1):29–54.

Nowicka, Ewa. (1989). The "Polish Movement of Friends of the American Indians". In: *Indians and Europe. An Interdisciplinary Collection of Essays.* Aachen: Alano Edition Herodot. pp.599–608.

Olindo, Perez. (1991). The Old Man of Nature Tourism. In: *Nature Tourism*. Edited by T. Whelan. Washington, D.C.: Island Press. pp.23–27, 30–38. Excerpt reprinted in *The Earthscan Reader in Sustainable Tourism,* Ed. Lesley France. London: Earthscan Publications Ltd.1997, pp.90–97.

O'Neill, Paul. (1981). *Das Ende und die Legende.* Time-Life Buecher "Der Wilde Westen".

Owens, Mark and Delia. (1985). *Cry of the Kalahari.* Glasgow: William Collins Sons and Co. Ltd.; Fontana PB.

Parker, Barry. (1996). "Cultural Eco-Tourism": A Bridge to the Past and to the Future. Unpublished Paper, October 1996.

Paskievich, John. (1995). *If only I were an Indian....* VHS Format Videocassette. Montreal: National Film Board of Canada.

Perkins, Frank. (1990). Earthwatch in the Kenya Desert. *Great Expeditions* 61:19–22.

Pfister, Robert E. (2000). Mountain Culture as a Tourism Resource: Aboriginal Views on the Privileges of Storytelling. In: *Tourism and Development in Mountain Regions*. Edited by P. M. Godde, M.F. Price and F.M. Zimmermann. Wallingford: CAB International. pp.115–136.

Pitts, Wayne J., and Paul E. Guerin. (1998). Indian Gaming in New Mexico: A Historical Overview With Implications for Tourism. In: *Tourism and Gaming on American Indian Lands.* Edited by Alan A. Lew and George A. Van Otten. New York: Cognizant Communication Corporation. pp.183–198.

Plaine, Martha. (2000). Spiritual Tourism. A new Spin on an old Tradition. *Communiquee* 4(11):14.

Plog, Stanley C. (1974). Why Destination Areas Rise and Fall in Popularity. *The Cornell Hotel and Restaurant Administration Quarterly* 14(4):55–58.

Powers, William K. (1988). The Indian Hobbyist Movement in North America. In: *Handbook of the North American Indian. Vol.4: History of Indian-White Relations.* Wilcomb E. Washburn, Volume Ed.; William C. Sturtevant, General Ed. Washington: Smithsonian Institution. pp.557–561.

Poon, Auliana. (1993). Global Transformation. *Tourism, Technology and Competitive Strategies.* A. Poon. Wallingford: CAB International. pp.85–92, 115. Excerpted in: *The Earthscan Reader in Sustainable Tourism.* Edited by Lesley France. London: Earthscan Publications Ltd., 1997. pp.47–53.

PriceWaterhouseCoopers. (2000). *Demand for Aboriginal Culture Products in Key European Markets 2000.* Prepared for Aboriginal Tourism Team Canada and Canadian Tourism Commission.

Prior, Colin, and Carolyn Fry. (2003). *Urvoelker. Vom Ueberleben Einzigartiger Kulturen.* Hamburg: National Geographic Deutschland.

Purvis, Andrew. (1999). Whose Home and Native Land? *Time*, February 15, 1999, pp.16–24.

Raitman, Laura. (2002). Spirits of the Arctic Tundra: Ecotourism in northern Canada enables aboriginal peoples like the Inuit to preserve and share their culture with the world. *The Ecotourism Observer* Fall 2002. Online Journal of the International Ecotourism Society. *www.ecotourism.org/observer/feature.asp.* 7 pages.

Record, Ian Wilson, (2003). Pine Ridge Renaissance. *Native Americas* Spring 2003:54–59.

Reimer, Gwen, and Andrew Dialla. (1992). *Community-Based Tourism Development in Pangnirtung, Northwest Territories: Looking Back and Looking Ahead.* A Report prepared for: Economic Development and Tourism, Baffin Region (Government of the Northwest Territories) and Hamlet of Pangnirtung. April 1992.

Reimer, Gwen. (1993). "Community-Based" as a culturally appropriate Concept of Development: A Case Study from Pangnirtung, Northwest Territories. *Culture* 13(2):67–74.

Robb, Deborah Jo. (2000). This is What Democracy Looks Like. *Encompass Magazine* 4(3):20.

Robbins, Mike. (1992). Community-Based Tourism in Remote Native Communities. In: *Community and Cultural Tourism.* Conference Proceedings, Travel and Tourism Research Association — Canada, 1992. Edited by Laurel J. Reid. pp.133–139.

Robinson, David W. (1993). Tourism Impacts in the Nepalese Himalaya: Lessons for Northern Canada. In: *Communities, Resources and Tourism in the North.* Edited by Margaret E.

Johnston and Wolfgang Haider. Thunder Bay: Lakehead University, Centre for Northern Studies. pp.61–80.

_____. (1994). Strategies for Alternative Tourism: The Case of Tourism in Sagarmatha (Everest) National Park, Nepal. In: *Tourism. The State of the Art.* Edited by A. Seaton et al. Chichester: Wiley. pp.691–695, 699–701. Excerpt reprinted in: *The Earthscan Reader in Sustainable Tourism.* Edited by Lesley France. London: Earthscan Publications Ltd., 1997. pp.176–186.

Rodriguez, Arnaldo. (1999). Kapawi: A Model of Sustainable Development in Ecuadorean Amazonia. *Cultural Survival Quarterly* 23(2):43–44.

Roe, Dilys. (2001). Community-Based Wildlife Management: Improved Livelihoods *and* Wildlife Conservation? *Bio-briefs* No.1, April 2001. London, England: International Institute for Environment and Development.

Royal Commission on Aboriginal Peoples. (1996). *Report of the Royal Commission on Aboriginal Peoples.* Volume 2: *Restructuring the Relationship,* Part 2. Ottawa: Minister of Supply and Services Canada.

Ryan, Chris. (1997). Maori and Tourism: A Relationship of History, Constitutions and Rites. *Journal of Sustainable Tourism* 5(4):257–278.

_____. (2002). Tourism and Cultural Proximity. Examples from New Zealand. *Annals of Tourism Research* 29(4):952–971.

_____, and John Crotts. (1997). Carving and Tourism. A Maori Perspective. *Annals of Tourism Research* 24(4):898–918.

_____, and Jeremy Huyton. (2000a). Who is Interested in Aboriginal Tourism in the Northern Territory, Australia? A Cluster Analysis. *Journal of Sustainable Tourism* 8(1):53–88.

_____, and Jeremy Huyton. (2000b). Aboriginal Tourism — A Linear Structural Relations Analysis of Domestic and International Tourism Demand. *International Journal of Tourism Research* 2:15-29.

_____, and Jeremy Huyton. (2002). Tourists and Aboriginal People. *Annals of Tourism Research* 29(3):631–647.

_____, and Steve Pike. (2003). Maori-based Tourism in Rotorua: Perceptions of Place by Domestic Visitors. *Journal of Sustainable Tourism* 11(4):307–321.

Sanders, A.J.G.M. (1989). The Bushmen of Botswana — From Desert Dwellers to World Citizens. *Africa Insight* 19(3):174–182.

Schalken, Wouter. (1999). Where are the Wild Ones? The Involvement of Indigenous Communities in Tourism in Namibia. *Cultural Survival Quarterly* 23(2):40–42.

Scheyvens, Regina. (1999). Ecotourism and the Empowerment of Local Communities. *Tourism Management* 20:245–249.

Schwartz, Ronald David. (1991). Travelers under Fire: Tourists in the Tibetan Uprising. *Annals of Tourism Research* 16(4):588–604.

Seiler-Baldinger, Annemarie. (1988). Tourism in the Upper Amazon and its Effects on the Indigenous Population. In: *Tourism: Manufacturing the Exotic*. Edited by Pierre Rossel. IWGIA-Document No.61. Copenhagen: International Work Group for Indigenous Affairs (IWGIA). pp.177–193.

Shackley, Myra. (2001). Sacred World Heritage Sites: Balancing Meaning with Management. *Tourism Recreation Research* 26(1):5–10.

_____. (2004). Tourist Consumption of Sacred Landscapes. Space, Time and Vision. *Tourism Recreation Research* 29(1):67–73.

Shelton, Napicr. (1983). Parks & Sustainable Development. 1982 World National Parks Congress. *National Parks* 57(5–6):16–21.

Sherman, Ben. (2003). Indian Country Tourism — Success Through Partnerships. *American Indian Report* 19(3):25.

Silver, Ira. (1993). Marketing Authenticity in Third World Countries. *Annals of Tourism Research* 20(2):302–318.

Singh, Sarina, et al. (2001). *Aboriginal Australia & the Torres Strait Islands. Guide to Indigenous Australia*. Melbourne, Oakland, London, Paris: Lonely Planet Publications.

Singh, T. V. (2001). International Symposium on Eco–Cultural Tourism 2001. Conference Report. *Tourism Recreation Research* 26(1):123.

Smith, Valene L. (Ed.). (1977). *Hosts and Guests: The Anthropology of Tourism*, 1st Edition, Philadelphia: University of Pennsylvania Press.

_____. (1989). Introduction. In: *Hosts and Guests. The Anthropology of Tourism*. Second Edition. Edited by Valene L. Smith. Philadelphia: University of Pennsylvania Press. pp.1–17.

_____. (1996). Indigenous Tourism: the Four Hs. In: *Tourism and Indigenous Peoples*. Edited by Richard Butler and Tom Hinch. Toronto: International Thomson Business Press. pp.283–307.

_____. (2000). Space Tourism: The 21st Century "Frontier". *Tourism Recreation Research* 25(3):5–15.

_____, and Maryann Brent (Eds.). (2001). *Hosts and Guests Revisited: Tourism Issues of the 21st Century*. New York: Cognizant Communications Corporation.

Sofield, Trevor H.B. (1996). Anuha Island Resort, Solomon Islands: a Case Study of Failure. In: *Tourism and Indigenous Peoples.* Edited by Richard Butler and Tom Hinch. Toronto: International Thomson Business Press. pp.176–202.

_____., and R. Alastair Birtles. (1996). Indigenous Peoples' Cultural Opportunity Spectrum for Tourism (IPCOST). In: *Tourism and Indigenous Peoples.* Edited by Richard Butler and Tom Hinch. Toronto: International Thomson Business Press. pp.396–433.

Songorwa, Alexander N., Ton Buehrs and Ken F.D. Hughey. (2000). Community-Based Wildlife Management in Africa: A Critical Assessment of the Literature. *Natural Resources Journal* 40(3):603–643.

Stansfield, Charles. (1996). Reservations and Gambling: Native Americans and the Diffusion of Legalized Gambling. In: *Tourism and Indigenous Peoples*. Edited by Richard Butler and Tom Hinch. Toronto: International Thomson Business Press. pp.129–147.

Stanton, Max E. (1989). The Polynesian Cultural Center: A Multi-Ethnic Model of Seven Pacific Cultures. In: *Hosts and Guests. The Anthropology of Tourism.* Second Edition. Edited by Valene L. Smith. Philadelphia: University of Pennsylvania Press. pp.247–262.

Steinberg, Michael K. (1998). Political Ecology and Cultural Change: Impacts on Swidden-fallow Agroforestry Practices among the Mopan Maya in Southern Belize. *Professional Geographer* 50(4):407–417.

Suchet, Sandra. (1998). *Indigenous Peoples' Rights and Wildlife Management: Experiences from Canada and Southern Africa, Lessons for Australia.* Progress Report, Ph.D. Fieldwork, August 1997–March 1998, Canada, Zimbabwe, Namibia, South Africa. Sydney: Macquarie University, School of Earth Sciences.

Swan, James A. (1990). *Sacred Places. How the Living Earth Seeks our Friendship.* Santa Fe: Bear & Company Publishing.

Sweet, Jill D. (1989). Burlesquing "The Other" in Pueblo Performance. *Annals of Tourism Research* 16(1):62–75.

_____. (1990). The Portals of Tradition: Tourism in the American Southwest. *Cultural Survival Quarterly* 14(2):6–8.

_____. (1991). "Let 'em Loose": Pueblo Indian Management of Tourism. *American Indian Culture and Research Journal* 15(4):59–74.

Taylor, Colin (1988). The Indian Hobbyist Movement in Europe. In: *Handbook of the North American Indian. Vol.4: History of Indian-White Relations.* Edited by Wilcomb E. Washburn, William C. Sturtevant. Washington: Smithsonian Institution. pp.562–569.

Taylor, George. (1995). The Community Approach: Does it Really Work? *Tourism Management* 16(7):487–489.

Taylor, John P. (2001). Authenticity and Sincerity in Tourism. *Annals of Tourism Research* 28(1):7–26.

Taylor, Ken (1999). Culture or Nature: Dilemmas of Interpretation. *Tourism, Culture & Communication* 2:69–84.

Timothy, Dallen J., and Kathy White. (1999). Community-based Ecotourism Development on the Periphery of Belize. *Current Issues in Tourism* 2(2&3):226–242.

Tirado, Michelle. (2003). Off the Beaten Path. Letting the World know about the perfect Vacation. *American Indian Report* 19(3):12–15.

Tourism Canada. (1988). *The Native Tourism Product*. A Position Paper. Ottawa.

Trask, Haunani-Kay. (1993). *From a Native Daughter. Colonialism and Sovereignty in Hawai'i*. Monroe, Maine: Common Courage Press.

Tsartas, Paris. (1992). Socioeconomic Impacts of Tourism on Two Greek Isles. *Annals of Tourism Research* 19(3):516–533.

Turski, Birgit. (1993). The Indianist Groups in the G.D.R.: Development — Problems — Prospects. *European Review of Native American Studies* 7(1):43–48.

Twyman, Chasca. (2000). Participatory Conservation? Community-based Natural Resource Management in Botswana. *The Geographical Journal* 166(4):323–335.

Uriely, Natan, Arie Reichel and Amos Ron. (2003). Volunteering in Tourism: Additional Thinking. *Tourism Recreation Research* 28(3):57–62.

Urry, J. (1990). *The Tourist Gaze: Leisure and Travel in Contemporary Society*. London: Sage Publications.

Usher, Peter J. (1984). Property Rights: The Basis of Wildlife Management. In: *National and Regional Interests in the North*. Third National Workshop on People, Resources, and the Environment North of 60. June 1–3, 1983, Yellowknife, NWT. Ottawa: Canadian Arctic Resources Committee. pp.389–415.

Vaiao, Leiataua. (1994). *Community-Based Tourism in Western Samoa*. Unpublished Paper. April 1994.

Van den Berg, Elvia. (2001). "At the Dqae Qare Game Farm in Ghanzi." SNV/Botswana. Retrieved from <www.cbnrm.bw> on June 24, 2004.

Van den Berghe, Pierre L., and Jorge Flores Ochoa. (2000). Tourism and Nativistic Ideology in Cuzco, Peru. *Annals of Tourism Research* 27(1):7–26.

Van der Post, Laurens, and Jane Taylor. (1984). *Testament to the Bushmen.* Markham, Ont.: Penguin Books (1985).

Veber, Hanne, and Espen Waehle. (1993). "....Never drink from the same Cup." An Introduction. In: *"....Never drink from the same Cup".* Proceedings of the Conference on Indigenous Peoples in Africa, Tune, Denmark 1993. Hanne Veber et. al eds. CDR/IWGIA Document 74, pp.9–19.

Vosa Flyman, Michael. (2001). Living for Tomorrow in the Southern Kalahari. SNV/Botswana. Retrieved from <www.cbnrm.bw> on June 24, 2004.

Wall, Geoffrey, and Veronica Long. (1996) Balinese Homestays: an Indigenous Response to Tourism Opportunities. In: *Tourism and Indigenous Peoples.* Edited by Richard Butler and Tom Hinch. Toronto: International Thomson Business Press. pp.27–28.

Waters, M. (1995). *Globalization.* London: Routledge.

Watson, Irene. (2001). Spirituality. In: *Aboriginal Australia & the Torres Strait Islands. Guide to Indigenous Australia.* Edited by S. Singh et al. Melbourne/Oakland/London/Paris: Lonely Planet Publications. pp.106–112.

Wearing, Stephen. (2001). *Volunteer Tourism: Seeking Experiences that Make a Difference.* Wallingford, Oxon: CABI International.

_____, and Monique Huyskens. (2001). Moving on from Joint Management Policy Regimes in Australian National Parks. *Current Issues in Tourism* 4(2–4):182–209.

Weaver, D. B. (1999). Magnitude of Ecotourism in Costa Rica and Kenya. *Annals of Tourism Research* 26(4):792–816

Weber, Will. (1991). Enduring Peaks and Changing Cultures: The Sherpas and Sagarmatha (Mount Everest) National Park. In: *Resident Peoples and National Parks.* Edited by Patrick C. West and Steven R. Brechin. Tucson: The University of Arizona Press. pp.206–214.

Weiler, Betty, and Harold Richins. (1995). Extreme, Extravagant and Elite: A Profile of Ecotourists on Earthwatch Expeditions. *Tourism Recreation Research* 20(1):29–36.

Welch, James with Paul Stekler. (1994). *Killing Custer.* New York, London: W.W. Norton Company.

Wells, Michael, Katrina Brandon and Lee Hannah. (1992). *People and Parks. Linking Protected Area Management with Local*

Communities. Washington, D.C.: The World Bank. The World Wildlife Fund. U.S. Agency for International Development.

Wesche, Rolf. (1994). Indigenous controlled Ecotourism in Ecuador's Amazon Frontier. Paper presented at the IIPT (International Institute for Peace through Tourism) Second Global Conference on *Building a Sustainable World through Tourism*. September 12–16, 1994, Montreal.

———, and Andy Drumm. (1999). *Defending Our Rainforest: A Guide to Community-Based Ecotourism in the Ecuadorian Amazon*. Quito, Ecuador: Accion Amazonia.

West, Patrick C., and Steven R. Brechin eds. (1991). *Resident Peoples and National Parks: Social Dilemmas and Strategies in International Conservation*. Tuscon: University of Arizona Press.

Western, David. (1997). Ecotourism at the Crossroads in Kenya. *The Ecotourism Society Newsletter*, Third Quarter 1997:1–2, 4.

Western Canada Wilderness Committee. (1993). *A New Leaf*. VHS Format Videocassette. Edmonton: Rainbow Bridge Communications.

Wheeler, Brian. (1991). Tourism's Troubled Times: Responsible Tourism is not the Answer. *Tourism Management* 1991, June, pp.91 96. Reprinted in: *The Earthscan Reader in Sustainable Tourism*. Edited by Lesley France. London: Earthscan Publications Ltd., 1997, pp.61–67.

Wight, Pamela A., and David McVetty. (2000). Tourism Planning in the Arctic Banks Island. *Tourism Recreation Research* 25(2):15–26.

Whitford, Michelle, Barry Bell and Mike Watkins. (2001). Indigenous Tourism Policy in Australia: 25 Years of Rhetoric and Economic Rationalism. *Current Issues in Tourism* 4(2–4):151–181.

Whittaker, Elvi. (1994). Public Discourse on Sacredness: The Transfer of Ayers Rock to Aboriginal Ownership. *American Ethnologist* 21(2):310–334.

———. (1999). Indigenous Tourism: Reclaiming Knowledge, Culture and Intellectual Property in Australia. In: *Tourism and Cultural Conflicts*. Edited by Mike Robinson and Priscilla Boniface. Wallingford, Oxon: CAB International. pp. 33–45.

Williams, Peter W., and Karim B. Dossa. (1995). *Emerging Market and Product Development Considerations: The Case of France and South* Korea. Paper presented at the *First Nations Tourism and Resort Development National Conference*, Vancouver, January 26–27, 1995.

_____, and Karim B. Dossa. (1996). *Ethnic Tourism: Native Interest Travel Markets for Canada.* Burnaby, B.C.: Centre for Tourism Policy and Research, Simon Fraser University.

_____, and Karim B. Dossa. (1999). *Aboriginal Tourism Markets: An Analysis of Germany, Japan and Canada 1999.* Burnaby, B.C.: Simon Fraser University Centre for Tourism Policy and Research.

_____, and J.K. Stewart. (1997). Canadian Aboriginal Tourism Development: Assessing Latent Demand from France. *The Journal of Tourism Studies* 9(1), 25–41.

Wilmsen, Edwin N. (1989). *Land Filled with Flies. A Political Economy of the Kalahari.* Chicago and London: The University of Chicago Press.

Woenne-Green, S., R. Johnston, R. Sultan and A. Wallis. (1992). *Competing Interests. Aboriginal Participation in National Parks and Conservation Reserves in Australia: A Review.* Melbourne: Australian Conservation Foundation.

Wood, Robert E. (2000). Caribbean Cruise Tourism. Globalization at Sea. *Annals of Tourism Research* 27(2):345–370.

Woodburn, James. (1997). Indigenous Discrimination: the Ideological Basis for Local Discrimination against Hunter-Gatherer Minorities in Sub-Saharan Africa. *Ethnc and Racial Studies* 20(2):345–361.

World Council of Indigenous Peoples, (no date.). Charter.

Wylie, Jerry. (1992). *The Manono Island Eco/Ethno-Tourism Project, Western Samoa.* Comments on the "Meet Us in Manono" Program developed by the Komiti Atina'e O Manono (KAMA) (Manono Economic Development Committee, Apia, Western Samoa) December 13, 1992.

Yasumura, Katsumi. (1996). Ethnic Tourism and the Problem of Social Inequalities in Mass Tourism. Revised version of a Japanese original, published in *Gendai Kankogaku no Tenkai (The Expansion of Contemporary Tourism Studies)*, Edited by I. Maeda. Tokyo: Gakubunsha.

Young, Lisa. (1997). Tourism threatens Arizona Hopi. *Windspeaker Classroom Edition*, March 1997, p.12.

Zeppel, Heather D. (1995). Authenticity and Iban Longhouse Tourism in Sarawak. *Borneo Review* 6(2):109–125.

_____. (1998a). Selling the Dreamtime: Aboriginal Culture in Australian Tourism. In: *Tourism, Leisure, Sport: Critical Perspectives.* Edited by David Rowe and Geoffery Lawrence. Rydalmere NSW: Hodder Education. pp.29–45.

_____. (1998b). Entertainers or Entrepreneurs. Iban Involvement in Longhouse Tourism (Sarawak, Borneo) *Tourism Recreation Research* 23(1):39–45.

_____. (1999). Touring Aboriginal Cultures: Encounters with Aboriginal People in Australian Travelogues. *Tourism, Culture and Communication* 2:123–139.

_____. (2002). Cultural Tourism at the Cowichan Native Village, British Columbia. *Journal of Travel Research* 41:92–100.

Ziffer, Karen A. (1989). *Ecotourism: The Uneasy Alliance*. Conservation International and Ernst & Young. First in Conservation International's Series of Working Papers on Ecotourism.

Author Unknown. (1993b). Indianism in Hungary. *European Review of Native American Studies* 7(1)37–42.

Newspapers/Newsletters

The Globe and Mail
High Country News
Newsletter of Far Horizons Archaeological & Cultural Trips
The International Ecotourism Society Newsletter/Eco Currents
Tourism in Focus (The Magazine of *Tourism Concern*)
Die Welt
Windspeaker

Further Bibliographical Resources

Agnew, Ella M. (1990). Who Owns What? A Lawyer interprets the new Canadian Copyright Act for Artists, Collectors and Galleries. *Inuit Art Quarterly* 5(2):24–29.

Allerston, Rosemary, and Chris Fournier. (1995). Art from Another World. *Up Here* 11(4):12–19.

Aloisi de Larderel, Jacqueline. (1993). Building a Partnership for Sustainable Tourism. In: *Going Green. The Ecotourism Resource for Travel Agents*. A Supplement to *Tour and Travel News*. October 25 1993. pp.8–9.

Ames, Michael M. (1987). A New Indian History for Museums. *Native Studies Review* 3(2):17–25.

_____. (1992). *Cannibal Tours and Glass Boxes*. The Anthropology of Museums. Vancouver: University of British Columbia Press.

Anderson, David L. (1993). A Window to the Natural World: The Design of Ecotourism Facilities. In: *Ecotourism: A Guide for Planners & Managers*. Edited by Kreg Lindberg and Donald E. Hawkins. North Bennington, Vermont: The Ecotourism Society. pp.116–133.

Anderson, Malcolm J. (1991). Problems with Tourism Development in Canada's Eastern Arctic. *Tourism Management* 12, September:209–220.

Ashton, Judy. (1993). Marketing Experiences in Aboriginal Tourism: Inbound Tourism's Perspective of Indigenous Tourism. In: *Indigenous Australians and Tourism: A Focus on Northern Australia*. Proceedings of the Indigenous Australians and Tourism Conference, Darwin, June 1993. pp.59–61.

Bachmann, Philip. (1988). The Maasai — Choice of East African Tourists — Admired and Ridiculed. *IWGIApp Document* No.61. Copenhagen: International Work Group for Indigenous Affairs (IWGIA). pp.47–63.

Bates, Bob. (1991). Impacts of Tourism on the Tribal Cultures and Natural Environment in Papua New Guinea. In: *Ecotourism incorporating the Global Classroom*. 1991 International Conference Papers. Edited by Betty Weiler. Canberra: Bureau of Tourism Research. pp.75–78.

Berno, Tracy. (1996). Cross-Cultural Research Methods: Content or Context? A Cook Island Example. In: *Tourism and Indigenous Peoples*. Edited by Richard Butler and Tom Hinch eds. Toronto: International Thomson Business Press. pp.376–395.

Blangy, Sylvie, and Megan Epler Wood. (1993). Developing and Implementing Ecotourism Guidelines for Wildlands and Neighboring Communities. In: *Ecotourism: A Guide for Planners & Managers*. Edited by Kreg Lindberg and Donald E.

Hawkins. North Bennington, Vermont: The Ecotourism Society. pp.32–54.

Boden, Gertrud, and Martina Gockel. (1995). Native North American Collections in Western European Museums. Replies to a Questionnaire. *European Review of Native American Studies* 9(1):49–54.

Boo, Elizabeth (1992). *The Ecotourism Boom. Planning for Development and Management. Wildlands and Human Needs.* A Program of World Wildlife Fund. WHN Technical Paper Series, Paper #2.

_____. (1993a). Wanted: Comprehensive Models of Ecotourism. In: *Going Green. The Ecotourism Resource for Travel Agents.* A Supplement to *Tour and Travel News.* October 25. pp.10–11.

_____. (1993b). Ecotourism Planning for Protected Areas. In: *Ecotourism: A Guide for Planners & Managers.* Edited by Kreg Lindberg and Donald E. Hawkins. North Bennington, Vermont: The Ecotourism Society. pp.15–31.

Bradbury, Alex. (1992). Staying in a Mayan Guest House. *Great Expeditions* 71:14–16.

Brandon, Katrina. (1993). Basic Steps toward Encouraging Local Participation in Nature Tourism Projects. In: *Ecotourism: A Guide for Planners & Managers.* Edited by Kreg Lindberg and Donald E. Hawkins. North Bennington, Vermont: The Ecotourism Society. pp.134–151.

Brim, Willie. (1993). Tjapukai — The Impact of Success. In: *Indigenous Australians and Tourism: A Focus on Northern Australia.* Proceedings of the Indigenous Australians and Tourism Conference, Darwin, June 1993. pp.47–48.

Brohman, John. (1996). New Directions in Tourism for Third World Development. *Annals of Tourism Research* 23(1):49–70.

Bronsdon Rowan, Madeline. (1987). Native Indian Youth in Museums: Success in Education at the U.B.C. Museum of Anthropology. *Native Studies Review* 3(2):87–97.

Butler, Richard W. (1975). *The Development of Tourism in the Canadian North and Implications for the Inuit.* Inuit Tapirisat of Canada, Renewable Resources Project, Volume 9. London: The University of Western Ontario.

_____. (1990). Alternative Tourism: Pious Hope or Trojan Horse? *Journal of Travel Research* 28(3):40–45.

_____. (1992). Alternative Tourism: The Thin Edge of the Wedge. In: *Tourism Alternatives. Potentials and Problems in the Development of Tourism.* Edited by Valene L. Smith and William R. Eadington. Philadelphia: University of Pennsylvania Press. pp.31–46.

Campbell, Bernard F. (1992). Community Tourism Issues. In: *Community and Cultural Tourism*. Conference Proceedings, Travel and Tourism Research Association — Canada, 1992. Edited by Laurel J. Reid. pp.22–25.

Campbell, Jeff. (1994a). The Soapbox (Opinion). *Aboriginal Business* 1(2):10–11.

_____. (1994b). Captain Greyeyes is Rolling on the River. *Aboriginal Business* 1(2):20–22.

Canadian National Aboriginal Tourism Association (CNATA). (1994c). Aboriginal Tourism Opportunities, Strategies and Issues. Paper presented at the IIPT Second Global Conference: *Building a sustainable World through Tourism*. September 12–16, Montreal.

_____. (1996a). Tourism as a Land Use Industry. Discussion Paper presented at the *Focusing Our Resources* Conference, Calgary, Alberta, April 14–16.

_____. (1996b). *Regional Aboriginal Tourism Development*. Discussion Paper presented at Aboriginal Tourism Team Canada Meeting in Calgary, Alberta, October 23.

Ceballos-Lasairain, Hector. (1993). Ecotourism as a worldwide Phenomenon. In: *Ecotourism: A Guide for Planners & Managers*. Edited by Kreg Lindberg and Donald E. Hawkins. North Bennington, Vermont: The Ecotourism Society. pp.12–14.

Churchill, Elizabeth. (1987). The Blackfoot Elders Project: Linking People and Objects in Museum Research. *Native Studies Review* 3(2):71–85.

Cohen, Erik. (1987). "Alternative Tourism" — A Critique. *Tourism-Recreation Research* 12(2):13–18.

_____. (1993). Introduction: Investigating Tourist Arts. *Annals of Tourism Research* 20(1):1–8.

Collins, Robertson E. (1993). Indigenous Cultures as a Tourism Attraction: An International Perspective. In: *Indigenous Australians and Tourism: A Focus on Northern Australia*. Proceedings of the Indigenous Australians and Tourism Conference, Darwin, June 1993. Commonwealth of Australia. pp.32–37.

Commonwealth Department of Tourism. (1994). *National Ecotourism Strategy*. Canberra: Australian Government Publishing Service.

Coull, Cheryl. (1996). *A Traveller's Guide to Aboriginal B.C.* Vancouver/Toronto: Whitecap Books.

Cousteau, Jean Michel. (1993). Ambassadors of the Sea: "Eco-Divers" discover new Worlds beneath the Waves. In: Going Green. The Ecotourism Resource for Travel Agents. A Supplement to *Tour and Travel News*. October 25, 1993. pp.20–21.

Cox, Bruce Alden. (1990). Historical Anthropology. In: *A Different Drummer. Readings in Anthropology with a Canadian Perspective*. Edited by Bruce Alden Cox, Jacques Chevalier and Valda Blundell. Ottawa: Carleton University. pp.31–37.

Dagnal-Myron, Cynthia M. (1990). "Where are your Moccasins?" A Guide for Tourists. *Cultural Survival Quarterly* 14(1):39–41.

Dann, Graham M.S. (1996). Images of Destination People in Travelogues. In: *Tourism and Indigenous Peoples*. Edited by Richard Butler and Tom Hinch. Toronto: International Thomson Business Press. pp.349–375.

de Burlo, Chuck. (1996). Cultural Resistance and Ethnic Tourism on South Pentecost, Vanuatu. In: *Tourism and Indigenous Peoples*. Edited by Richard Butler and Tom Hinch. Toronto: International Thomson Business Press. pp.255–276.

Deitch, Lewis I. (1989). The Impact of Tourism on the Arts and Crafts of the Indians of the Southwestern United States. In: *Hosts and Guests. The Anthropology of Tourism*. Second Edition. Edited by Valene L. Smith. Philadelphia: University of Pennsylvania Press. pp.223–235.

de Kadt, Emanuel (1992). Making the Alternative Sustainable: Lessons from Development for Tourism. In: *Tourism Alternatives. Potentials and Problems in the Development of Tourism*. Edited by Valene L. Smith and William R. Eadington. Philadelphia: University of Pennsylvania Press. pp.47–75.

Derek Murray Consulting Associates. The North Group and Norecon Ltd. (1994). *Northwest Territories Tourism Marketing Strategy 1994–95 — 1998–99*. Prepared for: Department of Economic Development and Tourism, Government of the Northwest Territories. July 1994.

Devine, Marina. (1992). No "Demon" Carvings from Baker Lake Arts and Crafts Centre....Yet. *Inuit Art Quarterly* 7(4):5–13.

Dieke, Peter U.C. (1991). Policies for Tourism Development in Kenya. *Annals of Tourism Research* 18(2):269–294.

Downie, Bruce. (1993). Katannilik Territorial Park: An Arctic Tourism Destination. In: *Communities, Resources and Tourism in the North*. Edited by Margaret E. Johnston and Wolfgang Haider. Thunder Bay: Lakehead University, Centre for Northern Studies. pp.51–60.

P Dragovich, D. (1993). Aboriginal Rock Art and Visitors to Mootwingee National Park. *Australian Aboriginal Studies* 1993, 2:58–65.

Downie, Bruce K., and David Monteith. (1994). Economic Impacts of Park Development and Operation: Katannilik Territorial Park, Lake Harbour, NWT. *Northern Perspectives* 22(2–3):7–17.

Duerden, Frank. (1992). A Critical Look at sustainable Development in the Canadian North. *Arctic* 45(3):219–225.

Duffek, Karen. (1987). It's Native: Where do you put it? A North West Coast Perspective. *Native Studies Review* 3(2):61–69.

Eadington, William R., and Valene L. Smith. (1992). Introduction: The Emergence of Alternative Forms of Tourism. In: *Tourism Alternatives. Potentials and Problems in the Development of Tourism*. Edited by Valene L. Smith and William R. Eadington. Philadelphia: University of Pennsylvania Press. pp.1–12.

Eagles, Paul F.J., and Elke Wind. (1994). Canadian Ecotours in 1992: A Content Analysis of Advertising. *Journal of Applied Recreation Research* 19(1):67–87.

Epler Wood, Megan. (1993). The Quest for Ecotourism Standards. In: Going Green. The Ecotourism Resource for Travel Agents. A Supplement to *Tour and Travel News*. October 25. pp.42–43.

_____. (1994). The Green Evaluations Program. An International Ecotourism Monitoring Program for Tour Operators. Paper presented at the IIPT Second Global Conference on *Building a sustainable World through Tourism*. September 12–16, Montreal.

Evans-Pritchard, Deirdre. (1989). How "They" see "Us". Native American Images of Tourists. *Annals of Tourism Research* 16(1):89–105.

Farrell, Bryan. (n.d.). Tourism as an Element in Sustainable Development: Hana, Maui. In: *Tourism Alternatives. Potentials and Problems in the Development of Tourism*. Edited by Valene L. Smith and William R. Eadington. Philadelphia: University of Pennsylvania Press. pp.115–134.

Feest, Christian E. (1995) "Repatriation": A European View on the Question of Restitution of Native American Artifacts. *European Review of Native American Studies* 9(2):33–40.

Fenge, Terry. (1994). Parks and Protected Areas in the North: Completing the Agenda. *Northern Perspectives* 22(2–3):1–2.

Finlayson, Julie. (1993). A Critical Overview of Current Policies and Programs. In: *Indigenous Australians and Tourism: A Focus on Northern Australia*. Proceedings of the Indigenous Australians and Tourism Conference, Darwin, June 1993. Commonwealth of Australian. pp.76–82.

First Nations Tourism Association. (1991). *"To know us is to love us". Native Cultural Tourism in B.C.* Discussion Paper.

Fisher, Eugene. (1995). The Voyage Out. *Up Here* 11(2):12–16, 49.

Fogarty, Lesley (Bangama). (1993). The Importance of the Indigenous Arts and Crafts Contribution to the Tourism Industry. In: *Indigenous Australians and Tourism: A Focus on Northern Australia*. Proceedings of the Indigenous Australians and Tourism Conference, Darwin, June 1993. pp.29–31.

Freeman, Don. (1993). Indigenous Employment in the Tourism Industry. In: *Indigenous Australians and Tourism: A Focus on Northern Australia*. Proceedings of the Indigenous Australians and Tourism Conference, Darwin, June 1993. pp.62–65.

Frick McKean, Philip. (1989). Towards a Theoretical Analysis of Tourism: Economic Dualism and Cultural Involution in Bali. In: *Hosts and Guests. The Anthropology of Tourism*. Second Edition. Edited by Valene L. Smith. Philadelphia: University of Pennsylvania Press. pp.121–137.

Gehreis, Barbara. (1996). *Danger, Tourists. London: Survival International.* Unpublished Paper.

Globe '90. Tourism Stream Action Strategy Committee. (1990). *An Action Strategy for Sustainable Tourism Development*. Vancouver, B.C. March 1990.

Go, Frank M. (1989). Appropriate Marketing for Travel Destinations in Developing Nations. In: *Towards Appropriate Tourism: The Case of Developing Countries*. Edited by T.V. Sing, H.L. Thuens and F.M. Go. New York: Peter Lang. pp.159–180.

Goddard, Carol. (1995). Sounds and Silence (Gwaii Haanas National Park). *Explore* 74:34–41.

Gonseth, Marc-Olivier. (1988). A Look behind the Tourism Facade: Some Considerations on the Development of Tourism in the Province of Ifugao (Philippines). *IWGIA*-Document No.61. Copenhagen: International Work Group for Indigenous Affairs (IWGIA). pp.21–46.

Gonzalez, Victor. (1993). Tourism and the Environment: A Policy Maker's Perspective. In: Going Green. The Ecotourism Resource for Travel Agents. A Supplement to *Tour and Travel News*. October 25, 1993. pp.16–17.

Goodfellow, Denise. (1991). Male Black Whip Snakes are well Equipped...or, can Cryptoblepharus Carnabyi Compete with Sun, Sand and Sex? In: *Ecotourism incorporating the Global Classroom*. 1991 International Conference Papers. Edited by Betty Weiler. Canberra: Bureau of Tourism Research. pp.224–227.

Gorio, Sylvanus. (1978). Papua New Guinea involves its People in National Park Development. *Parks* 3(2):12–14.

Government of Canada. (No Date). *Visitor Profile and Economic Impact Statement of Northern National Parks/Reserves and His-*

toric Sites. Summary Report. Environment Canada. Parks Service.

_____. (1992). *Facing Challenges, taking Leadership*. Final Report, Aboriginal Issues Management Team. Environment Canada. Parks Service. Prairie and Northern Region. May 1992.

_____. (1994). *Gwaii Haanas Economic Impact Study*. Parks Canada.

Government of the Northwest Territories. (1990). *Tourism: The Northern Lure*. Government of the Northwest Territories: Economic Development and Tourism.

Grant, Laurence, and Valda Blundell. (1992). Museums and First Peoples: Working to reconcile Competing Interests. *Inuit Art Quarterly* 7(2):52–54.

Greenfield, Jeanette 1996 (1989). *The Return of Cultural Treasures*. Second Edition. Cambridge: Cambridge University Press.

Gurung, Ghana, David Simmons and Patrick Devlin. (1996). The Evolving Role of Tourist Guides: the Nepali Experience. In: *Tourism and Indigenous Peoples*. Edited by Richard Butler and Tom Hinch. Toronto: International Thomson Business Press. pp.107–128.

Haas, Jonathan. (1996). Power, Objects, and a Voice for Anthropology. *Current Anthropology* 37, Supplement, February 1996:S1–S22.

Hall, Dana Naone. (1994). Preserving Hawai'i as a Hawaiian Place. Tourism, Development and Destruction of the Environment. *IWGIA-Document* No. 75. Copenhagen: International Work Group for Indigenous Affairs (IWGIA). pp.165–170.

Hancock, Lyn. (1995). Wild Power. Riding the North Nahanni River. *Above & Beyond* 7(2):35–38.

Hannah, Lee. (1992). *African People, African Parks. An Evaluation of Development Initiatives as a Means of Improving Protected Area Conservation in Africa*. Conservation International.

Hanneberg, Peter. (1994). Ecotourism or Ecoterrorism? *Enviro* 17:2–5.

Harper, Lynette. (1993). From Temple to Battlefield: Conflicting Ideologies in the Museum. *MUSE* 11(3):20–21.

Haywood, K. Michael. (1990). Revising and Implementing the Marketing Concept as it applies to Tourism. *Tourism Management* 7:195–205.

_____, D.G. Reid and J. Wolfe. (1993). Enhancing Hospitality and Tourism Education and Training in Canada's Northwest Territories. In: *Communities, Resources and Tourism in the North*. Edited by Margaret E. Johnston and Wolfgang Haider. Thunder Bay: Lakehead University, Centre for Northern Studies. pp.35–49.

Hemming, Steve. (1994). In the Tracks of Ngurunderi: The South Australian Museum's Ngurunderi Exhibition and Cultural Tourism. *Australian Aboriginal Studies* 1994, 2:38–46.

Herle, Anita. (1994). Museums and First Peoples in Canada. *Journal of Museum Ethnography* 6:39–66.

Heymann, Rudolph. (1993). Overview of the Realities of promoting Aboriginal Tourism internationally. In: *Indigenous Australians and Tourism: A Focus on Northern Australia.* Proceedings of the Indigenous Australians and Tourism Conference, Darwin, June 1993. pp.56–58.

Hinch, Tom D. (1992). Planning for Changing Markets: The Case of Native Communities in Alberta. In: *Community and Cultural Tourism.* Conference Proceedings, Travel and Tourism Research Association — Canada, 1992. Edited by Laurel J. Reid. pp.76–88.

_____. (1995). Aboriginal People in the Tourism Economy of Canada's Northwest Territories. In: *Polar Tourism. Tourism in the Arctic and Antarctic Regions.* Toronto: John Wiley & Sons. pp.115–130.

Hitchcock, Robert K., David Green and Megan Biesele. (1996). *Tourism and the Himba of Northern Namibia.* Omaha: University of Nebraska Press.

HLA Consultants and The ARA Consulting Group Inc. (1994). *Ecotourism — Nature/Adventure/Culture: Alberta and British Columbia Market Demand Assessment.* Main Report. December.

Hollinshead, Keith. (1991). "White" Gaze, "Red" People — Shadow Visions: The Disidentification of "Indians" in Cultural Tourism. *Leisure Studies* 11:43–64.

Horn-Miller, Kahente. (1993). The American Indian and the Problem of History. *MUSE* 11(3):44–46.

Howell, Benita J. (1994). Weighing the Risks and Rewards of Involvement in Cultural Conservation and Heritage Tourism. *Human Organization* 53(2):150–159.

Hummel, John. (1994). Ecotourism Development in Protected Areas of Developing Countries. *World Leisure & Recreation* 36(2):17–23.

Janes, Robert R. (1994). Personal, Academic and Institutional Perspectives on Museums and First Nations. *The Canadian Journal of Native Studies* 14(1):147–156.

Jarvenpa, Robert. (1994). Commoditization versus Cultural Integration: Tourism and Image Building in the Klondike. *Arctic Anthropology* 31(1):26–46.

Jasen, Patricia. (1994). Native People and the Tourist Industry in Nineteenth-Century Ontario. *Journal of Canadian Studies* 28(4):5–27.

_____. (1995). *Wild Things. Nature, Culture, and Tourism in Ontario, 1790–1914.* Toronto: University of Toronto Press.

Jules, Linda. (1994). Developing Tourism at the Secwepemc Native Heritage Park. *MUSE* 12(2):40–42.

Kafka, John. (1987). *Developing Tourism Resources in a Native Setting.* Proceedings of the First Annual Advanced Policy Forum on Tourism, May 1987, Whistler, B.C.

Kammerer, Cornelia Ann, and Patricia V. Symonds. (1992). AIDS in Asia: Hill Tribes Endangered at Thailand's Periphery. *Cultural Survival Quarterly* 16(3):23–25.

Kelly, John. (1994). Tourism in Hawai'i. *IWGIA-Document* No.75. Copenhagen: International Work Group for Indigenous Affairs (IWGIA). pp.172–182.

Koppel, Tom. (1996). The Spirit of Haida Gwaii. *Canadian Geographic* March/April 1996:22–33.

Kramer, Pat. (1994). *Native Sites in Western Canada.* Banff/Canmore: Altitude Publishing Canada Ltd.

Kurosawa, Susan. (1994). Red Sky at Night. *EcoTraveler* 1(4):42–45, 72.

Kutay, Kurt. (1993). Brave new Role. In: Going Green. The Ecotourism Resource for Travel Agents. A Supplement to *Tour and Travel News*. October 25. pp.40–41.

Larson, Scott. (1994). Heritage Centre injects Pride. *Aboriginal Business* 1(2):16–17.

Lawrence, Raymond. (1996). Frog Lake — Making it Happen. *Transition* 8(10):4.

Lea, John. (1988). *Tourism and Development in the Third World.* London and New York: Routledge.

Leonard, Doug. (1993). To Be Endangered or Empowered — That is the Question! A Case Study of Community Partnership. *MUSE* 11(3):28–31.

Lewis, Damien. (1990). Conflict of Interest. *Geographical Magazine*, December 1990:18–22.

Lindberg, Kreg, and Richard M. Huber Jr. (1993). Economic Issues in Ecotourism Management. In: *Ecotourism: A Guide for Planners & Managers.* Edited by Kreg Lindberg and Donald E. Hawkins. North Bennington, Vermont: The Ecotourism Society. pp.82-115.

_____, and Jeremy Enriquez. (No Date). *An Analysis of Ecotourism's Economic Contribution to Conservation and Development in Belize.* Volume 1: Summary Report. A Report prepared for World Wildlife Fund (US) and the Ministry of Tourism and the Environment (Belize).

Lorson, Scott. (1994). Heritage Centre Injects Pride. *Aboriginal Business* 1(2):16–17.

Lynch, Bernadette. (1993). The Broken Pipe: Non-Native Museums and Native Culture. A Personal Perspective. *MUSE* 11(3):51–54.

MacDonald, George F., and Stephen Alsford. (1990). Museums as Bridges to the Global Village. In: *A Different Drummer: Readings in Anthropology with a Canadian Perspective*. Edited by Bruce Alden Cox, Jacques Chevalier and Valda Blundell. Ottawa: Carleton University, The Anthropology Caucus. pp.41–48.

MacGregor, James R. (1987). The Opportunity for Native Tourism Development in North America (Excerpt). *Tourism & Recreation Workshop — Native Tourism Development*, Vancouver 1987.

MacIntyre, Wendy. (1995a). Healing Forest will keep Native Heritage thriving. *Transition* 8(5):6.

_____. (1995b). Award-winning Village Embodies Cree Values. *Transition* 8(6):1, 4.

Madsen, Ken. (1994). Exploring the Wild Bonnet Plume. *Up Here* (10(5):84–88, 104.

Mansperger, Mark C. (1995). Tourism and Cultural Change in Small-Scale Societies. *Human Organization* 54(1):87–94.

Maurer, Jean-Luc, and Arlette Zeigler. (1988). Tourism and Indonesian Cultural Minorities. *IWGIA-Document* No.61. Copenhagen: International Work Group for Indigenous Affairs (IWGIA). pp.65–92.

Mauze, Marie. (1992). Exhibiting One's Culture: Two Case Studies. The Kwagiulth Museum and the U-Mista Cultural Centre. *European Review of Native American Studies* 6(1):27–30.

May, Elizabeth. (1990). Tourism to the Rescue. *Cultural Survival Quarterly* 14(2):2–5.

Mazitelli, David. (1993). The Role of Governments in supporting ongoing Aboriginal Participation in the Tourism Industry: an Overview. In: *Indigenous Australians and Tourism: A Focus on Northern Australia*. Proceedings of the Indigenous Australians and Tourism Conference, Darwin, June 1993. pp.72–75.

McKercher, Bob. (1996). Differences between Tourism and Recreation in Parks. *Annals of Tourism Research* 23(3):563–575.

McMaster, Gerald. (1993). Object (to) Sanctity: The Politics of the Object. *MUSE* 11(3):24–25.

Metcalfe, David. (1991). Seven Spirit Bay: an Ecotourism Development in Western Arnhem Land, Northern Territory. In: *Ecotourism incorporating the Global Classroom.* 1991 International Conference Papers. Edited by Betty Weiler. Canberra: Bureau of Tourism Research. pp.199–207.

Michaud, Jean, Pierre Maranda, Luc Lafreniere, and Ginette Cote. (1994). Ethnological Tourism in the Solomon Islands: An Experience in Applied Anthropology. *Anthropologica* 36(1):35–56.

Millar, Jillian. (1994). Lobsters aren't the only Thing cooking in Maritime Tourism. *Aboriginal Business* 1(2):32–33.

Milne, S., S. Ward, and G. Wenzel. (1995). Linking Tourism and Art in Canada's eastern Arctic: the Case of Cape Dorset. *Polar Record* 31(176):25–36.

Mitchell, Ian, Michael Hall and Ngawini Keelan. (1991). The Cultural Dimensions of Heritage Tourism in New Zealand — ssues in the Development of Maori Culture and Heritage as a Tourist Resource. In: *Ecotourism incorporating the Global Classroom.* 1991 International Conference Papers. Edited by Betty Weiler. Canberra: Bureau of Tourism Research. pp.271–280.

Mitchell, Marybelle. (1990/91). The "Eskimo Art" Business. A History and Analysis of the Co-operative Movement in the Arctic. *Inuit Art Quarterly* 5(4):28–33.

Morgan, Jeremy. (1992). Authenticity and Wanuskewin Heritage Park. In: Community and Cultural Tourism. Conference Proceedings, Travel and Tourism Research Association — Canada, 1992. Edited by Laurel J. Reid. pp.140–142.

Morrison, James. (1993). Protected Areas and Aboriginal Interests in Canada. Discussion Paper. Toronto: World Wildlife Fund Canada.

Muehlen, Maria. (1990/91) Government Activity in Inuit Arts and Crafts. *Inuit Art Quarterly* 5(4):38–43.

Nepal, Sanjay K., and Karl E. Weber. (1995). The Quandary of Local People — Park Relations in Nepal's Royal Chitwan National Park. *Environmental Management* 19(6):853–866.

Neuspiel, Jan. (1992). Eco-Focus: the Himalayas. Tourism Impact in Nepal. *Great Expeditions* 72:28–31, 42.

Norris Nicholson, Heather. (1992). Cultural Centres or Trading Posts? *Museums Journal* 92(8):31–34.

Oelrichs Faila, Ian. (1991). Tourism: Protecting Indigenous Cultures from Modern Cultures by Managing the Landscape. In: *Ecotourism incorporating the Global Classroom*. 1991 International Conference Papers. Edited by Betty Weiler. Canberra: Bureau of Tourism Research. pp.79–85.

Pakes, Fraser J. (1987). "But is it Indian" — Indian and Non-Indian Interpretation of Plains Indian Art. *Native Studies Review* 3(2):27–46.

Parker, Barry. (1992a). The Development of Tourism in Aboriginal Communities across Canada. Paper presented at the 1992 *World Congress on Adventure Travel and Ecotourism*, September 20–23, 1992.

Parker, Barry. (1992b). Aboriginal Tourism: From Perception to Reality. In: *Community and Cultural Tourism*. Conference Proceedings, Travel and Tourism Research Association — Canada, 1992. Edited by Laurel J. Reid. pp.14–20.

_____. (1994). Aboriginal Tourism Opportunities, Strategies and Issues. Paper presented at the IIPT Second Global Conference on *Building a Sustainable World through Tourism*. Montreal, September 12–16, 1994.

Pearce, Douglas G. (1992). Alternative Tourism: Concepts, Classifications, and Questions. In: *Tourism Alternatives. Potentials and Problems in the Development of Tourism*. Edited by Valene L. Smith and William R. Eadington. Philadelphia: University of Pennsylvania Press. pp.15–30.

Pelly, David. (1995). The Torngat Mountains. *Above & Beyond* 7(2):7–11.

Phillips, Ruth B. (1990). The Public Relations Wrap. What we can learn from The Spirit Sings. *Inuit Art Quarterly* 5(2):13–21.

Pigram, John J. (1992). Alternative Tourism: Tourism and Sustainable Resource Management. In: *Tourism Alternatives. Potentials and Problems in the Development of Tourism*. Edited by Valene L. Smith and William R. Eadington. Philadelphia: University of Pennsylvania Press. pp.76–87.

Price, Martin. (1994). A Fragile Balance. *Geographical* 66(9):32–33.

Ray, Arthur J. (1987). Moose Factory: Heritage Planning in a Northern Community. *Native Studies Review* 3(2):99–121.

Reingold, Lester. (1993). Identifying the Elusive Ecotourist. In: Going Green. The Ecotourism Resource for Travel Agents. A Supplement to *Tour and Travel News*. October 25. pp.36–39.

Rice, Larry. (1995). This Native Land. *Explore* 73:52–56.

Rossel, Pierre. (Ed.) (1988). Tourism and Cultural Minorities: Double Marginalisation and Survival Strategies. In: *Tourism: Manufacturinbg the Exotic*. IWGIA-Document No.61. Copenhagen: International Work Group for Indigenous Affairs (IWGIA). pp.1–20.

Roville, Gerard. (1988). Ethnic Minorities and the Development of Tourism in the Valleys of North Pakistan. In: *Tourism: Manufacturinbg the Exotic*. Edited by Pierre Rossel. IWGIA-

Document No.61. Copenhagen: International Work Group for Indigenous Affairs (IWGIA). pp.146–176.

RT & Associates. (1989). Economic Development & Tourism Programs. A Review & Assessment. Prepared for the Legislative Assembly's Special Committee on the Northern Economy. Yellowknife: RT & Associates. May 1989.

Rudkin, Brenda, and C. Michael Hall. (1996). Unable to See the Forest for the Trees: Ecotourism Development in Solomon Islands. In: *Tourism and Indigenous Peoples*. Edited by Richard Butler and Tom Hinch. Toronto: International Thomson Business Press. pp.203–226.

Schulte-Tenckhoff, Isabelle. (1988). Potlatch and Totem: the Attraction of America's Northwest Coast. In: *Tourism: Manufacturinbg the Exotic*. Edited by Pierre Rossel. IWGIA-Document No.61. Copenhagen: International Work Group for Indigenous Affairs (IWGIA). pp.117–145.

Seale, Ronald G. (1996). A Perspective from Canada on Heritage and Tourism. *Annals of Tourism Research* 23(2):484–488.

Selengut, Stanley. (1993). New Priorities motivate Eco-Lodge Developers. In: Going Green. The Ecotourism Resource for Travel Agents. A Supplement to *Tour and Travel News*. October 25. p.22.

Shackley, Myra. (1996a). Too Much Room in the Inn? *Annals of Tourism Research* 23(2):449–462.

_____. (1996b). Community Impact of the Camel Safari Industry in Jaisalmar, Rajasthan. *Tourism Management* 17(3):213–218.

Sharp, John, and Emile Boonzaier. (1994). Ethnic Identity as Performance: Lessons from Namaqualand. *Journal of Southern African Studies* 20(3):405–415.

Sik-Ooh-Kotoki Friendship Society. (1995). *"Draft" Aboriginal Tourism Action Plan for the Southern Alberta Region*. Lethbridge: Sik-Ooh-Kotoki Friendship Society.

Smith, Valene L. (1989). Eskimo Tourism: Micro-Models and Marginal Men. In: *Hosts and Guests. The Anthropology of Tourism*. Second Edition. Edited by Valene L. Smith. Philadelphia: University of Pennsylvania Press. pp.55–82.

_____. (1990). Responsible Tourism: Some Anthropological Issues. *Tourism-Recreation Research* 15(1):45–49.

_____. (1992). Boracay, Philippines: A Case Study in "Alternative" Tourism. In: *Tourism Alternatives. Potentials and Problems in the Development of Tourism*. Edited by Valene L. Smith and William R. Eadington. Philadelphia: University of Pennsylvania Press. pp.135–157.

_____. (1996). The Inuit as Hosts: Heritage and Wilderness Tourism in Nunavut. In: *People and Tourism in Fragile Environments*. Edited by M. F. Price. Toronto, New York: Wiley. pp.33–50.

Sofield, Trevor H.B. (1993). Indigenous Tourism Development. *Annals of Tourism Research* 20(4):729–750.

Spalding, Julian. (1993). Interpretation? No, Communication. *MUSE* 11(3):10–14.

Stafford, Ed. (1994). National Park used to settle Land Claim. *Borealis* 5(2): 34–35.

Stanley, Dick, and Luc Perron. (1994). The Economic Impact of Northern National Parks (Reserves) and Historic Sites. *Northern Perspectives* 22(2–3):3–6.

Stenton, Douglas R., and Bruce G. Rigby. (1995). *Community-Based Heritage Education, Training and Research*: Preliminary Report on the Tungatsivvik Archaeological Project. *Arctic* 48(1):47–56.

Stewart, J. Kent. (1992). Aboriginal Tourism in Canada: Challenges in Community and Cultural Tourism. In: *Community and Cultural Tourism*. Conference Proceedings, Travel and Tourism Research Association — Canada, 1992. Edited by Laurel J. Reid. pp.9–13.

Survival International. (1994). Tourism and Tribal Peoples. *Survival Background Sheet*. London.

Task Force on Museums and First Peoples. (1994). *Turning the Page: Forging new Partnerships between Museums and First Peoples, Third Edition*. A Report jointly sponsored by the Assembly of First Nations and the Canadian Museum Association. Ottawa.

Telfer, David J., and Geoffrey Wall. (1996) Linkages between Tourism and Food Production. *Annals of Tourism Research* 23(3):635–653.

Thompson, Peter. (1995). The Errant E-Word. Putting Ecotourism back on Track. *Explore* 73:67–72.

Thumb, Tom. (1994). Observations and Opinions. *Aboriginal Business* 1(2):30.

Tiller, Veronica E. (Ed.). (1992). *Discover Indian Reservations USA: A Visitor's Welcome Guide*. Denver: Council Publications (CERT).

Tilmouth, Tracker. (1993). Tourism on Indigenous Land: a Land Council Perspective. In: *Indigenous Australians and Tourism: A Focus on Northern Australia*. Proceedings of the Indigenous Australians and Tourism Conference, Darwin, June. pp.26–28.

Tourism Industry Association of Canada & National Round Table on the Environment and the Economy. (n.d.). *Code of Ethics and Guidelines for Sustainable Tourism*.

Tutty, Darrell. (1993). Putjamirra — A Development Scenario. In: *Indigenous Australians and Tourism: A Focus on Northern Australia.* Proceedings of the Indigenous Australians and Tourism Conference, Darwin, June. pp.45–46.

Urbanowicz, Charles F. (1989). Tourism in Tonga Revisited: Continued Troubled Times? In: *Hosts and Guests. The Anthropology of Tourism.* Second Edition. Edited by Valene Smith. Philadelphia: University of Pennsylvania Press. pp.105–117.

Usher, Anthony J. (1993). Polar Bear Park and Area: Community-Oriented Tourism Development in Ontario's Arctic. In: *Communities, Resources and Tourism in the North.* Edited by Margaret E. Johnston and Wolfgang Haider. Thunder Bay: Lakehead University, Centre for Northern Studies. pp.17–33.

Waldern Hinds, Heather. (1994). Co-ops find Niche in Tourism Industry. *Aboriginal Business* 1(2):18–19.

Walker, Ernest. (1987). Indian Involvement in Heritage Resource Development: A Saskatchewan Example. *Native Studies Review* 3(2):123–131.

Wall, Geoffrey. (1996). Perspectives on Tourism in Selected Balinese Villages. *Annals of Tourism Research* 23(1):123–137.

Wallace, George N. (1993). Visitor Management: Lessons from Galapagos National Park. In: *Ecotourism: A Guide for Planners & Managers.* Edited by Kreg Lindberg and Donald E. Hawkins. North Bennington, Vermont: The Ecotourism Society. pp.55–81.

Weiler, Betty, Tracey Johnson and Derrin Davis. (1991). Roles of the Tour Leader in Environmentally Responsible Tourism. In: *Ecotourism incorporating the Global Classroom.* 1991 International Conference Papers. Edited by Betty Weiler. Canberra: Bureau of Tourism Research. pp.228–233.

Western, David. (1993). Defining Ecotourism. In: *Ecotourism: A Guide for Planners & Managers.* Edited by Kreg Lindberg and Donald E. Hawkins. North Bennington: The Ecotourism Society. pp.7–11.

Wheat, Sue. (1994). Taming Tourism. *Geographical*, April 1994:16–19.

White, Adam. (1993). *The Economic Benefits of Conserving Canada's Endangered Spaces.* Discussion Paper. Toronto: World Wildlife Fund Canada.

Wilkins, Charles. (1994). Wanuskewin. *Canadian Geographic* 114(5):22–32.

Williams, Peter W., and Alison Gill. (1991). *Carrying Capacity Management in Tourism Settings: A Tourism Growth Management Process.* Prepared for Alberta Tourism by Peter W. Williams and Alison Gill, Centre for Tourism Policy and Research, Simon Fraser University, November 29.

Wolfe-Keddie, Jackie. (1993). Tourism in the Eastern Arctic: Coping with "Dangerous Children". *Journal of Applied Recreation Research* 18:143–162.

Wuttunee, Wanda. (1991a). *Western Arctic Air Ltd.* Case Study. Lethbridge: The Centre for Aboriginal Management, Faculty of Management, The University of Lethbridge.

_____. (1991b). *Northern Emak Outfitting Inc*. Case Study. Lethbridge: The Centre for Aboriginal Management, Faculty of Management, The University of Lethbridge.

Wylie, Jerry. (1994). *Journey through a Sea of Islands: A Review of Forest Tourism in Micronesia*. Honolulu: Institute of Pacific Islands Forestry.

Young, Bruce. (1989). New Zealand — Maori Tourism on the Launch Pad. *Tourism Management* 11(2):153–156.

Young, Georgia. (1991). Educating the Destination Community about Tourism: Information and Participation. In: *Ecotourism incorporating the Global Classroom.* 1991 International Conference Papers. Edited by Betty Weiler. Canberra: Bureau of Tourism Research. pp.281–283.

Unknown Author. (1990/91). Who sells Inuit Art, and How? *Inuit Art Quarterly* 5(4):44–51.

Unknown Author. (1993a). Urgent Problems discussed by Artists. *Inuit Art Quarterly* 8(3):24–33.

Index

Index

A

Aberdeen, Lucinda *127, 129*
aboriginal tourism *see* indigenous tourism
Achuar, and ecotourism *224–226*
adventure tourism, compared to ecotourism
     174, 199
Africa *see also* Botswana; Namibia
     indigenous people of *5–6*
     indigenous tourism in *22–25*
African Government
     Ministry of Commerce and Industry
          (Botswana) *195*
     Ministry of Environment and Tourism
          (Namibia) *5*
Ainu *130*
Air Canada *32*
Alberta (Canada)
     market research of indigenous tourism
          in *79–89*
Alice Springs (Australia) *97*
Altman, Jon C. *131, 188*
Amazon, the *20–21 see also Ecuador; Peru*
     threats to *219*
Anangu
     control of marketing *169*
     and sensitivity to new age tourists
          169
     spiritual beliefs of *163–164*
Asia and indigenous tourism *16–19*
Australia
     Aboriginal tourism strategy (NT
          Tourism Commission) *94*
     indigenous tourism in *14–15*
     market for aboriginal tourism *93–97*
Australia and Canada compared *93, 181*
Australian aboriginal tribes *see also*
   Anangu
     Djabugay Aboriginals *128–129*
     Ngarinyin *146*
     Paakintji *123–125*
Australian Aborigines
     and authenticity in tourism *153–154*
     dreamtime (the dreaming) *15, 169*
     and employment in tourism industry
          37–38
     and involvement in tourism *113–115,
          137*
     joint management of national parks
          181–189
     and loss of traditional livelihood *37*
     spiritual beliefs of *145–147*
     as tourist guides *123–125*
     walkabout *3*
Australian Government
     Australian Commonwealth Department
          of Tourism *93*
     Australian National Parks and Wildlife
          Service (ANPWS) *182, 186, 189*
     Northern Land Council (NLC) *183*

     Northern Territory Tourist Commission
          94
     NT Government *182*
     Parks Australia *165*
authenticity of experience *87, 155, 158*
Auyuittuq national park reserve (Nunavut)
     193
     establishment of *238*
Ayers Rock *see* Uluru

B

Bali (Indonesia) and homestay tourism
     140–141
Basarwa *23 see also San*
     eviction and relocation of *194–197,
          200*
Bathurst Inlet Lodge (Nunavut, Canada)
     207
Belize
     cultural commoditization in *150–152*
     ecotourism in *213–218, 229*
     ecotourism sanctuaries and reserves of
          213
     Toledo Tourism Association *214*
Berbers *5, 23*
Bering Strait theory *3*
Berno, Tracy *142*
Birtles, Alastair *257*
Blackfoot Indians *2–3, 31*
Bolz, Peter *103*
Botswana *9, 23 see also Basarwa*
     community-based natural resource
          management in *23, 233*
     Remote Area Development Program
          194, 197
Buehrs, Ton *60*
Boyd, S.W. *202, 203*
Brandon, Katrina *248*
Brigham Young University *126*
British Columbia (Canada) *see* southern
   Canada
Buffalo Bill's Wild West *102–104*
Burchett, Chris *148*
Bush University (Australia) *146*
Bushmen *see* Basarwa; San
Butler, Richard W. *4, 8, 121, 202, 203*

C

Canada *see also* Alberta (Canada);
   northern Canada; southern Canada
     cultural authenticity guidelines *155*
     ecotourism in *204–207, 229*
     government promotion of community-
          based tourism *243*
     indigenous tourism in *25–33, 34*
     socio-economic conditions of
          indigenous people *36*

Index